TECHNOLOGIES FOR THE 21ST CENTURY

Volume 5
CONTENT AND COMMUNICATION

Martin Greenberger

Council for Technology and the Individual
Santa Monica, California

ISBN #1-886313-94-6

Published by
Council for Technology and the Individual
Santa Monica, California

The Fifth Roundtable in Multimedia

April 6-8, 1994

Organized by Council for Technology and the Individual, a foundation dealing with the human dimensions of technology

Discussions aimed at fostering an environment conducive to creativity, cooperation, and constructive competition

This volume is dedicated to those who look beyond the short term and see above the $$$

Sponsors of the Fifth Roundtable

Apple Computer
AT&T
Autodesk, Inc.
Bell Atlantic Corporation
Eastman Kodak Company
General Atlantic Partners
Hewlett-Packard Company
IBM Corporation
Intel Corporation
Interval Research Corporation
Kleiner Perkins Caufield & Byers
Lotus Development Corporation
Microsoft Corporation
NYNEX Corporation
Pioneer New Media Technologies
Robertson, Stephens & Company
Sega of America
SuperMac Technology
The Walt Disney Company

Contents

Multimedia Mosaic

A Story of Mystery and Suspense (with Game)[1]

The Beginning of the Middle

A story has a beginning, a middle, and an end.[2] The story of multimedia so far has a beginning and a middle, and the middle has just begun. It leapt onto center stage quickly and impulsively two years ago. It may last another two years, another two decades, or another century or two. The longer it lasts, the more interesting the ending is likely to be. It's not your typical story.

A story involves exposition, conflict, and resolution.[3] The exposition of multimedia — high hopes, exciting visions, early experiments — emerged gradually during the 1970s and 1980s. Then, in 1992, the pace quickened and conflict erupted. Competitive skirmishes flared up as companies vied to secure market share in the blossoming market for interactive CDs. Cultures clashed as once alien business and professional fields began to overlap and intermix. And a virtual battle of the gladiators took shape as big players rushed in to take a place and establish positions in a race to the New World — the world of the information superhighway.

As in Columbus' journey to the New World 500 years before, the superhighway initiative is intended to open up a territory of enormous opportunity.[4] The cauldron is coming to a boil. It's a time of definition, determination, and decision. Resolution lies ahead, but when and what is hardly clear at this point. No one grasps the full implications, although the press seems to think it does.[5]

The media is playing a conspicuous role in the unfolding drama. Readers can follow the narrative by glancing through a wide variety of newspapers and magazines. It's absorbing reading for sure, and there is no dearth of coverage. Journalists have a keen sense for a good story, and they are making the most of this one. But their accounts can be cursory and uncritical, even misleading.

The media love to create myths and then very quickly destroy them.[6] "Suddenly the brave new world that futurists have been predicting for decades is not years away, but months," one otherwise perceptive writer gushed a year ago. "By this time next year, vast new video services will be available at a price to millions of Americans in all fifty states."[7] We're still waiting. Now the focus in the press is on delays and failed expectations. "Hurdles Slow Information Superhypeway," a recent article declares.[8] This makes for a good story too.

The catchy puns and headlines, the selective use of material, the quotes from sources quickly telephoned (or nowadays e-mailed) are all designed to arouse the reader's interest and raise the heartbeat. Journalists are proficient. They write pointedly and on deadline. They know how to attract attention.

To get to the real and full McCoy, it helps to speak directly with the people involved, asking questions and listening to them talk among themselves. Not only that, it helps to examine social mores, and give a critical eye to education and other once sacred cows. It helps to reflect on human values, contemplate the adornments of civilization, and search for historical precedents. It helps to think about how we spend our leisure time and how we like to be entertained. No doubt about it; it can be a major undertaking. But these are weighty matters. How else do we begin to understand what's happening and where it's likely to lead?

Starting with the Computer

The real story of multimedia is part of a trilogy beginning with the automatic digital computer. The logical calculating machine has had its own fascinating history going back to Pascal, Babbage, Turing, Aiken, Von Neumann, and many other pioneers of what now almost seems like ancient history.

Treated with deference and unease during its first thirty years, the automatic computer was an important part of the world into which multimedia was born. A master of reason from the start, the computer quickly learned to read, write, do complicated arithmetic, store and retrieve prodigious amounts of information, manipulate text, understand languages, and play a variety of serious and recreational games. Before long, it was contributing mightily to all sorts of human activities, moving far afield from the numerical computations that first gave it a foothold.

But there was a problem. Computers, especially those of the larger and more powerful variety, were not very sociable. In fact, by the early sixties, during their puberty years, they were downright aloof and unreachable, even to those most closely involved in their programming. Frustrated but dogged, programmers at MIT, Dartmouth, and elsewhere labored diligently to make the giant machines of the day more accessible and useful. They built operating systems to distribute or *time-share* processing cycles in round-robin fashion among a circle of simultaneous users, much in the manner of a rotating switch with multiple contacts.

Project MAC was a groundbreaking project in time-sharing at MIT. It took its name from *Multi-Access Computing,* although the acronym had a second, also official meaning, one that put the focus on the user rather than the technology. *Machine-Aided Cognition* expressed the desire of project leaders to promote greater interactivity and a more personal relationship between user and machine.[9]

Some high priests of programming had indeed experienced a very special relationship with computers they had to themselves (at least part of the time). They knew how much better it could be. Ivan Sutherland, later to be a pioneer in virtual reality, worked nights at MIT's Lincoln Laboratory on a versatile machine made available to him for his doctoral dissertation. His *Sketchpad* program was completed in 1962. From one perspective, not a lot has happened since then. *Sketchpad* is one of the greatest things ever done.[10] It propelled the field of computer graphics onto a continuing ascent, and inspired much of what is now taken for granted in multimedia.

The time sharing of large computers offered a new paradigm for computer services. The image of a *computing utility* distributing computation and data on a broad scale took hold of the imagination.[11] It was 1961. Within three years, an even grander vision emerged, that of an *information utility*, a concept later realized in the on-line services we take for granted today, services such as America Online, Prodigy, and CompuServe.[12]

The information utility foreshadowed the grandest vision of all, the information superhighway, though the focus in the 1960s was more on person-to-computer and computer-to-computer communication than on the person-to-person (via computer) communication that prevails today. Personal messages, remote conferencing, and game playing were not what the original founders and sponsors of ARPANET had in mind. Their objectives had to do with computer resource sharing and packet switching.[13] What would they have thought of conference groups and MUDs? As ARPANET evolved into Internet, we found that what is often most important is that there is a person on the other end,[14] or at least the sense of a person.

Time sharing worked. It helped bring the computer nearer to people, and it gave rise to word processing and other innovations that would become extremely important in later years. A young faculty member at MIT, filled with enthusiasm for the new technology, wrote his talks and articles on a teletypewriter terminal in his Newton, Massachusetts living room. He was connected over switched phone lines to the time-shared computer at Project MAC, miles away.[15] That was heady stuff in 1964.

An analogy can be drawn with education. Thirty years ago, we were time sharing a mainframe computer with a bunch of terminals, like a teacher with a bunch of students in a classroom. Then we had a great breakthrough — the personal computer. Personal computers allowed people to sit and interact.[16] Today, we have the concept of distributed client-server computing. Nets and communication are the rage, and intelligence is dispersed from the center to the periphery. It raises interesting questions about the place of students. How will they rise to the challenge of these new technologies? What will they be able to do that they have never done before?[17] What should their job description be?

Personal computers came upon the scene in the 1970s. Within a decade, these useful desktop multi-purpose devices were gaining widespread popularity. IBM soon threw its weight behind the new arrivals, and the PC became a household word. The Apple and later Macintosh, equipment produced by an upstart rival, made a legend of Steve Jobs and his garage. The once formidable computer, like a machine with a mission, began appearing in unusual places, most notably the lives of ordinary people. On its now human scale, it was getting outright manageable.

Introduction of the PC was a giant leap forward and enormously liberating. But users had to relate to it primarily in machine terms. Spreadsheets and word processors were for certain much better than assembly language and COBOL, but they were not yet a comfortable technology for most people, like moms and dads for instance. Parents encouraged their children to become adept in a skill they may have considered beyond themselves, yet one they recognized was very important to the future. Computer literacy came to be regarded as an earmark of the educated person. In other words, people were still expected to adapt to the computer.

Taking Television to Task

In a different category were the increasing numbers of youths who were playing computer and video games for endless hours. They seemed to be wasting time. Worse, their intense absorption in fleeting images on the screen made them look like hopeless addicts, as far-gone as people glued to the TV. Interactive though it may be, the video game is not a joy to parents. Its very power over children makes it suspect. So does its astounding commercial success. The market for video games currently consists of one-third of U.S. households,[18] rivaling TV. In a sense, those in the video game business are also in the television business.[19]

Television forms the second part of the multimedia trilogy. It was already a major disappointment when multimedia came along. The promising technology that had been heralded with high hopes after World War II was being used more as a thought deadener than the mind expander it was supposed to be. Newton N. Minow struck a resonant chord when he spoke of a "vast wasteland" in his first public address as chairman of the Federal Communications Commission under President John F. Kennedy.[20] In the years since, the television set has been maligned as an "idiot box" and a "boob tube." Are executives in the television industry concerned? Some are; others not at all. The reason it's an idiot box, they demur, the reason it's a boob tube, is because the people are boobs.[21] They are couch potatoes. We're feeding them what they want.

Wait a second!. Not everyone is a couch potato. Some make channel cruising with the remote control a living-room sport, engaging in what a friend calls *interpassivity*. Others are not adverse to pressing the off button. Some don't watch TV at all (except possibly the Discovery Channel) and are proud of it. Significantly, non-viewers include members of the technological elite who are helping to bring to us the new interactive systems of the future.[22]

Not all members of the technological elite abstain. Three of them discuss their feelings about television. Says the first, a prominent game developer, "The big complaint when I was growing up was that we watched too much TV. We would sit and look at all the shows after school. Now the criticism is that kids play too much Sega and Nintendo."[23] Replies the second, unsympathetically, "We *did* watch too much TV, and video games are a plague."[24] Recalls the third, who considers himself a happy and productive member of society, "the whole time I was growing up, I was made to feel guilty about watching television four hours a day, as though I would turn out to be a drooling idiot. I suspect that the shoot-em-ups and fast-twitch games I keep hearing about are actually not that bad. They may be encouraging the children of our society to be interactive."[25] Unconvinced, the unsympathetic one quips, "You should have seen yourself if you hadn't watched so much TV."[26]

The average household has TV on six hours a day.[27] The average child spends four hours a day watching it. That's a hefty percentage of one's free time. The educational system in this country has changed enormously over the past generation because of women entering the workforce, single-parent families, and the use of television as a baby sitter.[28] We clearly need to pay close attention to what TV delivers, how it is consumed, and the role it plays in the development of children -- not to mention the effect it has on our own lives.

Interactivity — A Second Chance for TV

Promoting passivity is a major charge lodged against television, even though, as we have noted, not every viewer is a couch potato. Some viewers, in fact, get very actively involved, even finding an outlet for innovation and creativity. A case in point is the set of enthusiasts who write fiction about their favorite programs and characters, sharing their work with fellow aficionados. Consider Star Trek fans who take tapes of the old series, cut them up, and paste them together in new ways to create bizarre relationships and subplots never seen in the programs.[29] Their activity is low-tech, but it may be high in predictive value, an omen of the future.

An electronic form of video pasting, this one high-tech, was underway at the MIT Media Lab a half-dozen years ago. Some staff and students began digitizing video and working with video clips on their desktop computers.[30] MIT researchers had been experimenting with computer-controlled videodiscs since the late 1970s, their interest kindled by a project at IBM called Castle. The project began in Poughkeepsie in 1975-76. It was quite extraordinary. Steve Jobs hadn't even started work in his garage yet, and here was IBM building a real personal computer. The goal and strategy was to produce a transparent 12-inch floppy videodisc that followed the Bernoulli principle, with 10 hours of video stored in digital format.[31]

It was the dawning of the age of multimedia. Interest in the work at MIT spread to Apple, Voyager, and a growing number of other organizations. The goal was to use the computer to combine, manipulate, and package multiple media, taking advantage of the large silvery 54,000-image videodiscs starting to become available. These discs were in analog, not digital format. The first ten went to the FBI and CIA. The eleventh, the first one outside the classified community, came to MIT.[32]

Videotapes of work done in those days would look very similar to some of what is being done today, says an MIT pioneer, but "the mixing of audio, video, and data is not what multimedia is about.

It couldn't be less relevant. What multimedia is about is being digital. I bang my head on the wall and ask why it took us fifteen years to understand that. The FCC over the next five years is going to have dyspepsia because of what it means to be digital. We used to be able to point to parts of the spectrum and say, that's video, that's voice. Not anymore. It's all bits now, and bits are bits. What was done then, even though it looks on the surface like what people are doing today, was very, very different."[33]

Audio and video were brought into the digital fold gradually over a period of years, first with the highly successful audio CD, then with video digitizing boards, CD-ROMs, and a number of extended CD formats. Once video was residing in the computer with audio, graphics, and text, it was very natural to put it under user control. Work in that direction has been burgeoning.

The story of multimedia now takes on a new wrinkle. It could be the start of a magical love affair, where the TV enchantress brings fun and feeling to the life of the computer whiz, and he, in turn, brings thought and reason to her being. In the storybook version of this idealized romance, both grow; each benefits; both lead fuller lives; each becomes more desirable.

Or, it could turn out another way. Isadora Duncan, founder of modern dance and a pioneering feminist, preferred having children out of wedlock to entering into the restrictions of matrimony. She supposedly proposed to George Bernard Shaw that they have a child together, suggesting that with her body and his brains, it was sure to be a superb human being. Shaw, the curmudgeon, is said to have replied ungraciously that the child could instead have his body and her brains."[34] Might a similar fate await the offspring of TV and computer? Could each bring out the worst in the other?

On a more mundane level, the liaison with TV and the arrival of multimedia in full regalia can be considered the latest step in the computer's becoming more friendly and approachable -- more people-like. Fifty million personal computers were sold last year, four times as many in number as TV sets. The personal computer is becoming the hottest-selling piece of consumer electronic equipment in history.[35]

In truth, 1993 may be remembered as the year multimedia finally made it. There were approximately 7 million personal computers equipped with CD-ROM drives and soundboards at the end of 1993,[36] a year that saw widespread acceptance of CD-ROM technology, with over 4 million CD-ROM players shipped and an additional 8 million units forecast for 1994.[37] There are over 5,000 multimedia titles in development right now. Multimedia software sales in the fourth quarter of 1993 were $104 million. Hundreds of millions of dollars are being invested in this industry segment by the federal government, state and local governments, industry, venture capitalists, and investment plans.[38]

Will the multimedia PC be the avenue to the information highway, or will the primary interface be a computerized TV set? Knowledgeable people give contrary answers to the question. Some see it as the wrong question to ask, and give no credence to either position. They view the PC and its evolution, and the TV and its evolution, as ultimately co-equal partners. They believe that broadband networks will bring interactive services to both PCs and TVs. They do not think the two platforms will converge.[39]

An important part of the New World vision is the prospect that interactive multimedia will inject fresh vitality into the lives of couch potatoes, that video games will become a means for learning useful knowledge, and that no social or demographic group will be excluded from the joys and benefits of the new medium. Listen to one video game maker who wants to cultivate a significant new mass market. He is looking for ways to apply the video game technique to attract kids to use the technology for educational content. He also wants to expand the demographics. About 30 percent of his current audience is 6 to 12 years old, 30 percent is 12 to 18, 40 percent is over 18, and 80 percent is male. "This is where games now work," he notes. "There's a gold mine if we can find a way to embrace the rest of the spectrum. It's a huge potential market. If we can find the answer, we would instantly double our business. It's the big challenge."[40]

Content, Communication, and Control

Such are the hopes, social and entrepreneurial, for a new kind of content, taking full advantage of the technology, investing the user with control that is empowering, enjoyable, and uplifting. Some content can derive from the communication itself. Content is key.

A skeptic shakes his head. "Combining new technology and venture capital always seems to cause people to lose their minds. Nowhere else can someone get up at a conference and say, it's going to be about content, and get a round of applause. If you went to a bookseller's convention and said, we've determined that it's not the bindings, nor the packaging, nor the distribution, but the content that's going to drive this business, you'd be considered some sort of moron. *Of course*, it's about story. *Of course*, it's about touching people's hearts and opening their minds, by all of the tools and techniques that we've developed to do this over thousands of years of storytelling. The embarrassment of interactivity now is that it's a solution in search of a problem."[41]

So, how do we find the solution, or in the lingo, how do we identify a *killer application*? Let's brainstorm. Quickly give me your single best suggestion for future content, directs a top venture capitalist. Provide me with a blow-away idea that ought to be tried. Answers come in rapid-fire. Access to last Sunday's *60 Minutes*. A child reviewing past shows to do a paper on the Pharaohs of Egypt. Mystery services that nobody can be sure of (except for video-on-demand). Then come more adventuresome ideas: virtual community; intelligent television through interactive networks; interactive archeology; the videophone as a peripheral to the PC; interactive foreign languages; interactive history; confession and prayer (and penance); interactive government; interactive simulation. Finally, the questioner gives his own best answer: an interactive cancer channel to find out more about the dreaded disease and get helpful consultation. An associate adds a postscript on a lighter note: *karaoke*, the equivalent of singing in the shower, an application requiring privacy.[42]

The wonderful thing about the computer, with its images, sounds, text and interactions, is that it allows us to make all sorts of things. It's like a lego kit. Multimedia excels at handling different kinds of forms. What forms do we have? We have stories. What else? We can have surrogate travel, where a place becomes the organizing function. We can have a resource model.[43] And, of course, we can have games.

Games have been around for as long as stories. Games are not about exposition, conflict, and resolution. They are about competition, mastery, and winning or losing. The pleasure comes from winning. Look at what human beings like to do. Solitaire is fun, but gin is more fun, and poker's even more fun. It's no surprise that multiplayer games represent the top-selling video games of all time. The next step is network games. Ten years down the road, that's where it will be.[44]

Some say it's already there. Group play is so much more compelling than solitary play. People interact not with machines, but with people through machines. They want a personal experience. The greatest games in the world — chess, monopoly, Go — are just vehicles to understand the other person. Ultimately, games will do that in an interactive world.[45] More generally, interactive services will be an excuse to meet and socialize. They will be places that real people can visit together.

So, what is the killer application of the nineties? Simple, we are told. It's people![46]

The Next Chapters

This has been a start at the story of multimedia, but let's be honest. It's a biased and very personal account. It's the perspective of one who has lived the last four decades in and out of the computer trenches. The story would be very different if told by someone who lived those same years in the field of communications, consumer electronics, movie and television production, music, art, graphic design, entertainment, education, or publishing, all fields in which the emergence and impact of multimedia are being keenly felt -- often in dissimilar ways. Everyone interprets what's happening in personal terms. Every author has a *point of view*.[47]

Point of view is a familiar concept in literature and the movies. It is potentially even more important in interactive multimedia. The new technology is able to give each reader and viewer the ability to examine, experience, and shift between many points of view, all within the same environment, all under the person's own spontaneous control. It is also able to present the same point of view in different ways, using a variety of media.

If we were to guess at the elements that will be critical to the future of multimedia, *point of view* would be one, *control* would be another, and *communication* among people would be a third. On the same list of sure bets would be the *storytelling, mystery solving*, and *game playing* alluded to throughout this mosaic.

While on the subject of mysteries and mosaics, we should note the stunning success being enjoyed by the multimedia CD-ROM title *Myst*, and to *Mosaic*, the multimedia browser over the World Wide Web on the Internet. These two success stories carry with them lessons for the future.

If our story has a moral, it is this. The future will evolve in ways we can only dimly perceive today. The one thing we can be sure of is that we are likely to be wrong on some of the most important aspects, and will probably skirt some of the most difficult issues. Certain problems will be left to take care of themselves, or be bequeathed to later generations, along with the benefits.

We cannot leave the future entirely to evolution. Evolution solves problems, but it's hard to tell what problems it's going to solve and how.[48] Despite the perils of prediction, we must persist in our attempts to anticipate, plan, modify, and control.

Control, like content, is key. Thus encouraged and forewarned, read on reader, and decide the future for yourself.

Notes

[1] This chapter makes a start at telling the story of multimedia by placing a series of statements in patterned relation to one another. That's the *mosaic.* The statements are taken from the discussions in subsequent chapters of the book. The footnotes below indicate the chapter in which each of the statements appears, but not who made the statement. That's the *mystery.* Readers are challenged to fill in the names as they read through the book. That's the *game.* Multimedia must always have a game. We don 't know how the story will end. That's the *suspense.* But we do have a hint. The fundamental elements of *story, mystery, suspense,* and *game,* along with a top-selling CD-ROM called *Myst,* and a graphical browser on the Internet called *Mosaic,* are all playing important roles in the development of multimedia. That's the clue. After that, it's *point of view.*

[2] Chapter 2.

[3] Chapter 5.

[4] Chapter 8.

[5] Chapter 6.

[6] Chapter 8.

[7] Philip Elmer-DeWitt, "Take a Trip into the Future on the Electronic Superhighway," *Time* cover story, April 12, 1993, p. 50.

[8] Paul Farhi and Sandra Sugawara, "Hurdles Slow Information 'Superhypeway', *Washington Post,* April 7, 1994.

[9] MAC had a third unofficial meaning. *Maximum Assembly of Components* was an irreverent allusion to the fact that the project was a lavish user of hardware by the standards of the day.

[10] Chapter 4.

[11] John McCarthy, "Time-Sharing Computer Systems," in *Computers and the World of the Future,* Martin Greenberger, ed., MIT Press, 1962, p. 236.

[12] Martin Greenberger, "Computers of Tomorrow," *Atlantic Monthly,* April 1964.

[13] Robert E. Kahn, "Status and Plans for the ARPANET," in Martin Greenberger et al., *Networks for Research and Education: Sharing Computer and Information Resources Nationwide,* MIT Press, 1974, pages 51-54.

[14] Chapter 2.

[15] An amused visitor christened the wooden booth I built to soundproof the clacking terminal an "orgone box."

[16] Chapter 4.

[17] Chapter 3.

[18] Chapter 5.

[19] Chapter 5.

[19] Chapter 5.
[20] Newton N. Minow, "The Vast Wasteland," Address to the National Association of Broadcasters, Washington, D.C., May 9, 1961. See, also, Minow's speech on the thirtieth anniversary of the 1961 address, "How Vast the Wasteland Now?", Gannett Foundation Media Center, Columbia University, New York, May 9, 1991.
[21] Chapter 2.
[22] Chapter 6.
[23] Chapter 5.
[24] Chapter 5.
[25] Chapter 5.
[26] Chapter 5.
[27]Chapter 6.
[28] Chapter 3.
[29] Chapter 2.
[30] I had a thoroughly absorbing year working with Hans Peter Brondmo and Glorianna Davenport on digital video and *micons* while on research sabbatical at the MIT Media Lab in 1988-89.
[31] Chapter 4.
[32] Chapter 4.
[33] Chapter 4.
[34] An account of the exchange in the *Oxford Dictionary of Modern Quotations* refers to the woman as "a strange lady giving an address in Zurich." Other accounts specifically identify her as Isadora Duncan. Isadora and the rest of the Duncans were certainly not mentally deficient. Maybe Shaw was alluding to her views, not her mind.
[35] Chapter 2.
[36] Chapter 2.
[37] Chapter 2.
[38] Chapter 3.
[39] Chapter 6.
[40] Chapter 5.
[41] Chapter 5.
[42] Chapter 6.
[43] Chapter 2.
[44] Chapter 5.
[45] Chapter 5.
[46] Chapter 2.
[47] Chapter 7.
[48] Chapter 4.

It's a super-session of an opener for the Fifth Anniversary Roundtable in Multimedia, running six hours, with three moderators, six reviewers, and fifteen presenters. The presenters, in order of appearance, are Robert Abel, Burt Arnowitz, Scott Billups, Chuck Cortright, Steve Floyd, Claude Leglise, Jim Olson, Kristina Woolsey, Pavel Curtis, Stanley Frank, Bill Birrell, Frank Foster, Bill Gross, Hal Josephson, and Bob Stein. They discuss their work, comment on how multimedia is evolving, and speculate on future directions in the nature and creation of content.

It's a session in which the three moderators, David Bunnell, Lucie Fjeldstad, and Max Whitby pass the baton quickly to one another in a valiant effort to win the race with the clock. The scrappy reviewers, Stewart Alsop, Brenda Laurel. George Gilder, Donald Norman, Harry Wilker, and David Liddle question, critique, support, challenge, and help to illuminate the points of the presenters.

It's a session in which content is king, and the emperor is thought at times to be wearing no clothes. Kristina Woolsey brings up the familiar dichotomy of technology-driven versus market-driven content. Is the point of a piece to exploit technology or satisfy the consumer? She turns it into a trinity, adding design-driven content -- working to accomplish an identified objective. Pavel Curtis moves the discussion into the fourth dimension with socially-driven content, meaning communication among interacting people. Bob Stein adds still another dimension with editorially-driven content, use of the new media to help authors give expression to their ideas.

It's a session of caustic social criticism combined with a down-to-earth consideration of costs. Lamentations on the failure of the new media to contribute meaningfully to a thinking society (a theme echoed later in the Roundtable by James Billington) are followed by lamentations on the spiraling costs of production. Rising costs seem to contradict George

Gilder's contention that improving cost effectiveness will greatly broaden the production base, transforming the mass market into unlimited niche markets and leading to a new age in quality, choice, and satisfaction. Gilder's thesis is based on the model of the book business; his antithesis is TV. The place of text and the value of the book come up again and again in the discussion.

It's a session of striking contrasts and intriguing similarities. Stan Frank espouses the strategy of repurposing content, noting how much is available in the libraries of the world for underlying databases, and how expensive it is to "start from scratch." Bill Gross is equally insistent on doing just that, starting from scratch to develop wholly original material. Both men view what they are doing as adding value.

Finally, it's a session in which technology is cut to the knees by a series of equipment problems, as if to confirm the supremacy of content over technique, mind over matter. Fault is found with the large number of videotapes used by presenters, a style which some regard as an affront to the worth of interactive media, just as Kristina Woolsey acknowledges she once felt the use of a printed book in a multimedia product was a sign of defeat. Given the session's technological travails, those who choose the safe videotape route, as it turns out, are the lucky ones. They get to show what they intended. Multimedia pioneer par excellence Robert Winter is unable to show anything at all, except in private presentations from his laptop.

Like an evening ballgame that runs into extra innings, the session is prodigiously long. The late hour, adding to equipment frustrations, puts some players in a foul mood. The next morning, after a restless night of post-mortem, I apologize publicly to those directly affected (all of whom are personal friends) and to Max Whitby, who ably bears the brunt of the disarray as wrap-up moderator.

In summary, it's a session of content and discontent,[1] of fervent hope and mild despair. The Roundtable is resilient. With ups and downs, it moves on, participants joining forces to continue to push this promising field forward. Rolling with the competitive punches and skimming over the little episodes occurring now and then to liven things up, the participants work together, applying the technology to create a better world, better for their children and grandchildren, better for themselves. That's the wonder of this technology. It's developing so quickly that we should reap the harvest in our own time. What more elevating goal than that the fruit of our labor be sweet and unspoiled?

Robert Abel

Showing a video of his work on the human heart, Bob Abel speaks out on the need to go beyond what has been done with past media to take full advantage of the new technology.

We've come a long way since the First Roundtable. Lucie Fjeldstad and I were talking in the lobby about how remote things seemed four years ago, shortly before I started the *Columbus* project for IBM. If there is a secret for success, it is to make this medium different. The natural inclination is to move towards previous media rather than beyond, as with movies on-demand and electronic shopping. We must ask ourselves, as creators, what we can do to produce an experience that takes us further.

I started to do multimedia as soon as I got interested in it, rightly or wrongly. I made mistakes, and did some good things along the way. I learned not to make promises. Things are not what they seem to be, either on the superhighway or in the newspapers. They are subject to change. We live in an era of inevitable change. The greatest changes happen at the end of a century, particularly at the end of a millennium. And here we are at the end of the 20th century.

After six projects, I decided this past year that the best way to learn, as Stanley Kubrick said a long time ago, is to go out and ask a lot of dumb questions, hopefully coming up with some very smart answers. I went to the Library of Congress, where *Columbus* is permanently installed, watched people and talked with them. I never identified myself as having had anything to do with the project. I was like Lawrence of Arabia.

As I went through a variety of different areas, looking at art, medicine, education, business, and business-to-business, walking into places I normally would never go, I would ask in each case how they saw their field evolving. If I could get them to talk about their goals, I had a good shot at giving a creative assist. If I did not ask that question, I didn't have a chance. I met with frustration in many cases. We come from different backgrounds and see the corporate world at the end of the 20th century from different points of view. It is ironic that we have a communications gap in this era of so-called "convergence."

My rule of thumb on content is that it should be like something people have never seen before. By content, I don't mean art for art's sake. I mean 3D navigational capabilities, interfaces, and tools going beyond the normal PC paradigm. I mean working with teams of people on the words, sound, pictures, navigation, and interface, having partners who are building boxes and systems at the back end, while we are working on the front end. There are many parts. Society has not had to come together this much since the second industrial revolution at the end of the 19th century. We have to look beyond the technology. We have to look at a society in change, one that cannot go back, a society that has problems in education, drugs, gangs, crime, learning, training, jobs, economics. That's a lot to chew on for the coming year. It will be interesting to see where we are by the next Roundtable.

My company's work on the heart came out of rejection. In *Columbus*, we learned about *threshold guardians*, people who reject a good idea at first. We need the tenacity to stay with it. The Mayo Clinic was one of our many clients. The job we did for the Clinic was on the human heart. Seventy million Americans have heart disease. My father died of heart disease when I was very young. I asked the Clinic, "What are we doing to make the invisible visible?" I sat in the living room of a doctor who told me that he could set back heart disease. I was his student. He was my mentor. I told him I could make his vision.

I wanted to do a computer movement in 3D graphics. I haven't done computer graphics in eight years, but I had Indigo machines and friends in San Gabriel who could do it on weekends. The Mayo Clinic said it was not necessary. I replied that we would do it at cost — below cost! The Clinic said, "Just bring the book to life." So, we brought the book to life, but in our own way.

Stewart Alsop

I assume you used a lot of computers to produce your work on the human heart, but how is it interactive?

Robert Abel

In everything we do, we try to create an overview or context. In this case, the context is the healthy human heart. The challenge is to make clicking on a picture or icon the interface. If the problem is restricted capillaries, or a defective pulmonary valve, click on that.

You don't have to return to an environment of windows and still pictures. The way our new software works, all the videos are entrance points. You can dip in at any point without having to go back.

Brenda Laurel
Suppose I click on the ventricle during the animation?

Robert Abel
You get information related or linked to the ventricle, such as alternatives for treating the problem — surgery, medication, diet, preventive measures. The medical profession cannot treat everyone. People want to find out how they can begin to care for themselves with excercise, yoga, meditation, health, and nutrition. That's in there too.

Brenda Laurel
Is it in text, or are there experts talking in various media?

Robert Abel
There are experts talking in various media. Anyone who has had a serious illness will regard spending a half hour with the doctor as vital time, but may be almost too scared to listen. Knowledge is power. Now that we have digital video, what should we do with it? What we should do with it is make it possible to stop the news or video going by at 30 frames a second to see different points of view. This gets back to doing things with this medium that we could not do with prior media.

Stewart Alsop
What you're suggesting is that while the video is playing and I'm listening to the audio, I have the power to stop it at any point. The

video I'm watching is the result of some action I had taken in interacting with this health product.

Robert Abel
Right. There might be a reference to the healthy heart that relates to a problem you have. You click on it. The program recognizes shapes as well as concepts, even the context and the way you went about getting there. Did you go there first? Did you go there last? Did you fast forward through the first part?

Stewart Alsop
What form will this heart product take? Will it be on laserdisc?

Robert Abel
This gets down to a very basic question. We're looking at digital CD-ROMs and wondering if the laserdisc is still a valid medium. I don't think we need it anymore, except in a kiosk — an often-overlooked possibility. The idea is to put this information into digital form and get it out to the maximum number of people. Michael Schulhof of Sony, in describing the success of the Walkman, said most people know what they need, but not what they want. It's the role of the creative person to help people find out what they want, what will make their lives better.

Stewart Alsop
Although your works on Picasso's *Guernica* and on *Columbus* were startling, not many people could get access to them because they required so much equipment.

Robert Abel
I know. It was not a mistake; it was a reality. Having faced that reality, we determined to learn how to overcome the limitation.

Stewart Alsop

So we're going to see *Heart* from Bob Abel in an Egghead store soon?

Robert Abel

I hope so. And in other forms — DBS, you name it. We're trying to understand the limitations and strengths of each of the delivery systems.

David Bunnell

Before moving on to the next presentation, let me just say that I don't think the information highway is going to happen through the television set. It will happen, and is happening, through the computer. Fifty million personal computers were sold last year, four times as many in number as TV sets. We fail to recognize that the largest-selling consumer electronic device of all time is the personal computer, not the TV.

Burt Arnowitz

Burt Arnowitz reviews the evolution of multimedia from the perspective of his own company's creative output, while showing a video of a new suite of biology curriculum products called Concepts of Biology.

Arnowitz Studios created the first multimedia instructional system to be adopted in lieu of a textbook. Called *Computer Visions*, it has taken over 70 percent of the target market (90 percent in urban areas). Another one of our products, *The Animals*, has sold over a million units since it was introduced a year and a half ago — 85 percent being in OEM bundles. We are pleased with this commercial acceptance, yet still consider the main measure of our success the richness, depth, and quality of what we create.

Our overall design strategy calls for construction of a platform-independent digital asset, a *knowledge base*, that forms products for the current CD-ROM market as well as the future interactive television market. As an example, *Daring To Fly: From Icarus to the Red Baron*, is volume one in a series about the history of flight. Each volume will be delivered as a CD, but when we are done, all three products will exist in one knowledge base that can be accessed from the home through a video server on the information superhighway (or whatever it ends up being called).

We are using our design tools and knowledge-based templates for both the consumer and educational markets. This June we're delivering a suite of multimedia high-school biology curriculum products called *Concepts of Biology*. On a template that can be replicated, we created a multimedia resource that includes 2,700 illustrations, simulations with variable inputs and outputs, digital laboratories, and four hours of highly edited video material. Teachers can make multimedia lesson plans easily, and students can create their own multimedia presentations. The product line fulfills technology requirements in the classroom at multiple levels, and accommodates different teaching and learning styles. Teachers can use four laserdiscs with a teacher's guide as a resource, or four CD-ROMs, each containing all of the digital labs, digital renditions of the videotapes, simulations, and custom tools.

David Bunnell
With this in the classroom, can you get away from dissecting frogs?

Burt Arnowitz
That seems to be an issue. There isn't a dissection feature for squeamish people, but the product is designed to enhance wet labs in a normal biology curriculum. Dangerous or impossible things,

like environmental impacts over time, can be simulated in digital labs. The product can also be tied into field research and integrated with traditional labs.

David Bunnell
Isn't a teacher's showing a laserdisc on a television screen in front of class a different experience from the students' having computers on their desks and going through the software at their own pace?

Burt Arnowitz
Very much so. The trick is to design something that works on all levels, since there are not computers on everyone's desk in the classroom. We regard the laserdisc project as just a toe in the water. The same laserdiscs work with the full digital product. The software is delivered on a CD-ROM, which can contain the entire product or be used by the teacher to control a laserdisc presentation. This is not a video course. The laserdiscs are only for what they do best — illuminating and illustrating the instruction.

Brenda Laurel
How constrained do you feel by curriculum-based requirements and the vicissitudes of the adoption process? Is it a negative, or does it force greater creativity, in your view?

Burt Arnowitz
Well, it's a reality. We did the *Computer Visions* product for an adoption in the state of Texas. We had to satisfy very specific instructional and technological objectives. We started with a textbook, ended up throwing it out, then wrote the instructions ourselves, designing the pedagogy in an integrated-media instructional product that best fulfilled the possibilities of the technology. We took it on as a challenge. As long as we supported

the requirements of the curriculum, people could take or leave what we added.

The biology product was different. Holt, the publisher, really owns the market for high-school biology textbooks. It has very good books. We took four of its books, from general level to major level, and integrated the curricula in the product so there is a whole range of instruction designed with multimedia in mind. We did not take the curricula and say, "How are we going to add a picture to this little chunk in the textbook?" The textbook was just part of what we drew from to make the integrated product.

Brenda Laurel
Do you see a future where networking capabilites are integrated in such a way that students talk with each other and create a kind of content themselves, or do you feel the future of interactivity is still just allowing people to pick which part of the fire hose to drink from?

Burt Arnowitz
Holt is selling the product to teachers as the coolest way to manage resources, whereas our research tells us that 80 percent of the classroom use is by kids. They use these products much more than teachers. There's a misunderstanding of how these products will be utilized.

Everything we create can be networked. The *knowledge base* is a multimedia database, separate from the platform-specific code that addresses it. We're working now on a project about environmental science and environmental issues that will use the same template, but hook to a database on the Internet, allowing for collaborative classrooms all over the world, exactly what you're talking about.

Stewart Alsop

Burt, your background is video, Bob Abel's background is video, and Scott Billups, the next one up, has video in his foreground as well as his background. It seems thematic to have three of you in a row. You tend to default to projects that require a lot of machinery to support. What is the difference between doing really good video and really good interactive media?

Burt Arnowitz

Video is only part of the equation. The reason so many people with professional communications skills get into interactive multimedia is that if you come at it the other way, as a software programmer with a good application or technology, the key component is missing. Making multimedia requires collaboration. It can't come just from a television producer, or graphic designer, or software programmer. Everyone is involved. Still, it is the communication and production skills that give multimedia the professionalism and engagement that get people to use it, providing the look and feel that make for successful products.

Kenneth Silverman

You mentioned that 85 percent of the million units sold of *The Animals* went out bundled. As a publisher, what kinds of dollars do you see when a CD-ROM is bundled rather than being sold in individual units? What are the sales of a good-selling CD-ROM?

Burt Arnowitz

I've worn two hats. We created and produced the *The Animals*, but it was published by Software Toolworks, which paid for the production. We have a royalty interest in the product, but not much control over how it is sold. Bundled products usually bring in anywhere from $1 to $5, though *The Animals* can command $3 to $15 because of its richness. Wholesale it might take in $35.

As a publisher, we now have two products coming out under our own label: *Daring To Fly: From Icarus to the Red Baron*, and *Coral Reef: The Vanishing Undersea World*. These products are being distributed through Maxis, with whom we have an affiliate label deal. Our take-home, when everything is said and done, is about $12 to $13 per title. For purposes of business planning, we believe that 30,000 to 35,000 units would be a pretty good sell, but because of the explosion in the market, and based on Maxis' sales projections, it looks like the titles may do something over 60,000 units each on Mac and Windows platforms.

The good news is that the market is exploding. The bad news is that everyone knows this and is rushing to make product. There should be an important shakeout over the next few years.

Scott Billups

Scott Billups makes a pitch for the supremacy of storytelling, communication, and methodology. They are what make the real difference, in his view, even in this age of dazzling digital technologies.

I don't believe technology is capable of replacing methodology. There's a lot of hype out there. Right at the top is *multimedia* and *superhighway*. I don't believe any of it. It's bunk. I don't think there's anything new other than gradual innovation. I see nothing different in computer-aided production. Nothing is improving the way a story is told. A good story well told is a good story well told, whether told a thousand years ago or with a computer.

Some of the best interactive storytelling I ever experienced was when I was 5 and 6 years old. My dad was a Baptist preacher in West Virginia. He did two sermons on Saturdays and three on Sundays. As an only child, I had to go, because my mom played the organ. But they didn't require me to sit through all those sermons. I could play around the church. It was the one church in a very poor little coal mining community. There was an old guy there who could not stand being in buildings. He had lived his entire life outdoors. But he was a religious man. He would get his religion by osmosis, sitting on the porch of the church in a rocking chair. He could hear the singing, and that was enough religion for him. And he would tell me stories each Sunday. Every story started exactly the same way. I loved this man. If I looked off, the story would take a bend. If I got interested or excited, he'd develop that. I never heard the same story twice.

I have yet to see a multimedia title that can match him. *Multimedia entertainment* and *interactive multimedia* are oxymorons. The production process is a basic process. When I was a groveling intern for a cinematographer by the name of James Wong Howe in the early 1970s, I cut mats and backwound film in his Mitchell so that he could do composite plates. Now I do that on a computer. Even though I have some nifty tools, I don't see any real difference. All this ancillary mechanism that's starting to emerge is just a natural progression of the everyday production process.

The only difference is that the cost factor is down, so now anyone can come in and create bad content. The production community has traditionally been a very cloistered environment, replete with guilds and secret lingo. Anyone can now walk in and be part of it. There's a sense of power. Let's face it, communication is one of the most powerful forces on the face of the earth. It's what brought down Communism. The common man is now able to participate, due to the cost factor, not due to technology replacing methodology. The downside of many more voices having access to media is that we have a lot of bad media. The upside is that people who do understand conventional production methodology can now kick some heavy butt.

What I'm saying is that all this stuff that seems new and spectacular is really the same old thing. It's just a natural progression of the production process. Don't get swept away by the hype. There's no way a computer is going to turn you into an eloquent orator or improve your ability to write. It might do some spell checking for you, but it's not going to make you create a better script or help your resolution. A story has a beginning, a middle, and an end. The computer is not going to assist there either.

I represent the small studio — myself! It's just me, sitting at a computer with many friends out there. I'm involved in production on two major motion pictures with a cumulative budget of well over $40 million, three major theme parks, and a project for Nintendo. Last month, we created three titles for Acclaim, one of which had already raised $500,000 before it was released for production as a CD-ROM.

Do I think CD-ROM is cool? No, it's the 8-track of the digital age. Flashcards are two million times faster than CD-ROM. Two million times faster! CD-ROM is old technology, but it's one many people can grasp, so it's a viable production environment. It's a production tool. It teaches people how to communicate and set up structure. That's what's important. It teaches people how to organize their thoughts and communicate. It all gets down to communication.

Stewart Alsop
You never heard the same story twice from your old friend, and you have never seen anything as interactive as his storytelling. Have you seen anything on CD-ROM, aside from what you produced, that you thought was good?

Scott Billups
I didn't say that I thought what I produced was good. People came to me with wheelbarrows of money and asked me to please do this for them, and I did. That's my role as a production facility.

Stewart Alsop
So you haven't seen anything you think is good? There are titles out there like *Tuneland* and *The Living Book Series* from Bruderbund.

Scott Billups
I think some of the best attempts are represented by people in this room. The three best attempts I can think of, as a matter of fact, all come from people here.

Stewart Alsop
What would they be?

Scott Billups
I think Robert Abel has forged a path. He's out front and easy to take shots at, and we've all taken some good shots at him, but I doubt there's anyone else in the market that's pioneered as much as he has. Bob Stein, sitting in the back, has taken another area of the market, defined it, and developed a degree of sophistication on which we can all lean. As far as a single title that really communicates well, Robert Winter has done some spectacular stuff. That's my personal opinion.

Brenda Laurel
You say nothing has changed. I was talking the other day to Henry Jenkins from MIT who wrote a book called *Textual Poachers*.[2] He studies fan culture. Star Trek fans take tapes of the old series, cut them up, and paste them together in new ways to create bizarre relationships and subplots never seen in the programs. They do this with very low technology, VCR to VCR. Paramount, who owns these characters, hates it.

Your storyteller on the porch didn't own his stories and didn't copyright them, right? If he was telling weird stories about Mickey Mouse, Disney would have come and taken him away in a big truck. Stories were more interactive in the old days, because no one owned the material. People were able to rework it and share it back and forth in different ways. It may be true that many more people have access to production facilities now, as you say, but it seems to me that the privileged voice of the owners of story material and characters enforces an asymmetry. I wonder if the ownership of these intellectual properties can withstand the growing ability to produce things cheaply and quickly.

Scott Billups
It all comes down to the fact that the production environment is not as important as the ability to tell a story. Originality of thought, and being able to take a concept, develop it, and communicate it to another person is what's important. How we do it is irrelevant.

Doreen Nelson
I'm a professor working in the area of teacher training and school reform who sees the university as an enormous culprit in not focusing on methodology. I love what you said about technology not being able to replace methodology. I also love Brenda's

comment about the Star Trek fans who are able to cut and paste. There's something wondrous about that. As I look at your work, and at the things I'm starting to see today, I think about *success* in the context of social responsibility. You seem to have a lot of fun doing your work.

Scott Billups
Way too much. I get paid too much money to have way too much fun.

Doreen Nelson
I think that when kids can have lots of fun, like the kids Brenda was talking about, then we are providing a methodology with the technology, and it is really going somewhere. How do you think we educators and people in media can start to think together about social responsibility?

Scott Billups
For me, the whole gestalt of life is to create. Either we create or we hate. The more that people are in a mode of creation, the less they are in a mode of hate. Yet techno-weenies and computer-centrics trying to tell stories always end up with blood, guts, and sex. "Blow it up. Kill 'em. See some titties." It's all garbage, with few exceptions. The people who can tell a good story and know how to develop stories are just coming into their own with this technology. We're going to see some great content, but we'll also see a lot of garbage.

I work with Saban, not necessarily high quality, but very popular. They produce the Mighty Morphing Power Rangers, retrofitted old violent Japanese footage. But, "it sells," they tell me. The ceiling on the market is 12 year-olds. They want to expand the market.

"Okay," I say, "let's do it this way. Let's actually try to get some content in there." I'm not going to change them. I'm not going to change the whole format of the show. But I am going to be a positive force. That's all I can do — tweak things more to the positive.

Charles Cortright

Charles Cortright demonstrates an interactive music compact disc by the artist "formerly know as Prince." The disc is soon to be released.

Graphix Zone is a little company that has been doing marketing services, road shows, and seminars during the last five years for clients like IBM, Apple, Sony, Creative Labs, Intel, and Microsoft. We travel the world as a kind of unbiased-appearing evangelist for these companies. Two years ago, 17 of our 32 employees started in the business of interactive CD-ROM title development. We targeted the niche of entertainment/music. As we look at future prospects, we think entertainment titles are going to be at the top, especially when they are merged with a challenge and a game to produce a compelling journey.

The hardest part is finding the content. That's what we've been doing for the last year. Our initial product, to be announced in June, is based on Prince, a Warner Brothers artist. Warner Brothers and Paisley Park Enterprises, Prince's company in Minnesota, are our partners in this. It's the first of about five titles for this level of entertainer that we will be pumping out in the next 12 to 18 months.[3] Prince changed his name to a symbol last June, a sort of composite symbol that combines those for male and female. The title is a five to ten hour journey through a virtual symbol with different kinds of rooms.

There will be a lot of ambient sound in the finished product. The disc is a hybrid. It will run on the PC, Windows, Macintosh, and an audio red book player. Most of the renderings were done in Autodesk's 3-D Studio. Many are based on the Paisley facility in Minnesota. The graphics were done with Adobe and Electric Image products. There are secret passageways and hidden clues to be found. We deliberately did not put in any text other than the content itself. We did not want to say, click here, start playing music, stop here, play a video. We wanted it to be compelling.

There are eleven different rooms: a CD room, a music video room where you can watch videos, and a video challenge room with four full-length MTV Prince movies that are descrambled in the wrong order. The challenge, or the game, is to get them back in the right order. There are over 1,000 different views, quite a few animations, about 32 minutes of video, and a lot of 16-bit audio. It will be on the shelves June 7, Prince's birthday.[4]

Stewart Alsop
Are you publishing it yourself?

Charles Cortright
Yes, Graphix Zone is publishing it. The content is licensed and copyrighted from Warner Brothers Records and Paisley Park.

Stewart Alsop
I think it's a great title. I hope you'll send me a copy. It struck me as very similar in feel to *Myst*.[5] There isn't any overlap in designer though, is there?

Charles Cortright
No overlap.

Brenda Laurel
To do a title like this in the future, is there a need for new musical content produced specifically for the interactive format, or are you just repurposing songs that have already been recorded?

Charles Cortright
Prince has recorded a brand new hit song for this title called *Interactive*, to be launched at the same time. Prince is leading-edge. He sees this as a new medium. He'll be followed by many others, although some of the recording studios are cautious about this market because of the content issue you hit upon earlier. They want to make sure they stay in control.

Stewart Alsop
Scott Billups made a reference to computer nerds producing terrible content. As a computer guy, you have an unlikely background for growing a company that's dealing with a symbol. This may be an impolite question, but Prince has credibility and credentials as a creative artist. What do you bring to the party?

Charles Cortright
It's a good question. What we did in a completely unrelated business is what drew Warner Brothers Records and Paisley Park to us a year ago when they were looking for someone to develop this project. Luckily, I have some very creative ponytailed people working for me. We impressed them. We were very fortunate to land this. We now have three similar titles in development.

Stewart Alsop
Burt Arnowitz did not answer my question before on what makes interactivity different from other media, like video? Maybe you can, as a computer nerd.

Charles Cortright
It's because I'm not forced to sit down and watch something go from start to beginning.[6] I make the choice. I can go in whatever direction I want. I can look at what I want to see, and I can listen in a completely different way.

Stewart Alsop
But that means your story doesn't have a beginning, a middle, and an end.

Charles Cortright
That's right.

Brenda Laurel
It's music. It doesn't have to.

David Bunnell
What's the point of this product? I've seen so many adventure games where you go from room to room, and click on different objects to make things happen. It doesn't seem that new or particularly interesting to me, except that Prince is involved. What is new about it?

Charles Cortright
I didn't want to give too much away, but this is a journey for which you need to pick up certain clues along the way. At the end, there's a dome. Inside the dome is a lot of new Prince content. To get access to the dome, which might take from five to ten hours, you must pick up clues and bring certain items with you. As I said earlier, we wanted a title that was both entertaining, through music and video, and also challenging as a game. There is a payoff at the end.

Bruce Polichar
I want to ask Brenda about the interface. It seems to have a fluidity to it that is different from most of what I've seen. You've talked and written in a very interesting way about immersion, Brenda. What is your take on this?

Brenda Laurel
Obviously, I love it. I love that there are not menus. I love that it is trying to be POV. The point and jump-cut problem will eventually go away as we get more processing power or better look-up technology. I think it's the best compromise possible. I got a sense of spatiality looking at it. Filling a space with music is a killer idea.

Stewart Alsop
There's a genre of titles using a similar interface that includes *Myst, Seventh Guest*, and *Tuneland*. No visible controls are on the screen. The idea is to use the mouse as a navigational tool, either in real time or by clicking. It embodies what I was leading to in my question to Chuck. The difference is that interactivity is not predetermined. It creates an environment in which we can have our own experience. To do this, we need a screen without controls on it, and a world around which to wander. This title seems like a good example of that genre.

Brenda Laurel
The fact that there is individual viewpoint control makes the exploration of space with this product very different from exploring the body in Bob Abel's heart product. The sense of space is completely different.

David Bunnell
Chuck, how do you talk to a guy whose name is a symbol?

Charles Cortright

We can't use his name. For corresponding with his lawyer and Warner Brothers, the symbol had to be put in a keystroke. We refer to him as, "formerly known as Prince."

Steve Floyd

Steve Floyd demonstrates and discusses Revell's Power Modeler auto and plane kits, showing how multimedia can extend beyond the computer.

Software is typically bundled to sell computer components. I'd like to look at bundling with real-world objects not related to the computer. The Power Modeler series that we developed with Revell bundles CD-ROMs with toys you put together — not preassembled toys, but models. Many of us built model cars and planes in the old fashioned way when we were kids. Multimedia can help us combine fun and fantasy with real-world skills. Extending the computer experience is very important, whether in education or play, whether with children or adults. Combining a CD-ROM with a real-world toy is a first step in moving people off computers into other enriching activities.

There are two elements to this product. One helps enrich the modeling experience; the other builds on the fantasy of doing something with the model. We used focus groups extensively throughout the development process to find out what kids want to do. We found that when they build a car, they want the fantasy of actually driving it.

The interface tries to eliminate text on the screen. In the old days, the paper instructions for the assembly process came with weird diagrams. Every model kit has five or six different parts trees. It was often very difficult to locate the parts on the parts tree. Now, I can click on a part, like the main gear door, and immediately locate where it is on the tree. At the same time, I can click on the tire and see it assembled. I can control the assembly and stop it at any time. We're giving children the ability to use software and PCs to go beyond the play experience of a game to build real things.

Imagine how long it would take to produce written instructions instead of QuickTime movies showing the different steps in assembly. About 100 individual pieces go into one of these models. We found that the modeling experience is enriched tremendously if kids have success. One way to feel success is to begin painting the model the right way. When I painted models as a kid, I painted them after they were assembled. (I also got a lot of glue on the windshield. We've packaged warnings about using paint and glue around a keyboard.) We encourage kids to paint right way. To motivate them to paint their plane, we let them see what it looks like painted. For painting, gluing, and finishing — where typically parents are not around to help — we included soft-compressed video movies on the CD-ROM.

In using a child as narrator, we discovered that regardless of the age of the children we interviewed, they always felt that the narrator was two to three years older than they were. If we asked a seven-year old, the narrator was nine, and if we asked a seventeen-year old, the narrator was nineteen. The kids helped us design, both on a formal basis through the focus groups, as with any consumer product, and also on an informal basis. The kids played and we listened. We designed the product from their point of view, not ours.

I said there were two elements. The first is to enrich the real-life skills of building a model. The second is to experience some of the fantasy by flying a mission on the plane, or by driving a car to a racetrack, qualifying, and then racing. Kids sign in using their own name, so their scores can be recorded. We try to personalize the experience as much as possible for them. In contrast to a popular game like *Doom*, where the mission is to blow up and shoot everything in sight, we're trying to create an experience where kids can begin to examine and build their own story. The more they understand about the plane, the mission, the weapon system, the richer the experience will be. It's a real mission of mercy — a rescue mission modeling some real-world event going on now. It's not just a shoot-em-up game. It reflects human values.

Stewart Alsop
Is it a CD? Does it only work on a Mac?

Steve Floyd
It's a CD-ROM. Right now it's operating in a DOS environment, as opposed to Windows or Mac. We didn't feel the other platforms would give enough play for flying and driving simulations.

Stewart Alsop
Isn't that an issue for a kid who walks into a store and buys a model, only to discover later that he's got the wrong computer?

Steve Floyd
It's a major issue. What I think we're seeing is that it helps people justify buying very expensive hardware — $2,000 or $3,000 today for a high-performance home PC. At the same time, I'm a platform agnostic. It troubles me that we have to worry about all these cables, levels of software, and multiple configurations.

Brenda Laurel
Your product seems to address two specific, almost maniac markets: the model people and the flight simulation people. How much do they overlap, and how much do they have to overlap for you to build a combo product like this?

Steve Floyd
They don't overlap very much today, maybe 15 to 20 percent, although the demographics are very similar. Revell has well over a 70 percent market share in model building. The problem is that it's a stable share of a declining domestic market. The strategy is to get kids back into model building through the software. With the growing number of single-parent families, and with moms who never built models as kids, the computer in many ways becomes the babysitter, coach, and mentor for a great many skills. It troubles me that we don't realize the learning that is going on with the PC, which is the parent in many cases. We need to pay more attention to what it's feeding the children.

Brenda Laurel
Were you inspired by the airplane-repair videodiscs done by Boeing and others for the mechanic to take out and use? Have you seen any of them?

Steve Floyd
No, we haven't, although we've had two aircraft manufacturers come in to look at our product for their employees. It was kind of surprising.

Stewart Alsop
I'll think about that the next time I take off from LAX.

Brenda Laurel
Do you feel that the quality of game play in your flight simulations can compete favorably with the existing dedicated flight simulations that don't have models packaged in?

Steve Floyd
What concerns me about the commercial flight simulation packages is that they're very difficult to install and learn. It takes me a week to master them. We tried to balance what was operable with what would be fun. I think we compare favorably, on that basis, with some of the more sophisticated simulations.

Joe Fantuzzi
I'm curious about the business case. You said that models were a declining business for Revell. Does your product sell more stand-alone models for Revell without the CD? Also, what's the price?

Steve Floyd
I think bundling the CD-ROMs has minimum impact on model kits that are unbundled for several reasons. Buying software with toys is a totally new concept. Retailers don't know where to place the package. The package is large, and space on the software shelf is very competitive. Where do you put it in the store and how do you merchandise it? Also, people are not used to looking for it. It's only been on the market for six to nine months. In fact, the aircraft elements just went to golden master last Thursday. There's been very little impact in overall model kit sales so far. As for the price, recommended retail is $59.95, so the model kit is basically free.

David Niguidula
Once kids have made the model, are they doing anything different with it, or are they playing with the CD-ROM the whole time, with

the model sitting on the shelf? I'm curious if it's actually doing anything for their imaginations.

Steve Floyd
We've noticed two things. First, we were shocked in the home testing to find the kids almost all went to the model building first, and were willing to stay with it for a week or more before playing the game. We thought they'd start with the game playing. A smart parent could use the game as a reward. Second, kids still like to pick up model planes, insert firecrackers, throw them, and blow them up. This hasn't changed. Maybe that's good.

David Bunnell
In my mind, the real value is in the modeling. Is it necessary to have the flight simulator? Wouldn't it be just as valuable to teach kids how to build the model, then let them use their imagination, going "rrrrrrrrrr." Doesn't it steal from the imagination to do it on the computer, instead of playing with the model?

Steve Floyd
I'm not sure how to answer that. I have mixed emotions. As you know, it takes a long time and a lot of money to turn out a game, whether good or bad. It might make more sense to unbundle the two, sell the modeling side for a much lower price, and bundle it. There are plenty of games out there. The game could be built separately, or a business relationship developed to bundle existing games. That might make more sense from a business perspective.

Brenda Laurel
My impresssion as an outsider is that the main appeal of models is making them. When kids make especially elaborate models, don't they display them, rather than fool around with them?

Steve Floyd
That's true, yes.

David Bunnell
When I was a kid, I hung up the models I made from the ceiling. I didn't want them to get broken.

Stewart Alsop
You certainly didn't blow them up with a cherry bomb!

David Bunnell
No, I did that with frogs, not airplanes.

Stewart Alsop
So that's why you wanted the dissection feature in *Concepts of Biology*!

Doreen Nelson
I talked before about social responsibility. You may be surprised to hear me say that I think this application is socially responsible. It's socially responsible because you've returned the child to the physical domain. You're to be congratulated for that. Going from a two-dimensional surface on the computer to a three-dimensional surface to build the model is what IQ tests are all about. It will be interesting to see whether the students using your product improve their IQs as a result. This is what I was trying to address as social responsibility, not the subject matter. I happen not to like to see kids bombing each other, but Floyd's work is socially responsible in an educational sense.

Claude Leglise

With Lucie Fjeldstad taking over from David Bunnell as moderator, Claude Leglise describes the Indeo technology for displaying and using video at the PC, and makes a case for its importance in furthering the success of multimedia.

The ability to make money with the wonderful titles being developed will depend on choosing the appropriate high volume delivery platform. Which device will consumers ultimately use? Which device offers the high degree of interactivity these titles require? Which technology will make the titles inexpensive to produce and purchase? Which applications will justify the costs consumers incur? I propose that the personal computer, as we know it, is the platform of choice for the multimedia industry.

1993 will be remembered as the year that multimedia finally made it into the general press and public consciousness. A technology and set of capabilities that we have been talking about for well over five years suddenly erupted. Annual CD software sales exceeded $200 million for the first time, with half of the sales taking place in the fourth quarter. We're seeing a very high seasonality in both the title business and computer business.

There were approximately 7 million personal computers equipped with CD-ROM drives and soundboards at the end of 1993, including close to 2 million Macs. Sega CD made a phenomenal appearance on the market, soaring from essentially zero to a million in about a year. The number of CD-ROM drives installed in computers should double in 1994, and is likely to continue doubling every 18 months thereafter. Also, for the first time ever, over half the computers sold in the fourth quarter were installed in homes. As David Bunnell said earlier, the personal computer is becoming the hottest-selling piece of consumer electronic equipment in history.

Installed computers have processing power, memory, screens, soundboards, and CD-ROM drives. What's missing is video. Intel has been working for about 18 months now on the ability to play video clips on PCs for free. A little software embedded on a CD-ROM, or potentially on a network, will allow video clips to be delivered to any 486-based PC. This makes possible a full multimedia system on an existing installed base. Version 3.0 of *Indeo* (using Microsoft Video for Windows 1.0) was available for interactive applications last summer. Developers worked around the small video (the size of a postage stamp) by using artifacts of the production cycle.[7]

Indeo is software. One of the virtues of software is that it can improve rapidly, a lot faster than hardware can. From the little pictures that covered 1/16 of a screen at 25 to 30 frames per second a year ago, the technology had advanced to provide 320x240 pixels (1/4 of a computer screen) at 24 frames per second by last February. By the end of the year, we'll be able to provide 1/4 of a screen at 30 frames per second (full motion), and by the end of 1995, probably full-screen, full-motion, entirely in software.

This means that developers can create full-video, full-sound, fully interactive content for the millions of PCs out there without having to worry about the exact hardware inside the box. Ultimately, this will mean a constant screen experience for the user.

We've been talking about multimedia content for games and education. I want to move the discussion to business multimedia, an enormous potential area of application. What we are going to see in business multimedia is exactly what we saw in desktop publishing. Making 14 fonts available resulted in garish documents that looked like ransom notes, but desktop publishing enabled people to do what they couldn't do any other way.

In business, we create our own content for peers and friends inside the company, and for customers outside. We're already starting to see video and interactive equivalents of the ransom note. That's the bad news. The good news is that the technology is increasingly being used in business presentations, sales, and marketing; and it doesn't take a Steven Spielberg with Hollywood production values to use it.

In conclusion, the PC is evolving at an incredible pace as a multimedia machine through better chips, better busses, better video technology, and better CD-ROM drives. The level of quality that can be delivered on applications is steadily improving. This translates into abundant and growing opportunities for making money in selling hardware, software, and hot titles.

George Gilder
This is going to make analog look good. What's the point of doing it all in software? Scott Billups told us that we can get a two-million fold improvement from incorporating cheap hardware in the machine. Surely Intel is capable of producing good graphics.

Claude Leglise
It's the tyranny of the installed base. 37 percent of U.S. homes with an income over $40,000 have a computer. That's our target.

George Gilder
Then why not make them MPEG-compatible?

Claude Leglise
The problem with MPEG, JPEG, and other techniques that require hardware is that to play a title the consumer has to buy $200 to $300 worth of stuff.

George Gilder
The consumer already has to add a board for CD-ROMs.

Claude Leglise
The point is the CD-ROM issue is essentially taken care of, but it took ten years.

George Gilder
But the market today incorporates the CD-ROM player. Why don't you take this opportunity to upgrade the graphics massively, rather than producing images that are drastically inferior to what's going to be coming in game players, not to mention TV sets. You may actually make the PC look retarded.

Claude Leglise
The fundamental play is the installed base. We want to deliver new content to the installed base to create a business.

George Gilder
You're looking in a rear view mirror.

Claude Leglise
On the issue of quality, yes, the quality of video today on a PC is still inferior to what can be achieved on a TV set. But it's not going to be inferior much longer. Super VGA display with a resolution of 1024x768 is already planned for HDTV. We believe we will be able to fill a 10x7 screen in software within two years.

Donald Norman

Now it's my turn. You're not going to be any happier with me. I'm a people person, and a social person. We heard about culturally redeemable values earlier. For you, the whole aim of multimedia is to make money and service the installed base. But what is multimedia about? I thought Scott Billups captured it. It's about presenting something. If it's a story you want to present, the medium is not what's important; it's the story. Or a reference work, or an educational work, or even a game — what's important is the content. When you limit yourself to this big installed base, and to making money, that may be good for the stockholders, but not necessarily the nation...

George Gilder

It's not good for the stockholders.

Donald Norman

... and it's probably not good for the stockholders. For example, why on earth is the PC the medium of choice, except for the fact that Intel dominates in some of the hardware? Think about what a PC is. Is that what you want in your living room? It's not easy to use. It's multipurpose. It's complex, and it's made for computation, which is why it's called a computer. That's not what multimedia is about. It's about education. It's about entertainment. It's about enjoying ourselves. It's about communication. We're going to need a wide variety of devices. I'd love to see us explore what really will be used. I don't go to my personal computer to read a book, even though I've just published a book on CD-ROM. I want to read a book sitting on the grass, or on the toilet seat, or in my armchair. I don't want to go to the TV to balance my checkbook. I want the appropriate device for what I'm doing. I didn't hear a hint of this in all you said.

Claude Leglise
What platform did you target for your book on CD-ROM?

Donald Norman
It's a Voyager Expanded Book. I hope Voyager targets all of the platforms.

Claude Leglise
As a company, we're not qualified to pass judgment on the content. What we're qualified to do is provide technologies that make it possible to create very exciting content.

Lucie Fjeldstad
Claude, do you have any content or storytelling talent on the *Indeo* team?

Donald Norman
He has to think. The answer must be no.

Claude Leglise
Yes, we do. What are you getting at?

Lucie Fjeldstad
What I'm getting at is this. Coming from a computer background, as I did, you have to take the people who are going to paint the next picture, and mix them with the people who are going to create the paint brushes and the paint, or the next masterpieces won't be born by the computer industry.

Gary Andersen
My company publishes CD-ROMs. I'd like to speak up for the *Indeo* technology. We use it regularly. I agree about methodology

over technology, but if the story is good, *Indeo* is an excellent way to create product. We don't have to get hung up on the picture not being perfect. It's going to get there.

Michael Watts
I'm in the strange position of wanting to defend Intel. I don't want a technology channel deciding anything about the content, anymore than I want the makers of paper deciding what gets printed. The engine is what makes all of this possible.

Lucie Fjeldstad
But do you think Claude can provide a better engine if he incorporates people on his design team who are able to use that engine to create the content?

Michael Watts
Not really. Most of the design process has to do with silicon real estate and the laws of physics, not with the words that are finally put through the technology.

Claude Leglise
Lucie's question could be asked differently. Do you believe Weyerhaeuser would create better paper by involving book writers?

Donald Norman and **Lucie Fjeldstad**
Actually, they do.

Claude Leglise
It could be, but it's not as though we're developing the technology in a vacuum. Still, providing the means to tell the story is what we're interested in.

Philip Abram
We've talked about the PC as a delivery platform for multimedia, and as a development platform for title producers. Do you see any value in the PC's also being a development platform for end users, to enable them to develop their own stories and multimedia?

George Gilder
That's the most important role of the PC. In conjunction with the information superhighway, which Scott Billups has represented as hype, the PC vastly increases the amount of choice, and by so doing, fundamentally changes the cultural character of what is produced. As long as we have the bottleneck of only a few channels to the public, we go for shock, sensation, and prurient interest. But when the computer becomes a creative tool available to millions of users, the video and multimedia business can begin to resemble the book business.

Some 55,000 books are published every year in the United States. Because of digital desktop publishing in text, scores of thousands of magazines and newsletters are also published. Digital desktop publishing in video will evoke a similar efflorescence of video books, creating a video culture drastically different from that currently represented by television and Hollywood. The garbage in, garbage out that Scott Billups denounced is an artifact of the huge expense of creating programs. When it becomes cheap, every screenwriter (there are scores of thousands of them) will be able to create movies. People will get their first choice, rather than settling for what shocks or intrigues them.

Donald Norman
I'm not convinced. I think that individual publishing in video, audio, and text is critically important, especially in education, but it

will not produce quality. Look, I write books. It takes a single author three to four years at close to full-time effort to write a good book. When the book is finished, the author is not competent to publish it. It requires a publisher with a team of as many as twenty people to work on the book in various phases. Today, it's about a nine-month process for a commercial publisher to turn a finished text into a trade book.

With a video book, it's even more demanding. I've done a fair number of movies. I've also done videos, and I'm just finishing a CD-ROM book with Voyager, as I said. Even though I'm quite expert in technology, and I'm a good writer, I could not have done that CD-ROM book myself. Voyager's video team spent a full day shooting on a Hollywood sound stage, with fifteen people: sound people, light people, editors, producers, continuity people. After several months of editing, they returned to do a recording. Individual lone wolves are not going to get that quality. They will do a lot of learning, and they will get to appreciate quality, but they are not going to produce quality by themselves.

George Gilder
What was the total cost of that CD-ROM? Compare it to the cost of a movie, or a TV show. Prices are dropping drastically.

Donald Norman
But the critical element is the people talent. That's where the bottleneck is.

Peter Forman
I want to comment on the issue of MPEG versus *Indeo.* MPEG has no capabilities for enabling individuals to use (as opposed to view) video. It's a broadcast medium, in the same sense that television

today is a broadcast medium. It cannot be captured on the desktop or edited. *Indeo* can be. *Indeo* can empower individuals to use and become skilled in video as part of everyday communication. Scott Billups and others concerned about the lack of methodology in the use of this new technology belong to an elite group that has had access to very expensive equipment in the past, learning skills that the rest of us do not have.

You made the point yourself, George, that bringing down the cost enables new levels of human effort. MPEG does not do that. And it's not just the $200 on the delivery end. MPEG is not usable for the next two to three years by individuals learning the needed new skills to publish on their own. Software-based technologies like *Indeo* are much more enabling than MPEG. MPEG only enables the video server and the pipeline into the house.

George Gilder
MPEG is a compression and transmission medium. How the material is edited and processed before being compressed or transmitted is a separate issue, isn't it?

Peter Forman
But it still requires $75,000 to $250,000 for an MPEG compressor, or as much as a half million dollars or more for the very best compressors that are available.

Claude Leglise
I regard technologies as enablers in the history of mankind. What went through Gutenberg's mind when he invented the printing press? Was he inventing it with an eye on who was going to use it, and what was going to be written? I don't think so. The computer is fundamentally a very liberating technology, as are multimedia

technologies, in the sense that many users will get to do what they want. We will see ransom notes and stories poorly told, but they will be the expressions of people's feelings, and that's good. Our role is to provide the tools to do that; nothing more, nothing less.

Jim Olson

Jim Olson describes Hewlett-Packard's work with media servers and set-top boxes, the company's enabling technologies for video on-demand.

Hewlett-Packard is a newcomer in the video industry. We entered the global video marketplace about a year ago, introducing a number of products for people in the content preparation business. We now find ourselves in the broadband video delivery business, with our media server and set-top box technologies. Technology to us at H-P is the servant of the application and content provider, not their master.

Our customers in broadband delivery are also our partners. This is not a business where we throw hardware and software over the fence and expect content people and service providers to catch it. We're working with them. We've agreed to provide Pacific Telesis with the video servers for their broadband video delivery rollout starting at year-end; we've agreed with TCI to deliver digital set-tops for their applications; and we've agreed with Time Warner to provide Hewlett-Packard printers for real-time printing of coupons, brochures, and advertising media off the cable-TV system in Orlando.

One application we're supporting is news on-demand. When technology people like me who go to work at 6:30 in the morning come home at 9 or 10 at night, we'd like to be able to watch the news, not play games. The problem is that the news isn't on, so we go to bed. A lot of people in the world would like to see their news when they want it, not at 11 p.m. We are making it possible for Pacific Telesis, which is working on this problem, to store the news in MPEG for delayed broadcast. More people probably watch the news than view movies or play games these days. Delayed news may not be a killer application, but it could be one of the important applications in this industry.

Many service providers are starting with movies on-demand. Viewers would like to be able to fast-forward through boring introductions — faster than on a VCR. We think it is important to go at a 10 1/2 times, instead of a 3 times rate. Viewers would also like to be able to pause. The VCR takes a lot of heat as being difficult to use. It's really easy to use, only difficult to program. Almost everyone knows how to pause, fast-forward, and rewind on the VCR. Putting these functions on the screen will make our video server technology more acceptable. Our technology is built based on what customers say they want.

One of the most important media today is plain paper. People are not going to give up print media for audio-visual interactivity. They'll want paper too. We're working with Time Warner and others to connect printers to the cable-TV system in the home, allowing people to watch product demos when they want to, not when the advertisers want them to. With inducements like free coupons and brochures being printed out, advertisers will still have a pipeline into the home, a key part of the free-services trial in Orlando. Select a restaurant and have the menu printed on the H-P printer in your home. We don't think video on-demand will be paid for entirely by consumers. Orlando may show that advertisers are willing to pay dearly to fund much of the infrastructure.

Our video server technology is unique. Though we are the number two computer company in the country, we don't think the heart of the video server should be a computer. We're building the system from the ground up for Pacific Telesis and others. We believe that all components should conform to a standard open-systems environment. We're using MPEG and other standards to transport video on-demand to the home from the central office or cable head-end. We feel there needs to be industry agreement and a standard platform for delivery and interfacing among the various systems. We're a strong proponent of open systems.

George Gilder

Hewlett-Packard is one of the great computer companies. It's technology is among the most pioneering and fast-moving in the history of the world. Why go backwards to apply cosmetics to the corpse of broadcast TV? I already have two Hewlett-Packard printers attached to my personal computer. Why do I want one attached to a TV that can't render text in any readable form?

Jim Olson

The printer may not be attached to the TV. The printer in the study or family room may be networked to the cable system. We don't know the answer. That's why we're not introducing products to the marketplace for someone else to figure out how to use. We're working with Time Warner and others to test these systems. We're using many different kinds of printers. We'll be testing video capture as well as just graphics and text. There are many content issues associated with capturing images off a cable network.

Donald Norman

You missed an opportunity to respond that a printer should be wherever we want hard copy. We want a printer in the living room if we want photographs. We clearly want a printer in the study. It's like asking why we have an electric motor in the mixer, another in the electric clock, and still another in the grinder. Why not just one? Printers aren't the issue. The availability of information is.

Jim Olson
That's an excellent point. We think hard copy is a prevalent technology. It has become very important to Hewlett-Packard. But we need to understand how users want to use the media. We're not sure they want to have printers, like components of stereo systems, next to their TVs. We intend to find out. We've sold over 20 million laser and ink jet printers. We think the market in the home could be many times that, if we learn how to do it right. The possibility is there, but we want to work with content people, advertisers, and customers to figure out where to put these printers and how to network them.

Kenneth Silverman
Could you comment on the Time Warner Orlando trial? Where does it stand? Will it really go on the air at the end of this year? How do you read the other information highway rollouts?

Jim Olson
Looking beyond just video on-demand, we're very excited about Time Warner's full-services network. I think it will happen by the end of this year, later than planned. The reason for the delay is another server supplier. This has been made public. I reviewed our video print program just yesterday. We are about two weeks ahead of our original schedule to have printers in the home this month. As for the whole industry, I agree with those who say there is a lot more hype than reality. Things will happen much more slowly than the many articles in the *Wall Street Journal* suggest. We

view the video server part of the market as being about a billion dollars by the turn of the century, not six billion as some market researchers predict. We're taking a fairly conservative approach.

George Gilder

It's all downside on the TV and upside in computers. Sales of computers, multimedia processors, and CD-ROMs are all up strongly. It's your focus on TV as the vehicle that leads you to disappointing projections for your company.

Jim Olson

CD-ROM activity is a very substantial part of our PC business, but I did not come prepared to talk about it. Just last year, we became the number two computer company in the United States. By reinventing ourselves for the video business, and by listening to our customers, we plan on continuing to grow beyond that.

Kristina Woolsey

Kristina Woolsey discusses what she refers to as design-driven content, taking examples from Video Almanac, Life Story, and the new Viz Ability, a course on seeing, imagining and drawing.

Notice my black bag. Last year I could not come to the Roundtable because I had laryngitis. I sent media instead. Today, I have my media in this bag, but it doesn't seem to play. I do have my voice. What I'll try to do is give you a sense of the argument I want to make, then ask you to rely on your imagination for the rest. Multimedia is an incredible medium for tying together abstract concepts with concrete instances. I'll try to articulate some concepts, do some arm waving on the instances, and we'll see how it goes.

There are three basic approaches to multimedia. The first is from a technological perspective, where we maximize for the technology with exciting enablers intended to do what we think someone wants. The second approach is market-driven, leading to consideration of the installed base and what people are likely to buy. Previous presenters have given us a taste of each of these approaches. I'm here to introduce to the conversation a third approach, which is design-driven, asking what is it we want to accomplish and how do we do it? The design-driven approach can drive both technology and markets. In fact, the three approaches interact with each other. We need them all.

The word multimedia is interesting. I see people here whom I knew before we had that word, and we were doing the same thing then that we are now. But the word perseveres. One of its implied meanings is multiple media. The wonderful thing about the computer, with its images, sounds, text and interactions, is that it allows us to make all sorts of things. It's like a lego kit much more than a pencil, giving us the ability to use many different kinds of pieces to construct many different kinds of things. I want us to invent new things. That's exciting. Settling into lines of products with grand authoring tools or templates that stamp out the same kinds of products over and over is not good design-driven thinking.

Multimedia excels at handling different kinds of forms. What forms do we have? We have stories, which is a terrific oral culture. What else? That's the question I have been obsessed with for twenty years. We can have surrogate travel, where a place becomes the organizing function. We can have a resource model. We can organize alphabetically. And we can organize in other ways.

I can cite several of the forms from products I've built. Case number one is a product called *Visual Almanac.* The form of this product in its electronic version, which we fought very hard for, is simply collections, activities, and tools purposely placed in a box, a set of elements that can be combined in many different ways to make many different things.

Case number two is a product called *Life Story* with a very different structure. It's an annotated movie that can be interrogated in different ways, a traditional movie in terms of scope and sequence, but with remarks able to be attatched to it. It has three navigational directions. The user can enter the movie through science, drama, or people, then interrogate it and move around.

Another case is a little product called *Planetary Taxi,* a spinoff from the *Visual Almanac,* but with a very different structure. It's a game of taking passengers in a taxicab through the solar system.

Form is critical. It needs to come from what we intend to do. What does form entail? At the moment, electronic screens carry all the information. If we look at a CD, or a typical screen, we can't tell what's in it. We need to make the form explicit, because in an interactive domain, it matters if we get lost. We need to have signifiers wrapped around the structure of what we are doing. Typical screens do not tell us what to do. Putting in form indicators lets us know what to do with what is there, and also what to expect of it.

Another element we have to play with is text. In each of the major multimedia products that I have mentioned, we found that we had to create a whole book to go with it. We resisted incredibly, because we were demonstrating multimedia; adding a book to a multimedia product seemed heretical. Why couldn't we put it into multimedia? The answer is that the book provides a reflective format for categories of information that like to sit still ("on the lawn," as Donald Norman put it), whereas other things in these kits provide an interactive component. Electronics is good for an action-oriented piece; books are good for a reflective-oriented piece. That's one way in which we use text.

Another model is a textual wraparound, which says to someone, "You are teaching this course. Here's everything you want to know about DNA, and by the way, there's a CD in the back to help you learn it." The book now takes the front end. *Planetary Taxi* also uses text, in this case to provide hints for playing the game.

My punch line is the product I'm working on right now, to be released under the name *Viz Ability*. Our entire culture has little understanding of the notion of multiplicity of form. This product will take care of that. It will allow children to learn how to compose with media in the ways big boys and girls do, being able to take these elements and put them together. It's a course on seeing, imagining, and drawing.

I can take you to classrooms where kids with simple tools like *Premiere* and an 8mm camera are producing not movies, but magnificent, high-quality, visually-related works. It's happening very fast with these tools. *Viz Ability* is a kit for learning to do these things. It has a CD, with a whole set of electronic exercises that teach spatial imagination, visualization, perspective drawing, and idea diagramming. It has a little book that reflects on these matters and discusses cognitive issues, and a blank sketch book (the publishers love this one) for children to doodle in and carry around. Could it be electronic? Someday, maybe. Right now, we're providing a medium with which people can quickly learn these visualization skills.

George Gilder
Whose publishing these works — Claris?

Kristina Woolsey
No, none of these are published by Apple Computer. I have yet to get Apple into this business. *Viz Ability* will be brought out by PWS Publishing, an engineering publisher. Voyager has just introduced *Visual Almanac* as a second edition. *Life Story* is published by Sunburst, and the *Planetary Taxi* is also Voyager.

George Gilder
The only reason text is not usually presented electronically is that screen resolution is far inferior to that of paper. But over the next three years, screen resolution will rise to the equivalent of 300 dots per inch or better, at which point it will be as comfortable to read text on a screen as on paper. Books and magazines may not survive the emergence of news panels as light as a book to carry, whose screens are equivalent to paper in resolution and quality.

Kristina Woolsey
To get ready for these issues, I suggest we all design the best books we can, so there is a set of similar skills. We don't have to wait to do the design, though the usability factors might be different. I find I am starting to develop one kind of writing for the screen and another for a book. I don't know how different they really are. I suspect we will end up with a hybrid in the computer. For example, I would normally pause in a conversation to leave time for the other person to join in. Computer screens have the capability for leaving pauses. When I build a product I think is

good, it leaves a pause for the user to ask for something. It's a different kind of text, with more of a declarative function than a normal book.

Text on a screen should be used for invitation. We've forgotten that these things exist in a distributed domain. It's like a communication function. It's aberrant to have it all in one box. It happens to be economically nice for dispersion, but it ought to exist so that I can talk to you about it, even though I don't know you, creating my own videos for you to add to what you have, wherever you are. I think book publishing and electronic publishing will gradually merge. Each art will change into something different, just as the oral culture changed because of text. We no longer have to remember certain kinds of things.

George Gilder
What do you think of newspapers and the newspaper form?

Kristina Woolsey
Well, you know, I was going to make the extreme argument that text has no form, and then I realized that wonderfully written text has incredible form, and that's why we understand it and celebrate it. Some of us see the structure, others don't, which is the point I was making about multimedia. Newspapers are changing their form all over. The newspaper isn't going to stay the same, and then change into an electronic form. It's changing already because of the electronic mechanism of making it, as well as the potential for future delivery.

Lucie Fjeldstad
We all know that anytime there's a new medium, the market expands, but nothing goes away. Each medium has its own place.

Kristina Woolsey
Right, but I'm arguing that we have not just created a new medium called multimedia to go with broadcast, etc. That's too simple. I think the multiplicity of the media is what we've invented. It's not like the others. It's not a *next one* that previous media incorporate. It can be that, and other things as well. If we get confused by this, we will end up being incredibly shortsighted.

Donald Norman
Isn't it amusing that when you were forced back to the book, it never occurred to you that it is a medium that fits the definition of multimedia as well as the rest?

Kristina Woolsey
That's what I'm acknowledging here. It's one of the media I employed to deliver an intent. I laugh at myself when I realize that I first thought I was building something else, which I needed the book to round out.

Donald Norman
We are in a new genre, a kind of technological revolution. It's an exciting time of rapid development, even though it may take a hundred years and we don't know the direction we're moving. We are introducing new media. Technologies have what I call *affordances*, making things easy and making things hard. We tend to do the things that are easy and not the things that are hard. This affects what we produce, the way we think, and the kinds of structures we have.

We saw that paper has redeeming properties and is a very advanced technology. It has been around for 500 years, though today's paper making is very different than it used to be, as is today's book making. It isn't that the contrast is bad on screens, George. It isn't that we can't read screens as rapidly. I agree with you that in a few years we'll be able to read on screen. Dictionaries will no longer be printed on paper, since reference books are better on a computer. We can make an electronic reader that's cheaper, smaller, and lighter than a dictionary, and allows us to search. We don't read a dictionary; we search it. But when we want to create, a blank piece of paper or a notebook may always be the ideal medium.

George Gilder
You didn't write your book on a piece of paper, did you?

Donald Norman
But I read it on paper.

Kristina Woolsey
Yet paper doesn't hold movies. Multimedia lets images and sounds become equal partners with text, and allows people who are not high-level professionals use them all in discourse. Not everyone has to be a novelist or book writer.

Donald Norman
I want it all. I'm not against the computer, George.

Matthew Miller
Will *Viz Ability* be available soon? Will my kids be able to teach me to use it? Will it run on a PC?

Kristina Woolsey
We'll deliver it in October, according to our current schedule. We're in the middle of alpha and moving on to beta. It will come

out first on a Macintosh. Although it will just be a little product, it will be connected with a major change in schools. Its curriculum is as important as reading and writing, and needs to be integrated at all levels. This will take substantially longer.

George Gilder
Get a Mac.

Michael Backes
I'm swooning because you encapsulated what many people are thinking the media can be. I'd love to have you talk about the emerging grammar of this new media. My background is in motion pictures, a relatively mature medium that has had ninety years to develop things like a one shot. Multimedia doesn't seem to have acquired a grammar yet. I'm very interested in what your research suggests about how its grammar will evolve.

Kristina Woolsey
I think it is evolving. I'm working on *Viz Ability* with a new team of people whom I've known for a long time but not worked with on a product before. I keep telling them stories from other products. So there are grammars emerging from within local communities. Sometimes the dollars freeze them too soon, so that they are not generative enough, but that probably happened in film also. There are indeed rules. Often when we run into an interface problem, I have four examples of what we did in the past to solve it. We choose from those.

Apropos of motion pictures, we've created what I call *performance videos*. They are very short clips, just an in and an out that you compose as you click them. You determine the order on the fly. It's very nice for a presentation. When we show the product to small groups of people, they invariably say, if you knew about motion pictures, you would have done a dissolve, or a this, or a that. I work with a wonderful motion picture person. She can explain that we might have done those things, but this is a different medium. It does not require movies that have been created before. It can use sequences of interruptible images -- a different form.

The message is that it's very easy to get detoured from building a new grammar when multiple media is taken to be the addition of some motion picture and a little text. This relates to my comment earlier about text. The text changes when it goes up on the screen. It changes when it lives next to a motion picture. And it changes when it goes next to a button that let's us alter it, or lets us compose. We will not develop sophisticated new grammars so long as we import old ones.

Pavel Curtis

Pavel Curtis describes his killer application for the nineties, with an insightful commentary about the socializing nature of people, and with lessons from his experience in running LambdaMOO on the Internet.

I'm here to talk about the information superhighway, and also about the real world. It seems to me that some of the people at the top of American companies, who haven't even visited cyberspace yet, are in danger of forgetting certain important things about the real world.

Let's start with the highway. There's a large amount of confusion in the hype about the great information superhighway, as though the highway is the interesting part. Who cares about highways? Highway engineers do, but not the rest of us. Remember the old

Route 66 TV show? It wasn't the highway that was interesting. The people off the highway provided all the interest, all the stories. So let's get off the silly pavement and look at the people.

What about the people? People are really into communicating with each other, to the point of subverting any technology for multi-way communication, no matter how-ill suited to the purpose. Consider the so-called *broadcast* media, like radio. Radio talk shows are enormously popular, from nationwide syndicated programs like *Larry King Live* to the small-town, kilowatt, farm-station feature. Whatever the topic, whoever the guest, wherever the station, the lines are jammed with people trying hard to talk to lots of other people.

TV, the great pacifier? Not always. A few years ago, a group of German artists and technologists ran an experimental interactive television project visible throughout Europe. They patched together all kinds of technologies to create as many ways for people to communicate with each other as possible. People could call into the station on their touchtone phones. Some were patched into a shared audio channel, so they could talk to each other and anyone else watching the program. Others, in groups of two, were patched into a set of controls for playing on a piano keyboard. The twosome could make music together, responding or not to comments and suggestions from those on the audio channel. In another segment, instead of music, two callers could control a variety of picture-drawing tools to create art together.

These and the other interesting communications facilities created by the channel's operators were enormously popular throughout the time the channel was in operation. Even with on-line computing, the main point for many people is communication, regardless of the other services available. Consider France Telecom's nationwide videotex system, *Minitel*, whose chat lines represent approximately 20 percent of the services offered, and are among the most popular. According to CompuServe, which is the largest on-line service provider in the U.S., any service that involves one member interacting with another is more popular. The *New York Times* suggests that the real popularity of electronic magazines has little to do with reading, and everything to do with talking — and talking, and talking, and talking. Even on the massive global Internet, in spite of such data fire hoses as FTP, World Wide Web, and Gopher, approximately 25 to 35 percent of all cross-country traffic is strictly for interpersonal communication.

That's today, but what do the fancy new on-line services look like? In General Magic's Magic Cap system for PDA's, we walk the streets of a virtual city, where the cute virtual storefronts are rented out to real companies. We can go from store to store to find things to buy. Silicon Graphics and Time Warner have teamed up to do something similar with interactive television in Orlando. Again, we walk the streets checking out the storefronts, in this case, of a really well-drawn virtual city.

What's missing in both systems? What's absolutely crucial to their long term success and to the mental health of their users? *Other people*! That's right, we walk the streets of the little electronic metropolis all alone. It's the software equivalent of the neutron bomb. All the buildings are still there, but the people have been wiped out. These systems are going to be really depressing places to visit. Everyone knows cities are full of people. We can't help but feel terribly lonely walking these glitzy but utterly unpopulated streets. Real cities don't look like that. The city is a social place. It's a big mistake to strip that aspect away from it.

Now consider visions of the digital library of the future. All those resources neatly arranged, but no one to share our finds with; no one to compare notes with; no fruitful chance encounters with other patrons scanning the same section of the stacks; not even a real librarian to get help and advice from; just seemingly endless rows of electronic bookshelves to explore — all by ourselves.

But if we're an avid reader of *Wired* magazine, we know these things will be taken care of by intelligent agents — marvelous simulations of other people. Is this picture any better? Of course not. We don't need AI simulations of humans on the net, not when we already have 250 million intelligent agents in the United States. In real libraries, the very best reference materials are the ones that walk around by themselves: real living, breathing human beings. Whether or not we sit at the same table with anyone, the fact that others are there with us turns the library into a social space, alive with the potential for interaction.

Real bookstores are full of people too, people buying the same kinds of books as us, people at the next table in the attached cafe, people we arranged to meet at this cultural nexis of the community. Books aren't really the point. They're the excuse, the excuse to get together with others. In shopping, the situation is very similar. When we go shopping, we never do it in a ghost town, devoid of human contact. We bring a friend with whom to discuss the choices. We talk with the shopkeeper about the selection, and the weather. We get help in deciding about fit, matching colors, and possible accessories. We get opinions about suitability and price. We have company. A shopping trip often does not even result in a purchase, and this may not particularly bother us. To a large extent, shopping is not the point. It's the excuse, the excuse to go out and interact with other people.

Let's move on to that seeming holiest of superhighway Grails, video on-demand. From reading the papers, we get the impression that major corporations think movie watching is a solitary activity, a simple relationship whereby the TV screen puts out the content and the audience sits there alone in the dark taking it in. Nothing could be further from the truth. As was so clear in *Cinema Paridiso*, movie watching is a profoundly social activity. It just doesn't cut it to be watching *Jurassic Park* all alone, squeaking out little signs of distress as the jeep jerks down toward the heroes one nasty shock at a time. What really makes the experience work is being in a room with other people, with everyone's reaction feeding off of and into everyone else's. The audience in a movie theater laughs together, gasps together, cries together, even if they never look at one another.

If you're into this video on-demand business, maybe you can *begin* to get the picture of what I'm talking about here — the first *inklings* of the issues involved — if you realize that the most interesting application is not that my wife and I want to watch a particular movie tonight at precisely 8:43 P.M., but that we want to watch it together with our daughter, who lives across the country. The movie isn't the point. It's the excuse to get together.

Over and again I've made the same point. Companies have to ratchet back their corporate visions four or five notches and allow their cherished services to be the excuse, not the point. Create services as places that real people can visit together, and the customers will knock down the doors trying to get in. Bookstores have learned this; clothing stores have learned this; libraries have learned this; and movie houses have learned this. Maybe, with a little work, we in this industry can learn it too.

The title of my talk is the Killer Application of the Nineties? What is the killer application of the nineties? Simple. It's people!

Lucie Fjeldstad
I think I'll take him with me wherever I go. What about you guys?

George Gilder
A great speech and a great multimedia performance. But still, there is a $12 billion business in video cassettes, which people ...

Pavel Curtis
Which people very rarely watch alone. And they often bring friends over. And they are the occasion for lots of get-togethers. And people still go to the movies. And it's not just because movies are the first out. It's because *Jurassic Park* on a video cassette is a waste of two hours.

George Gilder
I think that's right.

Donald Norman
On the one hand, this is the kind of talk I would have given, although not as well. On the other hand, because it's the kind of talk I would have given, I know it's oversimplified. When I go to the movies, I want to experience and be captured by what the playwright, producer, and director have done. The people sitting behind me with different reactions get in the way.

As I said earlier, there is a new medium coming and the technology can be valuable. The real point is to figure out how to use it. We speak of an information highway, but information does not exist physically. We can't see it; we can't touch it; yet it is very important in our lives. We have to learn how to deliver it, access it, and work with it, while the focus remains on us.

Many of the stories we hear today, and many of the projections and market estimates that even my own company makes, are based on very unrealistic assumptions about how people behave. Our session has been extremely interesting. Claude Leglise started off with the technology drivers that we must have (despite what I said), because they are the enablers for what's coming next. Jim Olson then emphasized that we also have to look clearly at what the market wants; how people want to use the technology. But we cannot stop there. If we only ask people what they want today, with today's technology, they will want it faster, or better, but not with a qualitative difference, because they don't have the experience. The next step is the design-driven approach, which was Kristina's talk, looking at what it is we want to accomplish, and how we can do it with the technology. The final step is to back off and say, as Pavel Curtis has done, "Wait a minute! It's all about people, isn't it, people's lives?"

Lucie Fjeldstad
I'm glad I have Donald here. He just gave the summary. Any other comments?

Marc Canter
What is the threshold that makes you feel you have a person there, rather than a little drawing, or just words?

Pavel Curtis
Wearing one of my hats, I operate a social virtual reality on the Internet of enormous popularity, where the only medium is ASCII text. The people who use *LambdaMOO* have imbued it with

politics, art, egos, conflict — all the aspects of the human experience.

Marc Canter
Pedophiles?

Pavel Curtis
You bet! We've got them all. And they only have ASCII text. I think when there are people on both ends, the threshold you ask about is very low.

Marc Canter
It seems it could become a challenge of who can type the fastest and make the fewest spelling errors.

Pavel Curtis
Spelling errors turn out to be not important at all. It's just remarkable what people will forgive and figure out, even with the most garishly misspelled text. It doesn't even seem to be about speed typing. People just adjust to the medium. If it takes you a long time, then while I'm waiting for you to react to the last thing I typed, I'll type something new. It just folds in on itself. People manage to cope quite well. The important thing is that there's a person on the other end.

Marc Canter
Right. But doesn't it seem distracting, like in *Habitat*, where things are so goofy?

Pavel Curtis
If you use Habitat, and I have, you discover very quickly that you stop paying attention to what people look like after they first come

into the room, and only pay attention to what they're talking about. *Habitat* is graphical, but the graphics are largely unimportant.

Marc Canter

I find myself trying to second-guess whether the person who says she is a 12-year-old girl really is a 12-year-old girl.

Brenda Laurel

Most 12-year-old girls I know don't think they are 12-year-old girls, and hate someone to know they actually are. Pavel, you and I have had many conversations about how people like to construct personal identities on the net different from themselves, as Marc was just pointing out. I'm curious. Have you observed the construction of any cultural identities, or cultural groups in virtual communities, that are strikingly different from the kinds of cultures that exist in the actual world? I realize that's a very broad question.

Pavel Curtis

I think it is happening. Yes, it is a very broad question, and it's hard to answer with any authority, because we're just beginning to do social science in virtual worlds. But there is a political system on *LambdaMOO* that does not mirror any real-life system. People are adjusting to it and deciding it's a reasonable way to go. A whole culture is growing up around, for example, what the word mediation means in a virtual space. It's happening quickly and spontaneously. No one is deciding it should happen. It just does.

Stanley Frank

Max Whitby takes over as moderator as Stanley Frank describes the new directions of his company, with a video of a John Lennon title and a Sci-Fi CD on Space Station Babylon 5.

With so many high-quality, exciting multimedia titles available today, it's very easy to forget that our industry is less than four years old. At Compton's, we made a major commitment to multimedia publishing starting in 1987, resulting in a multimedia encyclopedia that added many features beyond those that could be accomplished with print alone. I will try to explain why we undertook to do this.

First, we knew that children had different learning styles. Some learned best by listening; some were visual learners. Print product alone was missing the mark in a sensory-intensive society. Teachers told us that kids in school didn't understand events in time. Which happened first, World War I or the Civil War? Many children did not know where the United States was in relationship to other countries. Could we help? More importantly, teachers wanted youngsters to be able to explore their natural curiosity at their own pace and in their own way.

So, we added pictures, sounds, animation, an interactive atlas, a history timeline, an on-line dictionary, and a natural language search and retrieval system. It was all easy to use, just point and click. At the time of release, in October of 1989, this was revolutionary. It gained immediate acceptance in schools and libraries throughout the United States, which is where all the CD-ROM players were at that time. There were none in the consumer market.

The features that we built into the original Compton's, unique then, are commonplace today. But we have added many new enhancements, including video sequences, slide shows, a navigational tool called *InfoPilot*, and more recently, full-screen, full-motion video. In addition, we continue to pour more than a million dollars a year into the underlying print database of the product to make sure that our content is always current and up-to-date.

Today, Compton's is available in nine different electronic versions and has shipped over two million units. We have also published sixty additional educational, reference, travel, cooking, and business titles. Two years ago, we entered retail distribution. Today, we are one of the largest distributors of CD-ROM titles. We are now exploring the promise of interactive TV.

As we know, 1993 saw widespread acceptance of CD-ROM technology, with over 4 million CD-ROM players shipped; 1994 is off to a great start, with forecasts of an additional 8 million units. 1993 also marked a shifting of the demographics of the marketplace, as the average age of multimedia PC owners declined from 42 to 37, and the major reason for purchase of a multimedia computer at home shifted from work-related to entertainment and education. This changing market dynamic was significant enough for us to form a new entertainment division for music and video-based titles. We have recently announced an interactive CD-ROM on John Lennon and a Sci-Fi title based on the Babylon 5 space station TV series. Both products are being produced jointly with Warner Brothers.

In the late eightees, we started with print as the underlying database, then added photos, audio, and finally video. Today, we recognize that the underlying database doesn't have to be print, but can be video to which text, photos, and interactivity are added. Or it can be music, to which text and video can be added. With Babylon 5, we started from the video, creating both a CD-ROM and a coffee-table book.

We're optimistic about the rapidly growing market for interactive products of all kinds. We see tremendous demand for high-quality multimedia software covering information, education, and entertainment for PC and interactive TV platforms. We plan to be a major player in both marketplaces.

Max Whitby
How do you feel about the protection of formats in interactive media? Having personally gone through the experience of a controversial patent case in the last few years, do you believe there are certain designs and styles of delivering product that it is right to have protected?

Stanley Frank
Let me start with the encyclopedia. The first thing we had to do was look at protecting the underlying database. Users wanted to print out the information. We responded by allowing them to print it out, along with an automatic copyright notice. We think that material needs to be protected for everyone's future safety, and also to ensure that people in print publishing, video, and music feel encouraged to participate in the interactive future.

Max Whitby
What about the patenting and protecting of designs, though? Do you have any comments on that?

Stanley Frank
Our patent is under review right now, so I can't comment on the legal aspects. But obviously, when we developed the property in 1989, we applied for a patent. We'll see how that plays out in the patent office and the courts.

David Liddle

I notice you recurrently use the term *underlying database*, which conveys the idea that starting from a reference orientation, you've added other kinds of products that are still primarily rooted in preexisting works. You're doing what we sometimes call *transmedia*, breathing interactivity and a different kind of life into products that already exist in another form. It's a natural focus for Compton's, but do you also have it in mind that your skills might be applied to doing original material solely designed for an interactive medium?

Stanley Frank

At the present, we are focusing on existing material. All the libraries of the world represent content. If we can add value, it can be repurposed quickly and economically, providing people with interactivity, video, and sound. The same goes for video and music. We're very high on music, which also provides an underlying digital database. In general, to the extent we can add value to an underlying database, we prefer to do it that way. Starting from scratch is very expensive and takes a long time. We think there are many valuable properties. We've licensed over 200 print databases that have been extremely popular in the original print format. We see ways to add value by bringing them to a digital platform. There's a lot to be done right now with what's out there.

Harry Wilker

With the encyclopedia, there is what I call deep interactivity. The sheer volume of information to be delivered, and the computer's ability to reference it randomly, constitutes a clear benefit to the user that cannot be obtained any other way. As you start moving out to other kinds of titles, how do you decide whether or not there's anything in the property that truly lends itself to interactivity? Or is it simply a matter of adding buttons to content so that it can be accessed differently?

Stanley Frank
No, we must be able to add value through providing additional information in different formats. Creative people in the print industry are used to maximizing the print format. If we now present them with an opportunity for creating product in what I call *electronic bindings*, as well as print bindings, they will soon be using the additional parameters available to publish products in video and interactive CD, as well as print. Creative people will pick up on the chance to make their product better. There are many possibilities. Our biggest problem, given finite resources, is getting to the projects in time.

Louise Velázquez
Music on video is a tiny market; people can watch it on TV. Much of the repurposed material I've seen on CD-ROM for different artists, whether Fleetwood Mac, Prince, or others not out yet, is extremely boring. The works were not created by the artist using the tools and grammar that ...

Max Whitby
Can I ask if you've seen Peter Gabriel's *Explora* disc, and whether you characterize that as boring?

Louise Velázquez
I think it's a fledgling effort. It's interesting the first couple of times, but not ten times. I hear your enthusiasm, but without the involvement of artists in the creative process, without their going

back and redoing their work, how is this different from a music video?

Stanley Frank

The consumer will be the ultimate judge. We feel the John Lennon title is going to be a blockbuster. Also, we are thinking of music in terms of a disc that can work either in the CD-audio player, for just the songs, or in the CD-ROM player as well, for information about the group, background, video, text, and so on. No one's vision is perfect, but we believe the music area is going to be very big, and we think we can make an important contribution to it.

Bill Birrell

Bill Birrell and Frank Foster, a double bill from Sony Pictures Imageworks, discuss and demonstrate their company's previsualization tool for filmmakers.

I've been very impressed with the level of discussion so far. This is my first Roundtable. I'm glad to be here and hope to be coming back again.

With production costs spiraling at an annual compound growth rate in excess of 10 percent, Hollywood clearly should be applying technology to help control costs. But Hollywood has always been a very slow adopter of technology, partly due to problems associated with the production process — short lead times and delivery schedules — true for the last seventy years. Our company was founded to facilitate the adoption of new technology. We are a full-service visual effects production company for feature films, television shows, interactive games, IMAX projects, and multimedia projects for Sony Pictures and other clients.

The creation of visual effects is by and large a problem-solving process. Some of the giants in the industry's development are sitting in this room. We regard effects primarily as tools for storytellers. The story is central. One of the key tools is our previsualization system, which, by the way, owes a great deal to Robert Abel & Associates, who were creating vector previsualizations back in the late 1970s. Frank Foster will say more about our system.

Frank Foster
We started investigating the use of multimedia for previsualizing motion picture scenes about two-and-a-half years ago in a research project at Tristar. In *Striking Distance* (originally *Three Rivers*), one of our first projects, we simulated about 30 minutes of stunt sequences with architectural precision, shot-by-shot, providing a very precise tool between the first unit (directors and actors) and second unit (stunts and shots not involving the principal actors).

We work on a PC-compatible platform using a variety of multimedia. About 80 percent of our work is based on Autodesk's 3-D Studio and AutoCAD software. We shot a project on location in Pittsburgh, taking data directly from the Pittsburgh Fire Department and Mayor's Office. We planned out a complete chase sequence involving an actual tunnel in Pittsburgh, based on the data from the city and car data that we have for the various models. Our system had to be fast, inexpensive, and reasonably portable. It had to be easy to use, and it had to have exact camera positioning and the ability to plan out lenses very carefully.

We have the ability with 3-D Studio to grab a camera, pan and tilt, move the camera around, select different wide-angle or telephoto lenses, adjust them, and place elements within the scene. We can very quickly add a mannequin to represent the actor, bring in a prop, and draw on a library of motion. We can shoot a background plate with live action, then have a computer graphics element in the foreground digitally composited later on.

After we're set up, the filmmaker comes in to work with us. We do not create on our own. We try to put the filmmaker's vision into multimedia, helping to express the vision and work it out clearly. An advantage of our system is quick playback from hard disk. In one program, we can load into RAM and run almost in real time. A hard-copy printout provides all of the measurements, and information on where the camera is placed. This assists the crew. Previsualization can also help the director decide if a zoom lens is adequate, or wheter a shot requires a dolly track. Determining this ahead of time can save a great deal of money.

Max Whitby
As a director, what would worry me about using a system like this is that I might get locked into something that looks great on the computer, then miss choices and opportunities on location that I would otherwise have considered.

Frank Foster
There's always flexibility for the director to experiment, especially when rehearsing the actors and refining the performance. What the system helps with is working out some of the technical and mechanical elements of the filmmaking process, so those concerns can be put aside. We don't try to make the movie in the computer.

Bill Birrell
The director is the client, not the studio. The director is in control of both the previsualization and how it is applied to production.

Previsualization provides a chance to experiment with different approaches very cost effectively, without a crew standing around at $10,000 an hour. Other approaches can be tried on set.

David Liddle
You made it clear that you don't make a prototype film with this system, although it's a possibility I find especially interesting. You seem to work through a number of different alternatives for the director. I notice the system is used in an ongoing way during the course of the film. It's kept live, rather than being used ahead of time to make up the ultimate cinematography and recipe for the film. In your use of it as a diagnostic tool during the production process, I see why it has to be portable, durable, and inexpensive. How well does that work out, and what are the ramifications for getting field-oriented people comfortable with this technology?

Frank Foster
A large part of what we are now doing is getting people comfortable with the system, and marketing it to filmmakers who are not yet accustomed to it. One of our main mandates is to make the technology available so that directors and filmmakers will use it, not only in previsualizing scenes, but also for planning title design. In fact, most of our title design is now done on the computer, all the way through to final execution. It's all digital, right up to the film.

But you're right; the process is ongoing. We initially thought we would be involved only in preproduction, then walk away and let them make the movie. But we're finding that they call us back. There's something they need to know, such as whether a motion-control camera will fit into a miniature correctly. They want to find out before being tied into the shot.

Bill Birrell

Computing is no longer the exclusive domain of the specialist. People with an interesting problem can now get over the lowered threshold, and feel competent and comfortable with the technology. Directors, who are not early adopters, are grabbing the mouse and starting to work on the previsualization themselves, with our artist.

The system also facilitates communication between first and second units. A significant portion of the picture is often shot by the two units simultaneously. The director, who has limited day-to-day input, has to use storyboards (an inaccurate form at best) as the most efficient way to get down ideas and communicate them. The system gives the first-unit director a way of indicating what is wanted from the second-unit director, and gives the second-unit director the ability to communicate back on what to expect.

Bill Gross

Bill Gross reveals the secrets of Knowledge Adventure's success with an analysis of the company's strategy and mission, and a demonstration of the title 3D Body Adventure.

I want to do three things very quickly: say who we are, reveal the secrets of our success, and describe how we've applied these secrets to make new ways of learning. We're the enriching-experience software company. We're trying to create the most enriching experiences for children and adults on the widest number of platforms possible. We started out making products for floppy disks, but 50 percent of our business is now on CD-ROM. Scott Billups said earlier that CD-ROM is obsolete. It might be in the future, and will be in the on-line business, but right now we can put 6 billion ones and zeroes on a piece of plastic and print it for 97 cents. This is so absolutely incredible, it is going to have a lasting impact on civilization. Even if CD-ROM becomes obsolete in a few years, it is great practice for what is coming. We have tried to utilize the utmost of performance and technological achievement in the CD-ROM environment for just that reason.

What have we done to succeed as a company? First, we have worked on a true marriage of content and technology. We're located at the center of the triangle of Arts Center College of Design, Caltech, and Hollywood. All of our programmers are from Caltech, almost all of our artists are from Art Center, and most of our writers, directors, and producers are from Hollywood. We have combined them in one location.

I believe technology will provide important differentiation in our industry for the rest of this decade, maybe always. By comparison, the use of technology in the movie and book business is more on a level playing field. In those businesses, technology does not afford as much of a competitive advantage. We believe that pushing the platform can enable us to make a much more powerful experience, and we work very hard at that. We develop all of our own technology in-house. I think anyone who wants to succeed in this business should work on having differentiated technology that is better than the standard tools.

We move very fast. We make titles in approximately four to six months from conception to completion. No one can touch us on that. We do it because we have very small teams. When I first started the company, we had just five people, working only for equity. We worked as a very tight, small entrepreneurial group. We're now doing exactly the same thing with multiple teams in the company. We've empowered each individual group. We don't pay people much, but give them a lot of upside in the projects. We work long hours and beat everyone else to market. Our products cost only 10 to 20 percent of what others spend to make their titles; not 10 to 20 percent less, but 1/10 to 1/5, and still with very high production values.

Another secret of our success is to grow quickly.[8] People are grabbing market share right now, which is very cheap compared to what it's going to cost. We've been growing at 300 percent a year for the last two years, and plan to do it again this year. It's very exciting, and also very stressful on the organization. But we've learned how to do it. We think it's a big advantage.

Going beyond development, we focus only on what we call *enriching-experience* software. We haven't ventured off into the game market, or into violent shoot-em-up products, and we're not doing *skill-and-drill*. We want people to come away with an experience that will add value and provide enrichment. It starts with the content. Almost all of our products are created from absolute scratch, with no porting of existing property.

In the marketplace, we listen to customers like crazy. We bribe them in every way we can to send back their registration cards, so we know who they are and can call them. My brother is in charge of quality assurance and technical support. Although he went to Caltech and is a developer, he's also very sensitive to what customers want. He talks to them all day long so that he can translate their ideas directly into our products. This provides a very tight feedback loop.

At the same time, we are working hard to build brands. We have an hexagonal-box series of Adventure products, currently with fifteen titles. *XYZ Adventure* is starting to mean something in the minds of consumers. We're building other product lines as well. In our line with IMAX films, we're adding depth and drill-down capabilities. We're doing very bold marketing and PR, and get a great deal of recognition for a company of our size. As merely a tiny start-up in La Crescenta, California, I'm amazed to be here at the Roundtable with major digital studios and publishers. We're proud of how much notice we've been able to get, yet we know there's much more to do. We're practicing for what's to come.

Our new product, *3D Body Adventure*, has 3D models of various parts of the body fully under mouse control. We can rotate body parts by moving the mouse left or right, open and close the hand with the mouse, identify body parts, and click on a part to look at it in more detail. The product also has flybys of body parts rendered on an SGI work station and decompressed in real time, with hypertext links that allow drilling down in multiple directions. It is designed to allow people to visualize things in new ways. This is done partly with content (we have a team of doctors and artists creating models) and also with technology, to enable things to be done that couldn't be done before.

3D Body Adventure provides depth and perception not evident from flat pictures in a book. In our *3D Dinosaur Adventure*, we have a dinosaur theme park in 3D, but the 3D is just a gimick. In *Body Adventure*, the 3D is used for enhancement of the educational process. We want to build other products where we take devices apart to show their insides in a way we couldn't do before. For example, we want to build a car engine that allows people to fly through the carburetor, pistons, and valves in full 3D, taking a look at how the engine works from the inside out. We want them to draw their own conclusions, have an experience doing it, and make discoveries that they would not have made otherwise. Our measure of success is goose bumps per hour, or goose bumps per dollar, and how much we can excite people to make discoveries on their own, giving them the aha! experience.

Max Whitby

There are an awful lot of names on the credits for *3D Body Adventure*. How long did it take? What did it cost?

Bill Gross

The product was started last September, and we just shipped diskette and CD-ROM versions in April. So, it was probably six or seven months. It cost between $150,000 and $200,000.

Harry Wilker

As a competitor, I'm envious of both your development times and your costs. How do you turn products around so quickly and still focus on the aha! factor editorially?

Bill Gross

We do it with kid testing every Tuesday afternoon. We bring in both registered users of our products and people who don't even know who we are. We expose them to a topic with books at first, then videos, then prototypes of the product. We have a very fast prototyping system, so we can find out what's turning people on early in the process. This helps us greatly.

I think a company is as good as its producers. Their personalities are in the products. The producer must have a vision for what it takes — a great story, a great discovery, a great aha! It has to come from the mind of someone who is passionate about it. That's what inspired me about Robert Winter's Beethoven product. It had such exciting analysis and content. It wasn't just Beethoven's Ninth on a CD-ROM, with some commentary on the side. A product has to have that passion or it's not going to work.

David Liddle

You said you felt companies had to build and control their own key technologies. I agree completely. You haven't given in to the prevailing cowardice on standards. You take the position that you can do something worthwhile and do it better, so why not take a chance that it may earn it's place. You deserve recognition for this.

Bill Gross

Well thanks, I hope it continues to pay off. I think it will, because many other successful products in the history of the PC business have also pushed their platform. They did not just adopt the lowest common denominator. I think we have to continue to come out with nonstandard technologies. Our compression is completely non-MPEG, and we had full-screen, full-motion displays, with no hardware assist, long before anyone else. Each time something new comes along, we try to leapfrog it. We have to keep doing this.

David Liddle

What we are beginning to learn in multimedia is that we sometimes have to take a bigger bite to do what we would really like to do. Is your company building a platform for its own use?

Bill Gross

That's exactly what we're doing. Here's another example. I loved Pavel Curtis' talk about people and community. We're working on that too, and want to embed it in our products. On the back of *Wired* Magazine, there's an *Absolut Museum* (a three-disc set available for $29.95) that we developed with Ogilvy and Mather for

Absolut Vodka. It has a 3D virtual reality zoomscape through which one can navigate. All the work we put into it was based on new technology. Taking the risk again, we connected a multi-user modem so that many people can be walking around in the museum, talking to one another and having a sense of community. Pavel Curtis is doing this with ASCII, but we want to make it rich and graphical. I urge you to take a look at that museum.

Max Whitby
Before moving on, I'd like to ask David Liddle whether he thinks there will be a wide range of small independent companies producing a huge variety of CD titles, or a consolidation over the next five years leading to a Hollywood-type studio approach?

David Liddle
Voyager, *Wired*, and Interval Research decided to run a contest aimed at experimental new work to see what we could do to stimulate some right angle thinking in this area. It's crystal clear that there's a mainstream business to be constructed out of repurposed work and conventional approaches to production. What's unclear is whether independent artists and small organizations can produce things sufficiently startling and interesting to gain economic momentum. My hope is that they can.

The movie industry in its early days filmed stage plays at the traditional audience distance under a proscenium arch. It took a while before the Russian, Sergei Eisenstein, decided that he could zoom in for close-ups. People would run screaming from the theatre at the sight of a nostril the size of a truck tire. But suddenly filmmakers came to understand what might be done with the new medium. I like to think we've learned from this and can now try more dangerous small-scale experments to jump-start the process.

Max Whitby

In the case of Hollywood, the studios formed quickly because it was simply too expensive for a small group of people to produce a movie themselves. These days, as we were discussing earlier, the technology is sufficiently low-priced and powerful for individuals and small groups to take control of it themselves. One of the interesting questions about the digital revolution is whether production will be absorbed by the current corporate structures or be dispersed among a wider community of creative people.

Hal Josephson[9]

Hal Josephson seeks to explain how creativity can be enhanced and performance maximized with 3DO technology, but a twist of fate intervenes and he has trouble showing the title Twisted.

3DO recently announced that it is entering the publishing business. It will publish a few titles this year, and is doing some affiliate label deals internally, something it did not anticipate. Software drives hardware. 3DO wants publishers to push the limits of what can be created. The company is internally creating new engines to enable things to be done with software that have never been done before.

Twisted, a creative breakthrough by Electronic Arts, is a good example. It's an interactive game show that doesn't involve violence. It's not the typical format of point-and-click or look-at-an-hourglass-until-the-video-comes-up. Using 3D cell animation, actors shot against blue screen are incorporated into computer graphic environments. In the software, you pick a character and become that character throughout the game. When you launch the title, you can set the level for adult or child, so you can play on the same game with your kids, a unique way to bring interactivity into the home. The game includes trivia questions and challenges from a challenge wheel, with the ability to move full-motion-video characters around in different environments. The platform is creatively optimized using audio cues to take you through the interactive content, eliminating the buttons.

Twisted is a first example of next-generation software using 3DO's software tool kit to optimize the performance characteristics of the machine. This gives the creative community the opportunity to do things not before possible on traditional CPUs, where the run speed is inadequate for transmitting high-bandwidth video information.

Bob Stein

Bob Stein is unable to get audio from the Voyager title, A Society of Mind. He decides not to go ahead with his demo, initiating instead a discussion that turns into a peppery and informative exchange.

I haven't slept in 24 hours and feel even crankier than usual. I've been to the Roundtable all five years, and it may be because I'm tired, but I don't think I've ever seen so much videotape. I like Bill Gross' stuff, but it's depressing that so little of what has been shown actually means something to people and makes a difference. Not that our stuff is any better.

It's always hard to make a cogent point in a few minutes. I'm hoping you've seen some of what we've done. Last year at the Roundtable, we showed the Beatles' *Hard Days Night*. It uses QuickTime with that little window in the corner. The first question everyone always asks when they see it is, can we make the window bigger? Yes, we can, but the window has text on the side. Every time we make the window bigger, the text disappears. I find this problematic, because I think text is important for the foreseeable future, especially if we want to have a dialogue in society that will make a difference.

We've been thinking at Voyager about how to integrate video and text in a way that will allow the two to live together in some kind of harmony. We did a project last summer with Marvin Minsky, a computer science professor at MIT, based on his book, *A Society of Mind*.[10] The producer, Ann Marion, who is here, and her partner Moe Shore, came up with a fabulous new way of doing video which makes video and text seamless on the page together.

Max Whitby
Bob is being extremely provocative. Would anyone like to challenge his crankiness?

Brenda Laurel
I don't want to challenge it; I want to reinforce it a little. I have to say that seeing John and Yoko making love on a computer screen in the new Lennon title is offensive to me. And if 3DO thinks that emulating a game show is the moral high ground because it's not violent, I've got news -- it's still cultural flotsam. I'm disappointed.

Harry Wilker
Voyager has been one of the companies that has avoided this flotsam. Bob, you seem to have a model that cares very deeply about the nature and editorial content of what you put out. What kind of a process and organization have you built to promote this?

Bob Stein
Voyager is basically an editorially-driven company. We have people who care about the ideas the authors are trying to express.

Like good editors, they exist to help the authors say what they want to say. It's very collaborative and integrative, trying to understand what the authors are saying and helping them say it in this new medium. We're editorially strong and technically fairly weak.

David Liddle
You make products for an intellectual audience and avoid a market-oriented approach, choosing what you think is worthy, then hoping that by doing a good job with it, there will be a market. That's very useful, because it sets a flag out on the turf, and there aren't very many other flags around. What's your sense of the expectations for multimedia? Do you think everyone is accepting the idea of its just being raw entertainment? Or is there a public perception that it ought to be intellectually worthwhile as well? Is there a *NewYork Times* kind of reader out there for this work?

Bob Stein
There probably is, but these issues go way past our industry and the technology with which we're working. They are deep and fundamental social and political questions. Yes, I end up making things for a relatively small part of the market, but I don't think it should be that way. I don't think we should have a society where only 10 percent of the people still think. It's not the kind of society we want to live in. In fact, the society will die if it continues this way. Extrapolating forward, it gets worse and worse.

On the other hand, I don't think Voyager is changing the world by making thoughtful titles. It's happening in the broader society, not in this room and not in this industry. I think we have a role to play; I'm not saying we can't help. But I'm not sure that if we all stop producing stupid things and create good things instead, it would make any difference, unless we could change the rest of society.

David Liddle
We tend to associate a technology with the most common interpretations made of it. It's clear from the work of Voyager and others, that this technology, with its ordinarily banal uses, is capable of being applied in much more meaningful ways. That's the flag planted by your works; it's why they are very important.

Max Whitby
George Gilder has written vividly on this subject.

George Gilder
People don't clearly understand the difference between making first-choice products and products for which people just *settle*. The multimedia industry is imitating the boob tube. Whenever I debate people in the broadcasting industry, they always come up to me afterwards and whisper in my ear, "You don't understand, George. The reason it's an idiot box, the reason it's a boob tube, is because the people are boobs."

I see the same sentiment emerging here. It's the effect of a top-down technology, with bottlenecks greatly restricting the amount of choice. Everyone has to *settle*. I have to settle for the choice of Expanded Books that Voyager offers. I don't happen to like most of them. I did like Gleick's book on Feynman, which was terrific, but I couldn't read it in the Expanded Book form. I just couldn't get through it. I had to buy a printed copy.[11] But that's an aside.

The key is that with the book business producing 55,000 books a year, everyone gets their first choice. The book culture is drastically different from the video culture today because people get what they want, rather than settling for some lowest common denominator that appeals to a miscellaneous TV audience. As soon as the multimedia industry can offer enough of a selection so that people will get their first choice, then the same people who are boobs when they are flicking through 50 channels (I'm a boob when I'm flicking through 50 channels) become intelligent purchasers and evoke excellent products.

This is why I think the information superhighway is central. It will allow creative people to circumvent the bottleneck and produce excellent products that are the first choice of the customer, rather than something customers settle for from among 50 possiblilites. This is how the technology can uplift the culture. Companies like 3DO that make products for boobs are going to fail. Companies that make products for the boob tube, which can't render text, are going to fail. It's companies like Voyager that are targeting an intelligent market which will eventually succeed.

Bob Stein
I think you're being a complete Pollyanna, George. It might be nice if it happened, but I don't see any reason why it should.

George Gilder
Look at the book business. There's incredible choice. A third of the most successful books are religious books, another third are technology books of the best quality possible, and another third are excellent literature of various kinds. A few best sellers reflect the boob-tube culture. They are translations from the tube by celebrity writers who emerge from this Madonna culture.

Bob Stein
Even if we accept the book business as something fabulous, which it isn't so much anymore, even if we take it as a paragon of virtue, its economics are entirely different from those of interactive media.

You're just not going to see 55,000 published works every year. Society is not going to fund them.

George Gilder
Why not? Joy's Law says that computer cost effectiveness doubles every year. On that kind of a learning curve, we're going to be able to produce excellent multimedia products at a cost comparable to the cost of producing a book.

Max Whitby
Bob, one of the ways this medium may be different from television is that the control of distribution need not be centralized. Have you considered putting any of your products on the Internet?

Bob Stein
Most of our titles would not work on the Internet, because they require too much bandwidth. I think the world is going that way, and expect twenty years from now to sell directly to the consumer, but we're in a transitional period of five to ten years before the high-bandwidth infrastructure is there.

Max Whitby
If one is looking for a wider range of choice, do you think the possiblity of an Internet type of distribution is a reason for hope?

Bob Stein
No, it doesn't deal with the fundamental question of cost of development. It makes it easier to distribute, and perhaps reduces marketing costs, but not development costs. Stuff we did five years ago costs us twice as much to do now, and may be costing others three or four times as much. I make stuff much more cheaply than Bill Gross, but the break-even is still too high. There's going to be

an unbelievable crash-and-burn in this industry, much bigger than people think. Selling 100,000 units will be very difficult for most of the titles being made, especially given their quality.

Laurin Herr
Why are your production costs increasing? Are people more expensive, or are your production values getting higher?

Bob Stein
It mostly has to do with people. Those who came to work for us five years ago with no experience, dying to be in this business, would work alongside of us for little pay in order to do something exciting. They can now go to R. R. Donnelley and make $125,000 a year. Or they can go to Silicon Valley and make $80,000 to $90,000. We still try to pay people $35,000 a year. It just doesn't cut it.

Bill Gross
I think a lot of it is the competitive environment. The ante is being upped every day. The customer is getting smarter and demanding more. We have to put more people on these products to make them stand out in the market.

Bob Stein
Yes, but I also think some companies are overpaying relative to what the return can be. There's a tremendous heterogeneity in this business: record people, video people, movie people, computer software people, publishing people, all from industries that pay their people differently. Hollywood's spending $2 million on a game is a small budget.

Notes

[1] A play on words taken from the talk at the Roundtable by James Billington.
[2] Henry Jenkins, *Textual Poachers: Television Fans and Participatory Cuture*, New York, Routledge, 1992.
[3] Four months after the Roundtable, Graphix Zone announced an agreement with Columbia Records to produce another Interactive Music CD-ROM (IMCD), this one on Bob Dylan.
[4] By the end of July 1994, the Prince title was first in sales and labeled "HOT" at Virgin Megastore in Los Angeles on both Macintosh and IBM platforms.
[5] *Myst* was produced by Robyn and Rand Miller of Cyan and was published by Broderbund.
[6] Cortright clearly means "from start to finish." The slip was too good to correct in the editing. It resembles one made by a high government official a while back, who declared, in presenting his carefully constructed plan, "each step is based on the next."
[7] The recent TurboTax CD-ROM for doing taxes employs the technology in its tutorial. A tax accountant gives advice about tax planning and how to prepare reports.
[8] Still another secret of Knowledge Adventure's success appears to be Bill Gross' persuasiveness. After meeting Ruth Otte, then president and COO of Discovery Networks, at the Roundtable, Gross lost no time convincing her to join Knowledge Adventure as president, which she did five months later.
[9] Five months after the Roundtable, Hal Josephson left 3DO to become president of the Interactive Media Festival.
[10] Marvin Minsky, *A Society of Mind*, Voyager Company Expanded Book, 1994.
[11] James Gleick, *Genius: The Life and Science of Richard Feynman*, Random House, 1993.

Transformation of Education

Questioning and Preserving Traditional Values

It has been argued that just as computer technololgy is flattening the hierarchies and breaking down pyramids, monopolies, and bureaucracies in industrial society, so too will it bring about the demise of education as we know it.[1] The cataclysm that befell the Soviet Union, the argument continues, foreshadows what's in store for a similarly bureaucratic school system.[2] It's just a matter of time.

How much time? How much change? How will it happen? What will be left? The panelists don't seem to expect a major transformation right away. Alan November suggests that giving a toilet a warmer seat or faster flush merely adds comfort and convenience, much as technology used in schools to warm and speed up the curriculum provides convenience but not fundamental change. He wants a new vision for education based on a new job description for students.

To Seymour Papert, school has little redeeming value. He deplores the adoption of a curriculum, segregation by ages, accreditation, the teacher at the front of the class, and the cutting of knowledge into little pieces. Maybe "child force" enabled by technology can set things right. John Grillos reviews the mission of education and considers its financial side, noting the increasing use of CD-ROMs in schools. Bernard Gifford describes a technology-mediated learning environment that is achievement-rich; Connie Stout reports on progress in networking teachers in Texas; and David Niguidula outlines the principles of teacher-centered reform at The Coalition for Essential Schools. Moderator John Kernan puts questions raised by panelists on the table, and a spirited discussion ensues.

Martin Greenberger
One of the highlights at each of the Roundtables is the session on education, a place where the new technology can make a major difference. Our highly experienced panel is led by John Kernan, who went off last year to start a new company. He had been CEO of Jostens Learning, the largest educational software company.

John Kernan
The topic that Martin has set out for us is the transformation of education, with a focus on traditional values. The idea is to explore ways we can use the new technology to make a positive difference in education, transforming the system, while at the same time preserving values we cherish from our own school days: the caring teacher, the friendships we made, the field trips, prom night, and so on. A great book I'm very fond of has the title, *All I Really Need To Know I Learned in Kindergarten.*[3] I don't remember seeing anything about the information superhighway or MPEG2 there.

Let's start with a little exercise. How would you compare today's educational system to school as you remember it? Is it better? (many hands) Is it worse? (many hands) Is it roughly the same? (many hands) That's about half of the participants for each of the three answers! Now, do you believe that the technologies we're talking about here at the Roundtable will have a positive effect on our nation's educational system? That's almost everyone. Keep your hand up if you have a clear vision of exactly how they will do this. Just seven people in the back (they may be out of earshot and only heard me ask them to keep their hands up). That's what I find at education gatherings around the country. Everyone is certain that technology is going to have a positive impact on education, but no one knows exactly how.

We have a distinguished and diverse set of panelists. I've asked each to pose a thought-provoking question. First, Alan November.

Alan November

I want to start with a familiar technology (brandishes a toilet seat). Imagine that your job is to transform and preserve what's good about this technology and this organizational design. I've been coast-to-coast studying how this system would be transformed if we applied supercomputer and multimedia technology to it. If you wanted to add features to this toilet seat, what would you do?

Here's what my research has shown. One, it has to have a gender recognizer. It has to know who's coming: the seat flips down or up without creating hassles in the family. It has to glow in the dark. If you have a 3-year old son, like I do, it has to be remedial, and it has to move to catch his stream, so he gets it right every time. Not only that, it has to be able to change color to match your bath prints. It ought to be ergonomic, adjusting for wide bodies, rising up or moving down for tall or short, and if you have a little trouble, it ought to be ejecting as well. Depending on your culture, it should vibrate just a little bit to help you. Maybe it ought to have some butt recognition, so it can do personalized multimedia, making magazines and newspapers unnecessary.

Last year in Singapore and Japan, 80,000 people spent $20,000 each on high-tech toilets. Twenty thousand bucks! Let's imagine that Nippon Telephone becomes a big investor in this technology and puts a touch pad in the bathroom wall. You punch in your personal code. The toilet has to know who you are before you go. The telephone line connected to the base of the toilet makes a call to get a complete urinalysis every time, and can check for colon cancer as well. The data flows to your doctor's office, where it is processed by a 120-day averaging algorithm. If something doesn't look good after a few days, the office calls you to come in for an examination. This is *real-time medicine* — not a check-up every two years, but in real time. Would this be worth $20,000?

The question applies to education as well. As I read the literature, there are only two ways to think about technology in the schools. We can take technology and improve what we're already doing, called *automation*. Almost all of what I see these days is automation. We're trying to improve current reality, like warming the seat or flushing the toilet faster. We're flushing the curriculum faster. An automated feature is not worth $20,000, because it hasn't given us a new vision of what schools can be. Until we put in the telephone line and have data flowing to the doctor's office, the business of the toilet stays the same, even with multimedia. It gets rid of human waste. The technologies are peripheral. They're just there for convenience — to make life more manageable — perhaps to self-clean. But when we add telecommunications in real time, the toilet enters a new business — wellness. Depending on your medical condition, it can extend your life by 10 or 15 years. That's worth 20,000 bucks!

So, my question is, what is the new business (not the new technologies, but the new business) of education? What problems can students solve, and what role can they play in life with these technologies that they simply cannot play without them? In improving tests, learning more stuff, learning more stuff faster, we're just automating the current reality. But stepping back from the technology, what is the role of students in a complex global economy? What kinds of problems will they be able to solve that they've never been able to solve before? A critical part of that question is, what role can they play? What is their job description?

Most people default to the doctor for their urinalysis. In fact, I'll bet most people have never even seen their urinalysis. They simply default to the highest level of education. But in the toilet example, you get the readout on an LCD panel in your bathroom before your doctor does. You now have much more responsibility for understanding your own body, and for maintaining your own nutrition and exercise. Your role fundamentally changes. Patients take on much more responsibility for their own health.

What will be the new role of children because of new technologies? What will they be able to do that they have never done before?

Seymour Papert

All my life I've thought of myself as a Young Turk bucking the establishment. Today, I may be in some sense the oldest person here. I thought I'd take advantage of this fact and reflect on the experience of having lived through the evolution of at least three waves in the development of computer technology. There's a common pattern that's very relevant.

Marvin Minsky and I cofounded the Artificial Intelligence Laboratory at MIT in the middle 1960s. In those days, artificial intelligence was this cognate enterprise that looked into such questions as, can a machine be made vastly more intelligent than a person? Then came the 1970s. An interesting kind of Gresham's law took hold.[4] Many critics say that AI collapsed because of a failure of vision. More likely, it collapsed because of its worldly success. All of a sudden it became possible to make a little expert system, a little robot, all sorts of little things that could be used tomorrow. This took the energy and the funding, and it dominated the atmosphere of the field.

I wondered yesterday, looking at both the title and the presentations in the session on successful multimedia, if there might be a similar phenomenon taking place now. I remember a much more grandiose vision at an earlier Roundtable, maybe not as cosmic as AI, but nearly. Now we're talking about instances of successful multimedia. Well, these are not bad things. They're very good things, and they are examples of ingenuity. But the visionary scale has come down to different proportions.

I remember during the 1970s when Alan Kay and I used to talk about what computers in education would be like. This was a grandiose vision of a revolutionary change in schools. Then in the 1980s, as computers began creeping in, I caught myself telling school establishments and administrators that, with this technology, I had what they needed. Wow! It's not what they need at all. It's poison to them. It's the kiss of death. It's the end of everything they stand for. It's the end of education as an organized entity — of the school as we've known it. That's the question I propose here. Is there any reason to believe that the school — with it's structure of classroom, segregation by age, and so on — will exist in 50 years? I like Alan November's example of the toilet seat, except that the toilet in some form is always going to be there.

Alan November
Who knows?

Seymour Papert
Well, who knows? But I think there's more reason to suppose that the toilet will be there in some form than that schools will be there. The central distinction I'd like to make is between school or education as an organized enterprise, on the one hand, and the learning environment (everything relevant to learning), on the

other. Obviously, the learning environment is going to go on, but I think the school has no redeeming virtue whatsoever.

We talk about socialization. Yes, I made lots of friends in school, but you know, Dostoyevsky[5] became a great writer on his own admission because of the major transformation he underwent after being thrown into prison in exile in Siberia. Solzhenitsyn[6] matured to great depths of spirituality and ability as a writer after being cast into Stalin's prison camps. The worst system can produce some good effects. I think that socialization in schools is of that nature. At school, socialization means that students in the first grade spend a whole year there learning how to deal with people of that age. Then the year comes to an end and they never see people of that age again. They have to spend the next year learning to deal with people of the next age.

Why do I think the learning environment will change so as to do away with school as we know it? Let me be clear. I don't mean there won't be new places where children gather together to learn, think, act, and work. We can't outguess the future. I'm only saying that what we've known in the past will go. It's about 100 years since John Dewey developed his plan to change school. It influenced how education works, but didn't really transform or do away with school. Why? Because Dewey had to rely on philosophical arguments. Philosophical arguments are never enough to change a deeply rooted social institution.

Today we have a force, in fact many forces for change. This whole technology movement is one. But there's a more potent force. It's *child force*. I recently visited with a grandchild who's three. I was amazed watching him select a videotape (he's got a collection of National Geographic videotapes), load it into the VCR, and look at it. He can't read, but he could tell what videotape it was. He's growing up with access to knowledge in a spontaneous, natural, self-directed way. It is inconceivable that this child will happily sit through anything like a curriculum where a teacher has an agenda of what to learn today. The whole concept of curriculum, accreditation, and segregation by ages is entirely a product of outmoded ways of disseminating knowledge. This kid is learning the difference. So that's my question. How long will it take before children say, "We won't take this anymore," and the school will collapse?

John Grillos

My firm is in the business of channeling money as growth capital into the most exciting companies in America. We expect to see some of these companies in education. As the two gentlemen preceding me pointed out, education needs to change. It must change either by evolution or revolution. There's a possibility that technology, at least working at the fringes, can help make that happen.

The topic of this session was a challenge for me because it refers to transforming education while preserving the traditional values of our schools — and I wasn't sure what these values are. Given that technology will probably affect teaching, I asked myself whether our goal should be to preserve teaching as we see it. I think not. So I tried to conceptualize what I thought the mission of education should be, and came up with a list of eleven things: (1) subject matter mastery (the three R's); (2) learning to think; (3) discipline; (4) peer interaction and cooperation; (5) learning leadership skills; (6) learning respect for the opinions of others; (7) learning to listen; (8) building pride and confidence; (9) getting close to intellectual excitement in learning; (10) ethics; and (11) morals.

That's a long list, but it appears to me that technology may play a role in only two of these areas: (1) core subject matter mastery, and (8) building pride and confidence. What technology can do, if you believe this mission statement, is relieve teachers of rote activities, allowing them to transform their job into more of the coaching and social interaction required to prepare our children for society. How can that happen? At a minimum, multimedia technology can provide a level of expertise and completeness that we can't expect from a teacher or a curriculum. Multimedia can individually paste things; it is multilingual; and it can provide instantaneous grading and feedback on the fly.

These are significant advantages, but they bring me back to the issue of money. Will technology add enough value in areas where it can really work to make a difference? Will schools be willing to pay for that value? In thinking about investing in education and how education companies will develop, we are not even sure if the education system will be able to pay for technical support. I've visited over 100 schools with computer labs. The vast majority of those labs are in the hands of people not well enough trained to use them. In almost 50 percent of the schools I visited, the computer labs weren't being used very much at all.

This leads me to ask whether multimedia will happen in schools? My answer is, without a doubt. I've never seen more horsepower behind an industry segment in the more than 25 years that I've been in this business. There are over 5,000 multimedia titles in development right now. Multimedia software sales in the fourth quarter of last year were $104 million. Hundreds of millions of dollars are being invested in this industry segment by the federal government, state and local governments, industry, venture capitalists, and investment plans. Millions of multimedia systems are being sold.

Seven million CD-ROMs were purchased towards the end of last year. By the end of this year, two million will be installed in our schools. With videodiscs, we struggled to get from 50,000 to 150,000 in a period of three years. I agree with those who said last night that the personal multimedia computer is going to be the hottest selling consumer electronics device in history. They're going into homes. They're going into businesses. They must go into schools, or education's credibility will continue to be questioned. Kids are using this technology in their homes. At the Roundtable last year, the average multimedia encyclopedia had a street price of well over $295. I think it's $49 now. A CD-ROM publisher can bundle a complete encyclopedia and dictionary in every one of its research CD-ROM titles for a couple of dollars.

So that brings me to my question: Will the multimedia school market be a viable economic proposition? I am of the strong belief that if we cannot make it a viable economic proposition, we will not be able to keep the private sector engaged in trying to develop multimedia technology, and we will not see the positive impact on schools. We won't get out of the chute.

Bernard Gifford
I've known Martin for over 20 years. He interviewed me in the early 1970s when I led the New York City Rand Institute. The Institute was trying to transform New York City government with the help of innovative analytical methods. If you've visited New York recently, you know how successful we've been.

Martin, like any good professor, poses a very provocative question: How do we transform education and preserve traditional values? I've been thinking about the issue. I'd like to make a couple of statements and then offer an example of a transformational solution that I think would enable us to use technology in creative and productive ways.

First of all, traditional value does not mean traditional behavior. I think we too often confuse our own habits, proclivities, and prejudices with traditional values. Traditional value does not mean teaching. It means learning. There's a profound distinction between the two. Traditional value does not mean schooling, but intellectual growth and development. Traditional value does not mean passive acceptance of received information, facts, and bits of knowledge, but the active participation of learners in the construction of their own knowledge. Traditional value does not mean technologically assisted eye-candy, but learner-centered, technology-mediated learning.

What we have in school today is the traditional teacher/textbook/student model, with prescribed directions of influence and interaction. What we've been doing in education for the last 12 years is bolting technology onto an existing teaching and learning enterprise. We have not changed it; we've tried to fix it through a form of technological grafting. This model is not additive; it's inconsistently implemented. We have no notion of what does and does not work. In fact, even researchers are quite often unclear as to whether they are adding technology to the capabilities of the instructor, the student, or the textbook. All three models have been tried. They all increase the cost of education, with mixed results.

Let me offer another model, a model in which the learner is placed at the center of the teaching and learning enterprise. This is a model that we're implementing — not just thinking or theorizing about — at Academic Systems. It is a model that places instructional text, the instructors, and a technology-mediated learning environment at the disposal of students. A technology-mediated learning environment is a system that allows students to go through a course at their own pace, at their own schedule, in accordance with their own diagnosed learning needs. It incorporates a learning management system and continuous real-time evaluation. The student's own learning drives the system and makes the instructor aware of acceleration or retardation.

What are some of the inherent advantages and disadvantages of traditional instruction versus the mediated-learning environment? Traditional instruction is a limited-media, limited-interaction model. Access is restricted to instructors. Instructors invest low-value instructional activities in the classroom. A mediated-learning environment, instead, makes productive use of interactive multimedia instructional technologies. It puts the student or learner at the center of the teaching and learning enterprise. It results in a productive use of teacher expertise and teacher talent. Most important, it generates measurable results. It is an achievement-rich system, rather than a technology-rich system.

How will this be implemented this year and five years from now? This year we expect to be installing a mediated-learning system in a few colleges and universities around the country. The digital video will come off of a Starlight-assisted file server. The courseware, the instructional management system, and the assessment system will come off of a standard server. Students will be able to receive information and learn at their own pace in an environment where the teachers pull them out, engage them in small-group instruction, and have them work on high-level problem-solving tasks. We think this model will take us from the bolt-on solution to one that gets closer to transformation.

In the long run, we are going to move away from the school, the college, and the university as we know it, defined by buildings and physical boundaries, to an institution defined by its capabilities to distribute interactive learning experiences. With the advent of the superhighway, we're going to see an emergence of colleges and universities that understand how the world is changing. They will distribute learning to businesses, to homes, and obviously on their own campuses. The chancellor of the Dallas Community College District predicts that by the year 2010 his district will be generating about one-third of its revenue from the distribution of learning using this model.

Not only is this model more effective in promoting student learning, it is far more efficient. Higher education is suffering from a cost disease today. Its costs, along with those of pharmaceuticals, have been increasing at rates 3 to 5 percent higher than inflation for the last 25 years. Only through intelligent utilization of interactive multimedia technology can we make higher education more productive and more efficient simultaneously. When the information highway moves off the front page of the Wall Street Journal into the homes, and to teachers and learners, we're going to see true distributive learning. My question to the panel is, how do we move from the bolt-on solution to a true transformational solution in education?

Connie Stout
I'm going to speak from the perspective of a classroom teacher. I taught for about sixteen years, the first year in a classroom that was long and narrow in an old school building in Fort Worth, Texas. With forty children to a room, it was difficult to achieve my goals. It struck me that if a teacher certified in 1890 walked into my classroom, she could have gone to the chalkboard and begun to

teach. If a doctor certified in 1890 walked into a modern operating room, he would be bewildered. Education has not changed much in the last 100 years.

As a teacher I was a troublemaker. I tried to do things differently. Eventually, I left the classroom for the State Department of Education, where I looked at what I could do to make an impact on education. I saw a need for communications, as there is in all states. In cooperation with the State Legislature, I developed the idea of a communications network to link schools, teachers, classrooms, and students. With State backing, I tried to obtain bids on the project. No one bid. They said, "You can't do it Connie." Eventually I went to the University of Texas, where they run THE Net, and to Texas A&M. Both said they would help. I knew then that we could do it, and we went ahead.

The network has now been operating for 2 1/2 years based on the Internet. Over 30,000 educators use it, logging in at a rate of over 150 interactions per month. Last February, when we put up our university interscholastic league assignment — which tells coaches what schools play each other — we had over 7,000 log-ins, showing that if we have something relevant, it will be used.

Our surveys over the network showed that teachers feel the system revolutionized their work, even though it's not high-tech and we do not have large workstations in our schools (we're not prepared for the information age; we still have Apple IIs and Radio Shack Model 4s). Still, our system gives teachers new-found freedom and makes students feel they can be very productive. A young teacher and her students at Peace Middle School in San Antonio, for example, used the network in doing tests of air quality. Teachers there had been very depressed. They had headaches and the kids were rowdy. The students found that the air had an inordinately high amount of CO_2. They told the school board there was a problem with the air filtering system, and got a completely new ventilation system for the school. They made a difference.

We also found that networking leads to new communities. At the University of Texas Health Science Center, the doctors in the hospital are working with nurse practitioners and parents to monitor the way kids with nutritional problems eat at home. The parents live all over south Texas. We put them on a network to provide a support mechanism. It's a wonderful application that does not require high-end technology.

Vice President Gore has charged us to have every school linked by the year 2000. My question is, how do we do it, and how do we use it? Will we use technology to impose an old teacher model, or will we develop new kinds of uses, as Alan November is suggesting?

David Niguidula

I work at The Coalition of Essential Schools, an organization that sprang up in the mid-80s to help with restructuring. We are not inherently high-tech, but some of us think about how technological applications might be useful. Everyone agrees that the Industrial Age model is not good enough; but who's going to change it? The people we trust to change the system are not the government agencies, vendors, textbook publishers, or high-tech conferences, but the teachers. Along with parents in the local community and students themselves, teachers have the most vested interest in what happens; and they are there for the long term.

Our organization is based on a few simple notions of teaching and learning called "Common Principles." We feel that the primary purpose of school is to help students learn to use their minds well. When a student graduates from school today with so many years of science, and so many of English, what does it mean? We're finding that in many cases it doesn't mean a whole lot. What we want is for students to demonstrate what it is that's really important. Our approach is to ask teachers what they want their students to know and be able to do — not just the gifted kids and not just the kids going to college, but everyone receiving a diploma. We call this a backwards-planning model. You people in business know about this, but it is a relatively new idea for teachers.

"What do we want our students to know and do?" is the easy question. We get the community together to try to figure it out. Two harder questions follow. First, how are we going to know? Every school in the country has a goals statement. Typically it includes goals like, "We want our students to be good citizens." What does this mean — that students know how to move a lever in a voting booth, or are able to read an opinion in the New York Times? What is it we want to see? What demonstrations? What indications?

Finally, given this vision of what we want kids to do, and what kinds of activities they may actually be involved in, then and only then do we consider how to arrange the school and put the structures in place. Going through this process rarely results in a decision to do 40 minutes of math, followed by 40 minutes of English, followed by 40 minutes of gym. The schools with which we work are in a very difficult transition. Everyone has a notion of how schooling should be, but the use of technology as a lever, as Alan suggested, has fallen far short of what schools could be doing. They need new visions of what's possible.

The Coalition is a grassroots organization. Our growth has been phenomenal — from a dozen schools ten years ago to nearly 700 now, with 150 of these schools having made a full commitment. We found that what is needed is an organization centered around children, with a vision of what teachers want their students to know when they graduate.

As we've heard, and I agree with this contention, most uses of technology are supporting the old paradigm of education. In the *Concepts of Biology* video that Burt Arnowitz presented, there were two segments. In the first, the teacher is at the front of the classroom showing this wonderful biology demo on a monitor, and all the kids are watching. What's different about that? It's just automation. Later in the tape it got interesting. Kids were working in small groups, interacting. Now we're starting to get somewhere; now the kids are involved. Almost all of the multimedia titles today are nothing more than glorified, slick texts and reference books. That's not what we need.

What we're looking for, and what students seem to be looking for, are new tools with which to create. In using computers in education, we started with BASIC, and then moved on to computer literacy, on the assumption that this is what kids will want to do when they graduate from high school. It is the same theory that was used when I was in elementary school. We all learned the New Math, and how to add in base 8, because this is what my generation was supposedly going to need when we graduated from high school. What students really need are new tools for creation. Teachers, as Connie mentioned, need new tools for communication.

The real question is how do schools and educational organizations have to change to use the new technologies well? How can the design of the new technologies and the development of titles accommodate a new paradigm of education?

John Kernan
Let's start with the last question asked. How do schools have to change to use the new technologies?

Alan November
I'm probably the only one on the panel that actually works in a school. We spend $12,000 a year per student in my school. In the last three years, of about 50 kids a year that we sent to an advanced placement exam, all but one scored a perfect 5. Now if we add technology to the curriculum, we're not going to get much better than that. We have maxed out the traditional model. And we spend a lot of money on educational technology — about half a million dollars a year, just in my school. But we have no incentive to change. That is why we will not use technology well. Without being in a marketplace environment like most people here, where we could literally go out of business if we didn't do well, we will never have any organizational incentive to change.

My contention is that we will not use technology well in schools until we have to — and we simply do not have to. Our students come to us almost no matter what we do to them, short of illegal acts. When there is school choice and parents can send their kids anywhere, and all of a sudden my students start leaving, then I'll become very interested in educational technology. I'll have an organizational motivation to change.

Seymour Papert
Yes, there has to be choice, but I think the choice is not anything like what you suggested. We have to focus, first, on what it is we

have a choice of, then on what we want in school. David Niguidula gave us an example. There's nothing wrong with what he said, except he didn't address the central issue. The central issue is not how knowledge and learning will be distributed, but what kind of knowledge will be learned, and what, in fact, we mean by knowledge?

The entire structure of school is determined by primitive technologies of the past — cutting knowledge up into little pieces, distributing them in an unsegregated way, with a curriculum, and a teacher in front of a classroom. This has shaped our concept of what knowledge children need, and of the very nature of knowledge. If we can't call this into question, little will change. According to the principles of John Dewey and open or child-centered schooling, the child should be in charge of the learning process. But once said, there is a fundamental contradiction in our then deciding what children are going to learn. As long as we decide what kind of knowledge they're going to have, we can't change the system.

At the height of "discovery learning" — the fad of the 1960s and 1970s — a friend told the story about a crestfallen teacher who had been superexcited about discovery learning. "Oh God," he said, "what do I do now? They discovered it wrong!"

Everything has developed, as Alan November suggests, into a coherent self-supporting system where each part snaps into place with the rest. The image of my grandson controlling his own search for knowledge is fundamental. It has to be addressed. The massive effect of the technologies is to give children access. The school is dead. It is not relevant to creating people like Solzhenitsyn.

Every baby learns to talk, walk, manipulate parents, laugh, and love in a natural way that's rarely like the way a researcher learns later on. The artificial kind of learning we call a school was simply proposed to get children to know things they didn't acquire naturally from the learning environment. As this need disappears, the institution of school will disappear. Our focus has to be not only on giving the new vision, but taking away the old idea firmly planted in society's mind of the need to learn the multiplication table, fractions, and everything else that's called the curriculum.

Bernard Gifford

Karl Marx 150 years ago said that after governmental perfection is achieved, the state would wither away. There's no evidence that the state is withering away. Nor do I believe that 150 years from now there will be any evidence that schools as we know them will have withered away. Unfortunately, Seymour, I think schools will still be here. The challenge for those of us who would like to utilize interactive multimedia to significantly improve teaching and learning, introducing radical incremental change, is to figure out how we can make the transformation from the bolt-on solution to a more learner-centered model.

The reality is that a learner-centered model in which interactive multimedia is used well will fundamentally change the nature of instructional work. It will increase the involvement and ownership of students in their own learning, improve the economics, restore far more control to the parents, and reduce many bureaucratic impediments to schooling. It does not represent a withering away of the school as we know it, but will, I believe, represent a considerable advance over the status quo. I agree that where we are today is totally unacceptable.

Alan Kay

My belief is that schools are never going to use technology well no matter how hard they try. McLuhan liked to point out that back in the 13th century at Oxford, education meant 30 students in a room writing down what one person said, usually someone reading from a book. When the students had done this enough times, they got their master's gown. Then the printing press revolutionized society. The only thing that did not change, McLuhan observed, are the 30 students in classrooms in North America still sitting and writing what someone else is saying.

The BOOK, which I used to call the Basic Organization Of Knowledge (solid state, 2 1/2 megabytes, high resolution, low power, low cost, large possibilities for serious discourse) has been done in by an organizational power structure that doesn't like subversive ideas. Even though the book created schools, schools acted against the essence of the book. The most powerful force is not the school, but access to the libraries, which our society is barely willing to pay for, once children understand the value of the book. When kids go to a library and begin looking up things for themselves, they start developing their own point of view.

The most important thing for those of us inventing new technology is to weigh the balance between institutional and subversive uses. Both Seymour and I were motivated years ago by Space War, which today would be called a video game. We started wondering if it would be as interesting for kids to learn how to make a Space War as to play it, but it's hard to impose what we think they need without coming down on them.

Most people trying to sell multimedia are catering to what they think people want — television-like things — without creating the deeper content needed for going to the next level. I don't believe it will ever happen in schools, but when there's enough computer-accessible content around, and people can make choices, many will wind up educating themselves. The educated people I've met in my life are those who have taken the responsibility themselves, away from school and parents, to find out more about what intrigues them.

John Kernan

I see that as almost idealistic. It would never even occur to many people in certain socioeconomic situations to take responsibility for their own learning.

Alan Kay

That's why almost everybody in America is limited by institutional schooling.

David Niguidula

I want to comment on the notion of getting subversive ideas into schools through technology. The most successful and commonly used multimedia tool currently in schools is HyperCard. It's a creation tool that allows students to break through the boundaries of disciplines and start connecting information. Is it a wonderful high-tech system in which we ultimately will all want to author? No, not necessarily. But it does permit students to create their own knowledge and link things together. When schools begin to accommodate to this mode of learning, we'll have made progress.

Donald Norman

For 30 years before joining Apple Computer, I was a professor at Harvard and at the University of California. I studied and wrote about learning and memory. Technology isn't the issue. The issue is the way we go about things, what it takes to learn, and the way we learn throughout our entire lives. We don't learn by being lectured to. That's the least efficient way to learn. It's the most efficient way to teach. That's the point. The reason the educational system is so hard to change is that it's designed for the teacher. I'll emphasize the higher educational process, which I know best, but this applies to all levels. It's easy for the professor to give a 50 minute lecture, but no one has an attention span of 50 minutes. William James in 1890 said his attention span was 10 seconds.

The way we learn is by trying something, doing it, and getting stuck. In order to learn, we really have to be stuck, and when we're stuck, we're ready for the critical piece of information. The same piece of information that made no impact at a lecture makes a dramatic impact when we're ready for it. We don't have to study it. It just hits.

How do we change the educational process so this becomes the normal way? It's not a technical issue. It's a social issue. The university system will never change until we change the reward structure. I became a very senior respected professor by publishing books and papers, and by going around the world giving talks, not by being a good teacher. The more I was a good teacher, the more it took away from my publications and therefore my promotion possibilities. I managed to succeed, but the reward structure was against me. We have to change the reward structure.

Technology is not the issue. I've gone to Seymour's classrooms, and Alan Kay's classrooms too. It's not the technology. It's the great teacher. What we need is a way of getting students engaged with the process, and bringing them to that special confusion where we can present the critical information.

Now, it turns out that technology can help, first of all with the economics, and secondly in allowing us to simulate, write newspapers, send them across the country, do science experiments, and study history, literature, music, and art. But it is mistaken to ask, what role will technology play? The real issue is the social structure of our schools in K-12 and in higher education. Nothing's going to change until we can change that social structure.

Connie Stout

I agree. Speaking as one who's been in the Texas State Department of Education, we set out to take care of this problem with site-based decision making. We found it didn't work as planned. I've had teachers come to me in tears because their principals go in to evaluate them. One principal said to a teacher, "I'll come back when you're teaching." She was in a room with children in work groups around computers. The problem is the reward structure that's in place.

We need to do some social marketing to get the parents behind us. Texas has a large textbook adoption system. Last year we spent $270 million on the procurement of textbooks (outdated, of course, immediately). One of the wonderful young elementary science teachers started a revolution when she proposed the option of offering either a textbook or an electronic media system. As a result, Windows on Science was adopted, the first adoption of electronic media. The parents revolted against it in the elementary school that my children attended, because the children were not bringing home a book. In this case, it was the parents who were holding back change.

With this system in place, how can education change? We need to teach children to be learners. I have real concerns about schools' changing. We gave money to schools for innovative projects to use technology, telling them they could waive most board rules. Only one school requested a board waiver, and that was to combine kindergarten and first grade. I agree with Don Norman. It's more than an issue of technology. We need to do social marketing. Going back to what David Niguidula said, teachers have to reform. But it's not just the teachers. The whole system has to be involved in order to get somewhere.

John Kernan
I've seen that from a practical point of view. The last company I ran, Jostens Learning, is a big educational software company. In order to get our message out, we had 25 full time lobbyists working just to break the textbook monopoly and get charter schools propositions through the legislature.

Martin Harris
In listening to this discussion, I started to personalize the issues and think about my own education and how I felt when I went to school. When I was old enough to understand that I was being socialized, I got really irritated. Are we willing to change the process of socialization so that the individual is more responsible? It's easy to just pass off. Though I'm a fairly aware parent, I do the same thing. I assume the school's taking care of my kid's education. Until such time as parents are willing to recognize that their children are being socialized in a way that is not good for their growth, the kids will not be learning how to learn.

John Grillos
I think personal responsibility is central to the issue. My feeling is that the institution will change in the same way our lives will change. The company does not take care of most people anymore,

and the school does not take care of their kids. As we expose people to the new technology and make it available to them, they will have to take on more of the responsibility for their own education. The technology will help them do this.

We'll still get educated for the same reasons we've always gotten educated — because social institutions put pressure on us to conform, or because we're motivated. Most of my learning happened after I left college. Most of it was without an instructor. It was done for one simple reason. I needed it. I was motivated to accomplish the objectives I set for myself. I had to figure out how to do it. One reason I've stayed in technology as long as I have (I will stay in it as long as I'm working, and perhaps beyond that) is because technology represents the potential of providing the information and the structure we all require to educate ourselves. At the end of the day, this is the business we're all going to be in. We don't have any choice.

The traditional institutions are broken. Companies and schools are no longer going to take care of us. We're making our healthcare systems portable; we've already made our retirement systems portable. That's because we're moving on. We're working out of our houses. We're changing jobs and careers every 2 1/2 years. We're taking on the responsibility to develop ourselves. We're going to have to do the same for our kids. I don't think the schools are fixable, but technology can play an important facilitating role as people take on more of a responsibility to educate themselves and their children.

John Kernan
I'm going to make Alan November's question our last. What's the job description of the child in the education system of the future?

Peggy Weil

To answer that question, we have to consider what people think the job description of a child is now. One we grew up with is, "Children are to be seen and not heard." On the Westside of Los Angeles[7], many consider their children ornaments — something to brag about ("My kid can do ..."). A more traditional view of children is that they are there to take care of us in our old age, in which case we want to teach them how to survive and negotiate adulthood. Our culture is mystified by kids. Many people barely tolerate them. If you fly with a child, you notice that people seem allergic to kids.

In marketing our culture to kids, there are two extremes. There's either Disney-type mass marketing (children are there to make Mom and Dad buy lots of stuff), which is candy-coated "edutainment" (a loathsome word), and then there is the dullest stuff in the curriculum (it's only good if it is hard and bad for you), which devalues learning for the sake of learning. We have to ask, "What do we think children are?" If they are natural problem solvers, which I think may be Alan November's answer, are we raising them to solve the mess we made?

Bob Stein

We're implying an incremental shift when we ask about an educational system of the future. I think we must first ask, what kind of society do we want, and given that, how do we want to educate the people in it? I have a problem with John Kernan's dismissing Alan Kay's comments as idealistic. It's not a good way to debate, and it devalues the ideas that Alan Kay, Seymour Papert, and Don Norman are putting forward. The problems of our society are deep and vast. Do we really believe that anything less than idealism can create a vision leading us forward? Nothing less than an ideal presentation of what we want to have will be sufficient to motivate us to change society as it has to be changed. Rather than dismissing the idealism, if it is based on good ideas, it should be applauded.

David Niguidula
Idealism is great, but we really have to figure out what makes sense for the individual child. An ideal is that every student should have help in learning what is needed next. That's what we should be working toward with the technology.

Alan November
A Martian coming to Earth to learn the job description of kids would think it was to prepare for tests and learn what big people, books, and computers already know. I propose a new approach, one that honors the wisdom and knowledge of children. Reverse the model. Kids know a lot, and can solve very complex problems that we don't give them, because we're so embedded in test preparation. The last thing I want to see is technology used to improve test preparation, although that may be the obvious and easy thing to do, and the way to make a quick buck. A much better path is to determine how we can make children feel they can contribute and become a valued asset to society rather than a drain. When asked what they're doing, most children, even when using technology, almost inevitably reply that they're doing what the teacher told them to do. What we would like to have them say is, "We are making a difference to the world."

It's the bane of good managers never to receive credit for their success. That should be the new job description for teachers. Let children think they have solved the problems themselves, brought the knowledge together, applied their own wisdom, and made an impact on society. They won't think the teacher taught them anything at all. This will take a very sophisticated application of cognitive, moral, and emotional development, along with organizational design and the technologies as well. I do think we need that kind of ideal to reach for.

Seymour Papert
I want to say the same thing from a slightly different angle. Don Norman claims nothing will happen until we change the social structure of the school. That's wrong. The social structure of the school won't change until something else happens. It won't change from the top down. We cannot design a new system and impose it! We have to see how something can grow out of the existing world. Bob Stein is absolutely right that idealism is what we need. What are the ideals? What is happening in the world that we want to support and strive for? Bob Stein's dedication to opening access to new forms of knowledge is, in itself, as important as an ideal.

Alan Kay says that individuals should take responsibility for their own learning. It was suggested that not many people do. I think that's wrong. Everyone does. All those children joining gangs, learning how to use guns, and selling drugs are also taking responsibility for their own learning. It just happens not to be the kind of learning that we think counts as real learning, and that we want them to take responsibility for. We have to connect social ideals of learning with what people are doing for their own intimate personal reasons.

Individual responsibility for learning does not mean we should not rely on other people. For example, I'm scaffolding with Alan Kay, as we've done over the years, taking one another's ideas and building on them. Schools treat children's forming collaborative relationships like cheating. Children are to be tested on what they know personally. Take a 10-year old who would like to design a complicated new machine. The fact that somewhere in the world there's another kid who shares this dream, and that through networking the two can be brought together, is an ideal that has nothing to do with the alleged educational objectives of school.

The idea that kids know a lot and we need to respect them is true, but not true. Kids are just people like everyone else. Everyone knows a lot. Yet our culture does not deeply respect individual ways of thinking, feeling, and learning. A deep respect for the right of individuals to be whoever they are is incompatible with the set curriculum and much of what goes on in school.

Bernie Gifford made an analogy with Marx. Marx was actually right. The state, as he described it, has withered away. What we now call the state is serving very different functions. I think school as we've known it also can and will wither away. But there will still be virtual or physical places where children gather for intellectual and personal interests, and to learn who they are.

Mark Stahlman

The problem with idealism is not that ideas aren't associated with reality; it's that most ideas are wrong, and most people aren't connected to reality. The educational system in this country has changed enormously over the past generation, having to do with women entering the workforce, single-parent families, and the use of television as a baby sitter. Television has become a primary educational force. We are now confronting the imminence of another set of new media. The job description for kids is to be participants in these new media.

Notes

[1]*Educom Review* interview with George Gilder, *Educom Review*, July-August 1994.
[2]L. Perelman, *School's Out*, Avon Books, 1993.
[3]Robert Fulghum, *All I Really Need To Know I Learned in Kindergarten*, Ivy Books, 1986.
[4]Known as bad money driving out good, Gresham's law holds that if two kinds of money in circulation have the same denominational value but different intrinsic values, the money with higher intrinsic value will be hoarded and therefore eventually driven out of circulation by the money with lesser intrinsic value. The law is named after English financier Sir Thomas Gresham (1519-1579), a founder of the Royal Exchange.
[5]Feodor Mikhailovich Dostoyevsky (1821-1881), the celebrated Russian writer, combined religious mysticism with profound psychological insight. His four great novels are *Crime and Punishment*, *The Idiot*, *The Possessed*, and *The Brothers Karamazov*.
[6]Aleksandr Isayevich Solzhenitsyn, Soviet writer and dissident born in 1918, wrote *One Day in the Life of Ivan Denisovich* and *The Gulag Archipelago*, revealing the horrors of the Soviet labor camp system. *Gulag* earned him the Nobel Prize for literature in 1970. After 20 years in exile, Solzhenitsyn returned to Russia from his home in Vermont at the end of May, 1994.
[7] The Westside is an affluent section of Los Angeles.

Creating Creativity

A Retrospective Look Ahead

Moderator Nicholas Negroponte calls it the panel with the highest IQ. He might with equal validity have called this the session with the most creative flair. For creative it is, in name, composition, and especially the way it approaches its subject. The discussion moves progressively from creativity in the university and laboratory, to creativity in the company, to creativity in forming a new industry, to creativity in the school, to creativity in the handling of supercomplexity, to creativity in the computer and in artificial creatures that learn — which leads, in a rousing finale, to the prospect of Darwinian evolution at microprocessor speed. What could be more creative (and stimulating) than that?

We are also treated to inside information. Negroponte confesses that he and his associates at the MIT Media Lab had blinders on for years about the true nature of multimedia. He has a novel way of measuring the level of creativity today; namely, the number of people involved simultaneously in both the content and technology sides of multimedia. Alan Kay gives testimony to the power of the shower and to the invigorating effect of interesting people, backing it up with stories of the people who influenced him the most. He calls the repurposing currently taking place in multimedia a "Burger King phase," and hopes for better, suggesting that the personal essay, where authors reveal their thought processes, offers a model to emulate.

John Warnock recalls his days at Xerox PARC, where creativity was not in short supply, but understanding how to take that creativity and turn it into something everyone could experience was. To Jim Clark, the real mark of a creative person is the ability to pursue and validate an idea. Danny Hillis looks to biological evolution as a paradigm for a creativity suited to building highly complex systems, such as thinking machines. He senses a general unease that multimedia may become just another broadcast television, instead of a richer, fuller mode of personal communication. Indeed, personal communication is what this session is all about.

Martin Greenberger

As a young faculty member at MIT 33 years ago, I put together a lecture series to celebrate the 100th birthday of the Institute. Called *Management and the Computer of the Future* ,[1] the series extended over an academic year, drawing interested crowds from the many universities, laboratories, and companies in the dynamic R&D area encircled by Route 128 — the Silicon Valley of the time.

The people involved in the lecture series — a virtual Who's Who of luminaries inside and outside of the computer field — included Vannevar Bush, Norbert Wiener, John Mauchly, C.P. Snow, Walter Rosenblith, Claude Shannon, Herbert Simon, Allen Newell, Grace Hopper, Alan Perlis, John Kemeny, George Miller, Howard Johnson, Robert Fano, John McCarthy, Marvin Minsky, J.C.R. Licklider, and many others. I've organized numerous events in the years since, but none until now has constituted a gathering of quite the august collective stature as that centennial celebration in 1961.

At that time, our moderator Nicholas Negroponte was just beginning his studies at MIT. Tom Stockham, then an assistant professor of electrical engineering at MIT, was on leave from the Institute as an Air Force first lieutenant; Alan Kay was playing jazz guitar in Denver, Colorado; Jim Clark was getting ready for college; John Warnock was an undergraduate at the University of Utah; and Danny Hillis was probably programming his first computer in a Baltimore kindergarten. Tom Stockham later moved to the University of Utah, were he became part of an extraordinarily fertile graduate program in electrical engineering and computer science. We'll hear about it in a moment. Its alumni include the same Alan Kay, Jim Clark, and John Warnock. Alan and John later went on to another exceptionally productive research environment at Xerox's Palo Alto Research Center, known as PARC.

I'd like to take this occasion to express our admiration and appreciation to these six men for the invaluable contributions they have made to the development of technology in the last two decades. Alan Kay, for example, has inspired much of what today we accept as commonplace in personal computing, and he continues to be a rich source of ideas and innovation. Nicholas Negroponte has led the pacesetting and farsighted MIT Media Lab, where I had the good fortune to spend a sabbatical year in 1988-89. Nicholas surely must have vision in his DNA. He's still as fresh and discerning in his thinking as ever. His penetrating insights would burn out most mortals. It must be his cool wit.

The three remarkable research environments represented on this panel — MIT, Utah, and PARC — illustrate the conditions for creative effort that have meant so much to progress in technology. As we look ahead to the next wave of advance, such creative environments may again play an instrumental role. My hope in assembling this uncommon panel was that its accomplished members might be able to draw on their experiences and past successes to help us set priorities for the future. Put them to work, Nicholas.

Nicholas Negroponte

Martin, thank you for the kind words, but it has taken me a few days to recover from the slight of being asked to be a moderator, and having the word "retrospective" in the title of my session. I feel like I'm being put out to pasture. I may not be burned out, but the message is that I'm over the hill.

I thought I'd take two minutes before starting this well-organized panel discussion to do something I've never done before in public — share with you how I actually got involved in multimedia. Like many of the people here, I came out of the computer graphics community. Some of us were more interested in images, others more in the interactivity intrinsic to computer graphics. I happened to be particularly interested in the television-based side of the subject. My work in this areas goes back to the early 1970s. I give thanks to Frank Carey, then CEO and later chairman of IBM. In 1974, twenty years ago, he told shareholders that IBM would get into the consumer electronics business.

What followed, in typical IBM tradition, was the creation of a task force. I think the statute of limitations allows me to talk about it now. Its code name was Castle. Castle considered a number of potential consumer products. The runner-up was a wristwatch, which IBM decided not to do. The winner was a personal computer with a videodisc built in.

The project began in Poughkeepsie in 1975-76. It was quite extraordinary. Steve Jobs hadn't even started work in his garage yet, and here was IBM building a real personal computer. The goal and strategy was to produce a transparent 12-inch floppy videodisc that followed the Bernoulli principle, with 10 hours of video stored in digital format. The designer created an amazing package. Somebody should try to find the pictures of it in the archives.

Tragedy struck in 1977. Through bad judgment, the project was divided in half. The personal computer piece went to Burlington, and later to Boca Raton. That's history. The other piece turned into the beginning of the DiscoVision joint venture that got off the ground about 1978. This too is history -- of a less auspicious kind.

How is it that the Architecture Machine Group at MIT got involved with computers and videodiscs before they were available publicly? The first ten videodiscs in the world went to the FBI and CIA. The eleventh, the first one outside the classified community, came to MIT. These 54,000-image discs took two years to manufacture. I could tell many stories. Some people here may have been involved in making the discs.

I've been doing multimedia now for twenty years. (I guess "retrospective" is the right word after all) Work done in those days looks very similar to some of what is being done today. But we made a mistake. The mixing of audio, video, and data is not what multimedia is about. It couldn't be less relevant. What multimedia is about is being digital. I bang my head on the wall and ask why it took us fifteen years to understand that.

Suddenly everything changes. I don't think even the smartest of us here comprehends the full consequences of being digital. The FCC over the next five years is going to have dyspepsia because of what it means to be digital. We used to be able to point to parts of the spectrum and say, "That's video, that's voice." Not anymore. It's all bits now, and bits are bits. It's a very interesting turn of events. If we take this retrospective look into the future seriously, we must acknowledge that what we did then, even though it looks on the surface like what people are doing today, was very, very different.

Now, when I'm not in the debilitated and humiliating position of being the moderator, what I've learned from being on a panel is that I should not be told what to say. I was recently on a panel where Larry King was the moderator. He sat there with his elbow on the table and grilled people. I won't do that.

We have five human landmarks from computer science here. I don't see them as Utah, PARC, and MIT. I see them as something different. Whatever multimedia means, it was very much on the fringe of computer science for a long time. People thought of it as somewhere between silly and sissy. That fringe status has now moved into the center. Very rarely have fringes moved that quickly into the center. When this happens, it usually absorbs the geniuses along the way who were in the center anyway. I think what characterizes all five panelists is that they have not just contributed to multimedia; they've been landmarks in other parts of computer science as well, and also in the world of thought.

I'm perhaps making a dreadful mistake by asking Alan Kay to go first. He sometimes can be long-winded. We'll ask you, Alan, to help get this animated group discussing, setting the stage in content while setting an example in time.

Alan Kay

I'm trying to imagine how it would be to leave out the vowels in the interests of time. It works in Nicholas' transcoding idea, but not, I'm afraid, when I'm talking.

John Warnock and I were both graduate students of Dave Evans at the University of Utah. John spent a little less time as a graduate student than I did. He only spent about six weeks. He won't tell this story, so I will, since we're talking about creativity here.

John was a mathematician working as a systems programmer in the university computing center . One of Dave's graduate students walked in one day and asked John about techniques for dealing with large arrays of numbers. John asked, "Why do you need to work with large arrays of numbers?" The graduate student started explaining about hidden-surface algorithms and the immense data structures they used. Right in the middle of this explanation, it occurred to John how it could be done without any storage algorithms at all. In fact, he did it himself over the next few weeks and got some really fantastic pictures. Soon afterwards, he wrote the shortest graduate thesis that I think has ever been accepted for a Ph.D. at Utah.

John and I graduated together. I did it the hard way. I actually had to sit down and do some work! But one of the nice things about the University of Utah, and most places that encourage creativity, is they are astoundingly like kindergarten. My education started out with a real kindergarten, and that was a lot of fun. Then came sixteen years of torture, and finally, graduate school. Had I been more ambitious, I probably wouldn't have gone to graduate school, but the thought of going to work seemed even more appalling then going back for another year or two of school. I just happened to wind up at a graduate school that was run like a kindergarten, as were most graduate schools with ARPA funding. Nicholas came out of one; so did Danny Hillis. Although these kindergartens were unstructured, there were themes in the air. This makes for a potent combination.

Dave Evans, the founder of the University of Utah computer science department, was a shy person. He had a chuckling, hesitant way of talking. At meetings, when we asked what his opinion was, he'd often laugh and say, "I don't know anything." That always used to bug us, but now I know what he meant. The reason he had so many good insights was that he actually understood when he didn't know something. As a result, he was very open to new ideas.

The model of creativity that Arthur Koestler calls *bisociation*[2] recognizes that thinking takes place in a certain context. Once in a while, someone reveals our thoughts in a different context. If it is a joke, we say, "Ha, ha." If it is science, we say, "Aha!" If it is art, we say, "Ah!" In each case, we allow ourselves to see something out of its original context. The best kind of environment for creativity is one that allows this kind of rumination, where thoughts can pop occasionally to other contexts, then pop back again.

Ivan Sutherland developed Sketchpad in 1962. From one perspective, not a lot has happened since then. Sketchpad is still very impressive. When Ivan was asked what techniques and resources helped him to be creative, he replied that lots of water on top of the head must have helped him, because he got most of his ideas in the shower. I resonate to that. I've gotten most of my ideas in the shower too. I once tried to get Xerox PARC to install a shower in my office. They wouldn't do it because it looked elitist, even though I pointed out that it only cost $2,000 for a shower, and they were willing to pay $45,000 to provide me with a personal computer and the accompaniments. They didn't go for it. They gave up one of the cheapest pieces of research equipment they could buy.

In truth, every idea I've had is in the context of knowing other people — people like Nicholas Negroponte, Seymour Papert, Ivan Sutherland, Tom Stockham, fellow graduate students like John Warnock, and "youngsters" like Danny Hillis. What I'm interested in has a way of popping around. For example, anytime Seymour disagrees with me, I wind up agreeing with him. It happened again today. I got up and said something that I thought was reasonable. Actually, it was reasonable! This is the other thing. I think he really agreed with me. But just for the heck of it, he decided to disagree, and I happened to like the way he disagreed. That's what happens around interesting people. It doesn't matter whether they agree or not. There's a way of agreeing or disagreeing that's going to help the next set of thoughts.

What got me going with computers was not programming, which I had done for a few years as a job, but a combination of other things, such as Bob Barton's view of the computer as a medium — something grander than a vehicle or tool — and Seymour's notion that the computer was really to help us think about thinking by giving us ways of building and debugging our own ideas. These notions got me wondering about the real content of computing, and the serious things we should be able to do with computers.

The advent of the essay and of printing gave us a way of arguing that we never had before. This made an enormous difference. Our country is partly the result of the ability to argue, rather than having to accept dogma. The only way to have a coherent civilization previously was for everyone to have to believe the same thing. Science is not possible under those conditions, because then knowledge comes from authority rather than experiment. To have science, we have to agree on how to argue; the same for democracy. We don't specify how everyone is to live, but how we're going to argue about it. These are powerful ideas. Whenever a new medium comes along, we should ask what it is good at representing? With what new forms of thought does it help us? Each new medium has a way of helping us think about certain things, and hiding thoughts about other things.

Adults seemed very shaky to me when I was a kid. I worried about the teachers I had in school. They seemed to know very little, and weren't really interested in much. I thought it was my inability to perceive, and I would change my mind as I grew older. But as I grew older, adults looked worse! I think the job description of children is to save the world from the previous generation. What we should be teaching them is how to think better than the previous generation learned to think.

Let me end with what I think is the crux. The most interesting aspect of Piaget's stage theory[3] is not that each stage obtains at a certain age. He didn't mean that. What is most interesting is that the ability to think about things in the best ways we know, which appears around the age of twelve to fourteen, requires an appropriate set of precursor experiences. In other words, we don't automatically start thinking in powerfully detached and abstract ways unless we have an intuition constructed from a large variety of concrete experiences about the world. The reason to try to do something about the early learning experience is precisely to make sure that children don't miss out on the precursor experiences they will need in order to be powerful thinkers later on.

When I look at a piece of multimedia, I ask myself whether it's a carrier of powerful ideas. Is it a carrier of deep experiences? Does it provide a way of arguing and discussing that we did not have before? Does it embody what 21st-century thinking, or 21st-century content, or serious discourse is going to be about? Right now, it does not. It's hard to find anything really impressive. We seem to be in a Burger King phase in multimedia.

There's a wonderful place to get hamburgers here in Brentwood, just the way they used to be: fabulous taste, charbroiled, rare, absolutely fantastic! They cost $6.50. There's the problem. To sell a hamburger for 99 cents, you basically have to take cardboard, flavor it, and set up a big marketing campaign to convince people it's the same thing that used to be called a hamburger. Much of what's going on in multimedia today is this kind of repurposing.

Take television. Television has changed debates from being about something important over an extended length of time, to two minutes of response and one minute of rebuttal. We have to guard against this. It's what Don Norman termed Gresham's law. It's easier to make crap than good stuff. Crap in the marketplace, like the de facto standards for certain operating systems I can think of, can make it difficult for better things to come along.

So, what does creativity mean? Looking at the past, it means being in an environment where argument isn't treated as bullets, where we don't have to agree with everyone to get really good ideas from them, and where there are systems that allow us to represent our ideas. I hope multimedia will eventually turn into this.

Nicholas Negroponte
As I said, I took a risk. The quality of the bit stream was high, but its length was a bit too long. Tom, it's your turn. You might have to set a new precedent with respect to time.

Thomas Stockham
I don't know how I got mixed up in this. I don't think I heard the word multimedia until about six months ago. That's where I'm coming from. But the reason I'm glad to be here is because I'm surrounded by people with whom I've been associated in the past. The only thing I've done myself that is related, and that I really enjoyed, was making digits work with sound. It is what has given me the most satisfaction. Since doing that, I've gone off in other directions.

These students at Utah were a special bunch of people. They were selected by Dave Evans, a very bright person who operated in an unconventional way. If there's a problem with education, it's with convention. There wasn't convention in the selection of the ten to fifteen students in computer science brought to the University of Utah for a period of five years starting in about 1968. I wish we could put together a similar group again by having a formula for how it's done. But that day came and went. It's very hard to have happen. Several of the people sitting here, including myself, were part of it. I was a little older, and I was the teacher for some. It was a thrill for me. I would just say, yes, this can happen. But it's rare, and it takes something magical to have it work.

John Warnock

Since this discussion is about cultivating creativity, I would like to take a different tack. I was very fortunate in the 1972 to 1982 time frame to work in the world's greatest sandbox, Xerox PARC. We were surrounded by incredibly talented, enormously bright, energetic people. We were endowed with a flow of money and financing. We could build nearly anything we wanted to build. Many great ideas occurred. Creativity was not in short supply. What was in short supply was an understanding of how to take that creativity and turn it into something everyone could experience.

Similarly, our problems with multimedia and education are not a shortage of ideas or directions to go, but of knowing how to build an impedance match (a term I learned from Tom Stockham) between the creative process and the real world.

For the last ten years, I've been trying to build an organization to turn creative ideas into real things that get used by people. It's been a very rich experience for me and I've learned a lot about how it's done. The trick is to promote creativity by allowing one side to have a disdain for the status quo. On the other side, we have to understand how people work and what their prejudices are, so we can plant an idea into the social structure in a fundamental way and get it adopted. This transition is the hard part. It's building the right set of tools and establishing the right incremental learning process to make change.

To get multimedia to happen on a broad base scale, we will have to take the authors of information today, who are used to print and video media, and incrementally move them in an evolutionary way from their accustomed authoring environment to one in which they can work in the future. This isn't achieved by giving them a brand new tool, but by an incremental process they can follow to move toward a more creative environment. The challenge before us is to make that transition over the next five to ten years so that all of the authors of books and information have the same model of the book of the future, and the same creative ideas on what that means, while still maintaining the impedance match.

I love creativity. I try to promote it inside my company wherever I can, and I try to use it in getting new ideas into products wherever I can. Yet, in retrospect, it seems to me that the greatest service we can perform for creative people is to put their ideas into widespread use.

James Clark

I don't really understand creativity. I just know it happens. Thomas Edison said that creativity was 1 percent inspiration and 99 percent perspiration. I've done an awful lot of the 99 percent and I'm not sure how much of the 1 percent. Ideas are easy to come by. We sit here and have them every day. To me, the real mark of a creative person is having the ability to validate an idea in some fashion, whether by writing a paper, proving a theorem, or building a company. I happen to fall in the last category. Personally, I don't consider three-dimensional graphic workstations a very novel idea. It seemed to me perfectly obvious, since the world is three-dimensional. If I hadn't done Silicon Graphics, I doubt anyone here would know who I am. People think of me as a visionary. I don't see that.

Around 1986, I suddenly got the multimedia bug and realized that technological trends were leading in the direction of all digital. I tried to motivate people in Silicon Graphics to pursue competing platforms that would be at the leading edge of the multimedia revolution I was sure would take place. After two or three years of hard pushing, sometimes yelling or cajoling, I managed to get the company to do that. I then got excited about broadband telecommunications and the propogation of computing technology into low-cost devices, such as set-top boxes. I cajoled again and managed to get other companies to give us lots of money so that we would develop our technology for these purposes.

In none of this do I observe any particular genius. I don't see in myself the kind of flair that I ascribe to the people I think of as highly creative. I just see a lot of hard work. That's a big part of it. An idea isn't worth much unless it's pursued.

Danny Hillis
We were charged to make this a retrospective that draws lessons from our successes. I think what is much more interesting are the lessons learned from our failures. I'd like to concentrate on that.

I'm interested in the kind of creativity that involves creating things much more complicated than any one individual can comprehend. This may sound corny, but I'm still interested in making a thinking machine — a machine that learns, reasons, creates. This was always my goal. It's what I would have liked my company to do. Yet, after years of very hard work, somehow all we've succeeded in doing is making a very fast computer.[4] That bothers me. On the other hand, I've learned some lessons about why it's so hard, and I think there's hope for the future. What I'd like to talk about is how the creative process could be very different in building much more complicated things.

The way we build a computer is an extrapolation of the standard engineering process going back to antiquity. We basically divide the problem into parts — an I/O system, a processor, an operating system — and assign each part to a different group of people. We define the interfaces between the parts — how they're going to work together — and then those people go off and create within those interfaces. For a very complex system of objects involving hundreds of millions of lines of code and billions of transistors working together, we find that people rapidly lose a sense for the entirety of what they're creating. They only have a picture of a tiny piece. This limits what the system can do and leads to a fragility in what is created. People hold back on their creative instincts to make sure they don't violate the interfaces or exceed their responsibility.

These days the details are so complex that parts are assigned to computers as well as people. Much of the design of the supercomputer is now done by computer. We break away the layout of a chip and hand it off to a computer. Many complex objects are built this way. The result is that not only does no single individual understand the entire design, all of the individuals collectively don't understand it. We only use the computer to help with the bookkeeping, and to help automate that same process of engineering that goes back for hundreds of years — doing little pieces, or filling in for a person where possible.

Another example of something very complicated is a Boeing 777. An airplane has a zillion different kinds of parts in it to make it fly.[5] Those parts are put together by people who don't know about the other parts. But Boeing is very proud of its automated design system. I was told the system looks for interferences between two things built for the same place, and automatically generates all the forms to be filled out when that happens.

Are we doomed to this way of building things? If so, I don't think I'll ever see a thinking machine. I don't think we'll ever get to create something that complicated, since it surely is infinitely more complex than the airplane or a supercomputer, and we are already at the limits of that way of engineering.

But I think there's hope. Biological evolution produces things much more complicated than airplanes or supercomputers, with a great deal of robustness. Biological systems do have a certain modularity of parts, but violate this modularity wantonly whenever there's a good creative idea. A certain patch of skin might make an effective eyeball, or a sweat gland might produce milk for babies. Evolution is able to be creative in a much more profound sense than an engineering organization. The computer may offer a way to mimic this kind of creative process. There are hints of this just beginning to happen.

For example, I already can literally throw random sequences of instructions into an environment where programs are selected according to their ability to solve a problem. The instructions evolve to solve the problem in ways no human programmer would ever do, because of the complex interactions between the pieces and the difficulty of specifying boundaries. In some recent work, creatures were basically thrown into a world and allowed to develop nervous systems. They learned how to swim, walk, or jump, producing some very complicated biological solutions. It's difficult to say how these creatures work, but they're very effective and robust at walking, swimming, or jumping.

I believe that the power of technology coupled with people may let us start designing and creating things in a whole new way. In a very profound sense, computers could then become new amplifiers for mind and creativity, not just bookkeepers taking care of details. I sense we're at the cusp of this right now.

Nicholas Negroponte
Well, that's a hard act to follow with questions. Let me do something quickly to separate the first part of this session from the rest. This may seem simplistic, but the world of multimedia is to some degree divided into those involved with enabling technology and those involved with content. How many people here consider themselves involved with content? How many with enabling technology? How many with both? (Over half!) Just so I'm not a liar, how many with neither? (One a/v person back there. Do you work for the hotel?)

Here's why I ask. After not having taught in a classroom for fifteen or twenty years, I've recently been hauled out of my retirement from teaching. I tried to explain to my students why this particular time in history is so fascinating. I had them consider the difference between the inventions of television and of photography. Television evolved over a period of ten to fifteen years. It was a technical imperative, passed off to be used as it could.

Photography was different. Its invention and evolution were by photographers. The people who propelled and moved the technology were the people who used it.

Computing has now come around to that point. People in multimedia are like the photographers. That's why I think it's an interesting period. The creators of innovative content are also involved in the enabling technology. Over half the people here claim they're involved in both. I think that's true. It probably is one of the most important measures of the creativity of the time — a theme of this session — suggesting a rich time, a rich place, and a rich group of people.

Now is the time to ask these gentlemen the questions you've always been wanting to ask — anything from their net worth to what they're doing. And be provocative. It hasn't been too provocative so far. I've noticed a few people are sleeping. Time to wake up and ask whatever you want. Marc Canter, I cannot think of a better person to start. Although his voice is so booming, can we get him a microphone? Are you going to sing it, or speak it?

Marc Canter

I'm going to sing it. I've asked John Warnock this question in private, and now I'll force it out in public. To my chagrin, Adobe/ Aldus is the leading multimedia company, yet it doesn't think of itself as a multmedia company. No one can do multimedia without either Photoshop or Premiere, much as I wish they had to use MacroMind products. Since I'm here representing Kaleida Labs, I'm going to be very unabashed and say that I think Adobe should build its next generation of products using ScriptX. This would usher in a new generation of object-oriented tools, and we wouldn't need so many people building enabling technology. Instead, they could build little components that sit on top of Adobe's suite of tools. Adobe would make a lot more money, and we'd have object-oriented standards. Smalltalk, which we've been waiting twenty years for. would become viable, and we'd have a robust industry. So, that's my question. Will you do it? Why not?

John Warnock

All we disagree on, Marc, is how to do it. We have to go from being like photographers — creators and users of the technology — to a situation where everyone is able to be a user. Nicholas is quite right. We're now involved in both sides of the equation. We're figuring out what silver halide's all about, and we're also taking pictures. The rest of the world — the information authors and educators — don't want to learn about silver halide. But they have to learn enough of the process to move their skill set from print or video publication, where they are today, to multimedia.

First, we have to give them tools to do their jobs better. When they feel comfortable with these tools, then we can start saying, "Hey, guys. It's a small step to incorporate a little video or sound, and to use this photograph as a piece of video, or this text in an interesting way on your display." The right evolution is to release these existing tools incrementally over time and move people gradually into being the multimedia authors of the future. Building a brand new metaphor or way of doing things, and requiring everyone to adopt it in order to be a multimedia author is unrealistic. It forces too much of a discontinuity in the way people create information.

James Clark

Can we have a little controversy? I just want to observe that Postscript was a brand new thing. I think that refutes what you just said.

John Warnock
It was a brand new thing that worked with existing software conventions.

Marc Canter
What we're really talking about is the business model. Postscript was a revolutionary business model. Everybody wants to have the Postscript business model. Everybody wants to have a little piece of everything, right?

Alan Kay
Not everybody.

Marc Canter
Adobe's creativity and a huge amount of its time has been spent in Acrobat — Postscript version 2 — trying to recreate the business model it understands. John Warnock's statement to me was, "Let's stick with the safe stuff where we can make lots of money. Since everyone knows about print and video, we'll keep selling more. Photoshop is really a tool for photo image processing. We know what that is. It's not multimedia. People don't like multimedia. It's a bad word." What I'm saying to John is, forget about Acrobat. You can't recreate your phenomenon a second time. Okay?

John Warnock
You just watch, Marc, but thank you for sharing.

Marc Canter
My point is, we're really terrified of a world where everything's a plug-in. We don't know what the new business model is. We don't know exactly how we're going to make money. Certainly Kaleida doesn't. Yet, we know it's the right way to do it. I don't think

anyone here doubts that object oriented is going to happen. The problem is we don't have companies like Aldus and Adobe showing us how to do it. How much does it cost for a plug-in? How much are you charging? What's the licensing for ScriptX? We don't know. We're looking to you for leadership, not just to show us how to do Postscript 2.0, or Acrobat.

John Warnock
We'll take this off-line, Marc.

James Clark
In response to what John said, I do believe there is going to be something completely new in multimedia publishing that takes the world by surprise.

Brenda Laurel
I want to make a connection between this panel and the previous one on education. I didn't hear any of the panelists say that what made them creative was a stirring presentation, a lecture by a professor, or a great book. Instead, it was being in a context of other smart people fumbling around with similar ideas. It was having a relationship where the authority of the mentor came from the relationship and from trust, not from a charge to pass knowledge down. The previous panel did not consider this issue at all.

With authored interactivity, we give children the illusion that they have choices, all of which have been thought of by the author. Marty Harris told us how irritated he became when he finally discovered in school that he was being socialized. When children learn that what we've been calling interactivity is another name for authority and privileged voice, we may find that we've produced a level of cynicism from which we cannot recover. If we want to create an educational environment of mentors, collegiality, and communication of like-minded (or not like-minded) people working on similar problems, then a stand-alone, totally preconceived, well-designed, well-produced multimedia product is exactly what we don't want. We need to be thinking about how people can communicate with each other, forming communities like the ones that grew these panelists, and finding mentors even when they don't exist in Muleshoe, Texas.

John Warnock

One of the best ways to do that generally is by effectively increasing the ability to communicate with one another. I never took a course from Tom Stockham, yet I think of Tom as one of my best teachers. Alan Kay was exactly right about being around smart people. Smart people feed on ideas. The neat thing about the University of Utah was the excitement about getting the next piece of the puzzle. There was also that excitement at PARC. Everyone talked about getting that next piece. It was a very productive, creative environment. I agree with Brenda that well-crafted multimedia is probably not the right answer. Creating better, more visual, richer communication between people is where it's going to be at.

Alan Kay

Brenda has been interested in various forms of rhetoric over the years, and so have I. The personal essay is a model of something we can pass around, which is not the same thing as trying to pass down revealed wisdom. The essay is not like a textbook. It was invented as a literary form in about 1550, a hundred years after the printing press. I must say, as much influence as Seymour Papert has had on me in person, the papers he wrote, especially around

1970, had even more of an influence. I could spend hours with them trying to form a point of view. Seymour was trying to convince, but he wasn't trying to tell. His papers in the form of personal essays were incredibly useful.

Jerome Bruner's essays in psychology are also in that form. Bruner wrote essays in order to understand better what he was trying to think about. With these ruminations, we get to follow the thought processes of someone who can really think. I'd like to see more multimedia attempting to do this, rather than trying to teach directly. The closest that I've seen so far is the Marvin Minsky CD that Ann Marion did, with an essay on *A Society of Mind*, previously published as a book but much better in CD form.[6] The CD has glimpses of Marvin's personality, which I think helps to understand his writing better. I may be wrong, since I've known Marvin for many years, but I think knowing Marvin helps to understand where he's coming from when reading his prose.

Danny Hillis

We're touching here on a issue that everyone is talking about quietly in the halls. There's two ways multimedia could go. The fear is that it will become a one-way kind of broadcast, in which interactivity means choosing from a menu which store to enter, which video to have beamed, a pretty trivial type of interactivity. The danger is that a telephone company mentality will prevail — an installed base of capital, a certain service, people paying a monthly fee to get that service, information delivered and dumped out.

A very different view of multimedia is for it to become a mode of communication where people work together, virtual communities develop, and new ideas flourish on how to have businesses not controlled by the deliverers. The telephone company does not control what kinds of business can be done over the telephone. Nor were telephones conceived from a model of all these kinds of business. Telephones were successful precisely because they were a generic enabling technology that allowed people to do a whole bunch of things nobody ever imagined doing. Multimedia done right could act in the same way. Done wrong, it would just be another broadcast television, where people choose from menus on their screen and services are provided. This would be a disaster.

Philip Abram

Excuse me if I go back to the photography analogy. In all of the cases we've talked about, whether photography, Postscript, telephones, or even broadcast television, the technology got out of the way of what people wanted to do with it. To quote George Eastman: "You push the button; we do the rest." Postscript is beautiful. We don't need to worry about the magic. Is there a multimedia Brownie in our future? Is there a multimedia camcorder? Is there a telephone type of technology, where people won't have to know what they're using, only what they get?

John Warnock

If that doesn't happen, we will not have succeeded. The human interfaces have to be built so that they are totally natural.

James Clark

As much as I hate to say it, I think the interface may already be here. It's called a PC. The PC is generating installed base like nothing else in the world. My sense is that it is certain to become a dominant interface, one of possibly two. The television world will have to get really serious in a way I haven't seen yet, if it is to catch up. Television people are wedded to an old infrastructure and an old way of doing things. They think they have plenty of time. I don't think they do. The personal computer could very well evolve into the de facto standard for interfacing with all multimedia.

Jonathan Seybold
We've talked about creativity in schools. We've talked about creativity in the university environment. I want to take it one step further and talk about creativity in a business environment. Three of you have founded companies.

Alan Kay
Five! Five founded companies. I did, and so did Tom Stockham.

Thomas Stockham
I learned my lesson.

Jonathan Seybold
Okay. I'm curious about your views on how one fosters your kind of creativity in a commercial business environment? What are the secrets there?

James Clark
In the case of Silicon Graphics, we had a lot of good creative people. The process is not as easy to define as you might expect. It has to do with an attitude about disagreement. There is no autocracy in my ex-company. Those who tend to be autocratic basically get killed. They just don't win. We did things to encourage creativity, but it was really the culture that encouraged it. The founders were all from an academic setting. They didn't hesitate to challenge and to express polite disagreement. Those who came from a more rigid or structured corporate setting didn't succeed. They felt uncomfortable, and either left or changed.

John Warnock

Highly structured organizations are the enemy of creativity. You need flat, open communication. Promote it. If people start to build turf, stop them. Constantly communicate ideas between all parts of the organization. Never put down an idea. Treat it as a positive possibility, not an impediment. Create an atmosphere where communication is rewarded, and people can have crazy ideas. 3M is one of the most innovative companies I've ever known. It's a huge company with 80,000 employees, 65,000 products, and an amazing ability to generate ideas.

Danny Hillis

You don't have to foster creativity. People are inherently, incredibly creative. The paradox, for a lot of good reasons, is that organizations try to limit creativity. To avoid having people create more things than they can possibly follow up on, organizations build in pruning and suppressing mechanisms. This occurs by necessity. They actively suppress creativity. The trick is to not let these pruning and suppressing mechanisms get out of control. There's a danger they will take on a life of their own. My sense is that creativity is natural to everyone. All we have to do is avoid suppressing it to the degree that we can.

Alan Kay

The problem is that what works for a startup doesn't work later on. Let me take Jim Clark as an example. I don't know anyone who was more focused on what he wanted to do. He and his associates were working for years on a chip set. The sponsors would change, but the project went on. It went through three or four different sponsors in different places. There was nothing else they wanted to do. When they started Silicon Graphics, they did not try to do higher-level languages, or compilers, or any of the other things they might do if they were a larger company. This focused creativity is well suited to startups. We find the same kind of creativity with Danny Hillis doing the Connection machine, and John Warnock developing Postscript. The incubation period on Postscript was remarkably long. Some day the history will be written.

A startup requires great creativity and incredible focus to get going. The problem is that as the organization gets bigger, it doesn't want to do just one thing anymore. Focusing on one thing starts working against it. When I was working on the Smalltalk system, it was good in the beginning to hire people who were completers; but it killed us in the middle when I wanted to change the system. The completers wanted to complete. They were going to complete with me or without me. The needs are different in each phase of a company's life.

Danny Hillis
We could call that the NASA effect. To accomplish an almost impossible task, NASA had to prune, focus, and stay absolutely pointed at its goal of getting someone on the moon. When it achieved this spectacular result, it was left with an organization that was perfectly tuned to put a person on the moon, but not to do anything else. The Manhattan Project is another example. At my company, we're facing a similar challenge right now. Having accomplished an exceedingly difficult task, how do we widen out and do a broader variety of things. It's a very tough problem.

Christopher Herot
I want to repeat a story that John Warnock's former adviser and employer Dave Evans told me over lunch a couple of years ago. We'll see if John says it's really true. Evans said that one of the reasons for Postscript's success was that John had carefully

shepherded the intellectual property through a number of different employers. Evans & Sutherland didn't have a proprietary interest in it, so they let him take it away with him to Xerox PARC. At PARC, John carefully gave a seminar to establish that it wasn't Xerox's property; it was his idea before he got there. When Xerox's lawyers came after him as he started Adobe, he could prove it was his own idea.

Everyone here seems to agree that for a creative idea to work its way to the marketplace, someone has to stick with it for a long time and stall the skeptics. I wonder if it's also true that the idea has to be taken through an incubation period at some big corporation or university, the kind of organization that is exactly the wrong place to bring it to market. How do these ideas manage to make their way to the marketplace? Do they have to move through different organizational structures before becoming a commercial success — something everyone gets to experience?

John Warnock

Postscript actually went through four implementations. It was a design system at Evans & Sutherland; it was called JAM at PARC, and was later reincarnated there as Interpress. The final implementation, after six or seven years of experience, was done in the most flexible way that we could manage at the time.

Focus is very important. We have to allow creative ideas to be propagated, but as Danny suggested, still focus on what we believe are the winners. We have to pick and choose. At Adobe, we have a technique for testing ideas before making large financial commitments. It is to have an "arrow shooter" with an idea shoot an arrow into the woods. We assign a very fast prototyping programmer (one of the Bob Sproulls of the world) to find the arrow and build an existence proof. It doesn't cost much to have one programmer try to build a prototype of an idea. If this shows feasibility, we initiate a process of "road building" to construct a superhighway to that idea, using all of the heavy-duty, industrial-strength engineering and process needed. That's when real money gets committed. Picking and choosing where the scouts go and where the roads are built is the tricky part of managing a large company and keeping it profitable.

Alan Kay
Do you have some secret cache of Bob Sproulls?

John Warnock
We have six programmers ("scouts") who are very fast prototypers.

Doreen Nelson
As I listened to the panel, I noticed a kind of squeamishness with regard to creativity, as if you're not entitled to talk about it. That upsets me. I build cities with kids — real cities, not computer cities, although I did write the teacher's guide for *SimCity*. The reason I build cities is because of the parts and wholes that Danny Hillis is talking about. There's a creative process in the way cities work that can be laid out for people. I'd like the members of the panel to think with us about these parts and wholes — the wholes we can't see. What can we do to bring these ideas to bear in education?

Alan Kay
It doesn't bother me to talk about creativity. I'm closer to Jim Clark on this than I expected to be, though I'm not as reticent as he. I do believe that ideas are everywhere, but I think we should not be satisfied generally with early versions. We need a threshold, and we need more than just a pragmatic reason to improve an idea.

Many of the creative people I revere refuse to talk about their creativity. Ivan Sutherland is an example. Ivan used to take on a different career every three or four years. He's done five or six by now. He'd get restless. He was such a genius, he could start making first-class contributions within the initial year of a new career. I'll never forget explaining to him an early machine I designed that Evans & Sutherland was thinking of buying. I said, this is just like what you did in Sketchpad. He had done Sketchpad for his doctoral thesis only five years before.[7] He couldn't remember! Sketchpad is one of the greatest things ever done, and I knew it better than he did at that point. He had completely flushed it from his mind in order to be working on interactive 3D graphics.

Another example is Bob Barton, one of the great machine designers of all time. I had to take him out and get him drunk to have him talk about what it was like to do his magic. (This was tough, because he was six feet four and could drink a lot more beer than I could!) Occasionally, someone is introspective about the process. But so much of it is subconscious, accidental, and incubational, plus the 99 percent that has to be added to make an idea into something real, that it's very hard to say anything intelligible.

I was associated with Doreen Nelson for years. What she does with City Building Education is one of the best ways to get kids thinking in larger terms. She has as good a key on this as any of us.

Mark Stahlman
Creative destruction is at the core of the professional experience of many people here. The real creative challenge is to find new business models and invent a new industry. Could the panel talk about the creativity that goes beyond creating a company, the creativity required to create a new industry around new media?

Danny Hillis
It's not so much creativity as sheer stubbornness. The ideas of the people who change the business are not that much different, or better, than the ideas of those who do not. But people who are stubborn and focused can endure setback after setback, and hop from one company to another. What distinguishes many of the people at this table is they kept with it, while the ideas of lots of creative people who were not that stubborn didn't go anywhere.

John Warnock
Oh, you have to be stubborn! But if we're building a new industry, in the final equation we must deliver value. People have to perceive that it is good; that this is the way they want to live their lives; that these are the tools they want to use; that it makes for a better world. We must build an economic infrastructure for which people are willing to pay, one that has deliverable value. The proper business model is one reflecting that. Demand for the goods and services has to be dominant enough to attract the necessary money, or we will not succeed.

Alan Kay
While I was working with Seymour Cray's lab in 1965, I read an article by Gordon Moore in *Datamation* that said integrated circuits were on an exponential path. I didn't think anything about it at the time. Three years later, when visiting one of Seymour Papert's earliest LOGO installations, I thought that kids should have a computer they could take around with them, and remembered the article. It wasn't a question of inventing a personal computer. That seemed inevitable. It was, how good could we make it?

Not long after writing his paper, Moore became one of the three founders of Intel. His prediction had been based on what was then an unpopular technology, because it was so slow. At lunch a couple of years ago, I asked him why he decided to do it this way. He said that bipolar was too hard to fabricate and did not lend itself to prediction. He picked this other silicon technology, that happens to be the one all computers are made from today, because it was easy to fabricate. He was able to show that by making it sufficiently small, he could get it to run fast enough to make it competitive. He backed up his conviction by personally starting a company that made the technology work.

This story repeats itself over and over. Someone gets interested in something for its own sake, then goes out and becomes one of the forces in making it happen. Marc Canter should stop complaining to John Warnock, and go out and do it himself.

Matthew Miller

I commend Danny Hillis for his comment that underlies and ties together much of the discussion yesterday and today. A biological metaphor drives many creative processes. The best ideas arise not by design, but by a process of unbiased selection that can benefit from accumulated change. As Kristina Woolsey and Pavel Curtis indicated, we need design, but with a multiplicity of interaction.

The education panel asked, how do we get creativity in the schools? How do we use the technologies? Even the language describing how we hook computers together shows our biases. Thirty years ago, we time-shared a mainframe computer with many terminals, like a teacher with many students in a classroom. Then we had a great breakthrough — the personal computer. Personal computers allowed people to sit and interact with themselves, like a good stand-alone multimedia application, which is an interesting but probably irrelevant evolutionary dead-end.

Now we've taken a great leap forward — client/server computing. With intelligence at both ends. let them talk to each other.

But the client/server model with children as clients and the teacher as server leaves out moderation and guidance. After all, self-organized activities can go in directions we don't approve of, like the gangs in Los Angeles. Connie Stout told us that networking leads to new communities, environments in which creativity can flourish, with new and different things arising spontaneously, made useful by a mentor, CEO, teacher, or (in a synthetic universe) a guide, who throws away what does not compete well and keeps what does. Then let them breed, interact, mutate, and mature.

I want to hear Danny's point of view on where all this is heading, given the ability to do breeding and maturing in machine cycles, as opposed to having to suffer through human generational times.

Danny Hillis

I don't want to talk about this technology as if it's there, or about to be there, like multimedia. It's true that a lot of the important things we deal with in our lives are created by this emergent evolutionary process. So when we go into the lobby, there may be an orange coffee pot and a brown coffee pot. No one decided that orange coffee pots would be for decaffeinated coffee. That just happened when people started to associate orange with Sanka, or something like that. After a while, it became associated enough that society made the decision. Nor did anyone invent schools, as Seymour Papert would tell us. Many parts of our society were not designed in the classical sense. They emerged.

The question is whether with the computer we can reproduce this process on a much faster time scale to try out far more alternatives.

Right now, with ordinary parallel computers and high-speed networks, we can do the equivalent of hundreds of thousands of years of biological evolution in tens of minutes. But evolution doesn't work toward a goal. It creates things of great complexity and robustness, which will solve problems presented by the environment they're in, but it is often not what we want.

For example, with the creatures that were learning to walk, Karl Simms gave them the problem of getting from here to across the line. The first thing they did was grow very tall, and then fall forward. This solved the problem, but was not what he had in mind. So he put limits on how tall they could grow. Well, his simulated world had a bug, and energy wasn't fully conserved. What the creatures learned was that by hitting themselves, they could actually scoot over a little bit. They started moving in jerks and jolts. So he fixed that bug. But, still, the finite integration in the simulation had significant round-off error. The creatures discovered that by vibrating very quickly, they could get the accumulated error large enough to move across the line. The moral of the story is that evolution solves problems, but it's hard to tell what problems it's going to solve and how it's going to solve them.

Alan Kay
There's a million different species all happily living today on Earth, solving the same problem in a million different ways.

Nicholas Negroponte
On that note we should quit, with thanks to what is probably the panel with the highest IQ at the Roundtable.

Notes

[1] Martin Greenberger, ed., *Computers and the World of the Future*, MIT Press, 1961. The book of lectures and discussion was given this revised name in its second and paperback editions as the scope covered turned out to extend well beyond issues of management.
[2] Arthur Koestler, *The Act of Creation*. 2d edition, London: Hutchinson & Co. Ltd., 1976.
[3] Jean Piaget. 1896-1980, eminent Swiss child psychologist, was noted for his studies of intellectual and cognitive development in children and his formulation of stages of development. Seymour Papert worked with Piaget for several years before coming to MIT.
[4] Thinking Machines, a highly-respected pioneer in making massively parallel computers, filed for Chapter 11 on August 17, 1994, after being able to attract new investors following a failed public offering.
[5] Hillis told how when he was once on a plane with Marvin Minsky, they picked up a little folder that read, "This airplane has three million tiny parts in it helping to make your travel safe." It didn't make them feel all that safe.
[6] Marvin Minsky, *A Society of Mind*, Voyager Company Expanded Book, 1994.
[7] Ivan Sutherland, "Sketchpad: A Man-Machine Graphical Communication System," *AFIPS Conference Proceedings*, pages 329-346, 1963.

"Will large film companies move rapidly and decisively to produce interactive multimedia?" asks moderator David Horowitz. The panel has its doubts. Strauss Zelnick believes that although many studios already have stakes in multimedia, most product for the foreseeable future will continue to emerge from small, specialized independents, many licensing valuable studio properties. As production values become more critical in the longer term, some independents may be taken over by studios, or form alliances with studios, or look increasingly to studios for financing and distribution.

Zelnick does not see much of a future for interactive stories, but Michael Backes expects talent from Hollywood to play a central role in developing new genres of interactive storytelling. Bran Ferren argues that the story must remain uppermost; he has no wish as a viewer to assume the prerogatives of writer or director. Gilman Louie insists that interactive entertainment isn't about telling stories, but creating real-time, three-dimensional playgrounds where players make the rules. Doug Trumbull indicates that, for him, what it's all about is getting people inside of the screen, something he hopes to do in a variety of location-based settings.

Shinobu Toyoda reviews the current state of video games, and points to theme parks as a fruitful environment for future interactive entertainment. Games may be the principal genre today, but as with previous art forms, the contours will develop in ways we cannot anticipate or foresee. Panelists are bullish on the prospects for multiplayer games via network and cable, enabling cooperative as well as competitive participation among widely scattered players.

Martin Greenberger
Back in 1990, at the time of the first Roundtable, we reflected on multimedia's "two cultures," to use the phrase C. P. Snow popularized in the period after Sputnik.[1] As the computer and TV came together, Silicon Valley was meeting up with Hollywood and New York. Programmers and engineers lined up on one side of the technological divide, artists and entertainers on the other. The talents, backgrounds, and value systems of the two cultures were clearly different, but there was also common ground. We guessed the divide would narrow and the cultures would find productive ways to work together.[2]

Much has happened in the last four years. The force of technology and its potential in entertainment have become abundantly clear. An attractive new business has come into focus. Attitudes have shifted; resistance has weakened. The two cultures are indeed working together. It has become the rule rather than the exception.

This session will consider the role to be played by corporate Hollywood and the major studios in the context of entertainment, both in the home and outside the home. Our moderator, David Horowitz, was once a practicing lawyer. When a lawyer has learned, it is said, he no longer needs to practice. David was a quick learner in the entertainment industry. He will draw on his wide experience to provide a framework for the discussion.

David Horowitz
We're here today to talk about interactive entertainment. In the course of our discussions, we'll endeavor to flesh out the concept and adumbrate its many forms. The hotly discussed and debated new interactive medium stems from major breakthroughs in technology, as has every innovative form of mass communication

since Gutenberg. First, there is digital technology, which accounts for the increasingly large installed base of personal computers and CD-ROM drives in consumers' homes, along with the advent of FMV-capable 32-bit home entertainment systems connected to the TV set. A second recent breakthrough is switched broadband communications technology, whose commercial imminence is still a moot question both inside and outside of this conference.

A central issue for this session, as its title indicates, is the extent to which the film industry and the major Hollywood studios will be major players in the new medium. There are conflicting signals coming out of Southern California. On the one hand, we have a major industry figure like Barry Diller jumping in with both feet, and seeking to pull a major studio in with him. At the other end of the spectrum are certain studio heads who disdain a precipitate rush into interactive entertainment, maintaining that control of content is key. Since they are sitting on content, the medium will have to come to them.

Historically, the studios have been slow to adopt new video technologies. Whether it's out of fear, lack of vision, or inertia is hard to say. When TV came along in the 50's and 60's, only one major studio moved quickly into the new medium to actually produce television programming. That was Columbia Pictures under the Screen Germs banner. The new medium was largely ceded by default to new independent production entities and one former talent agency, MCA, which did not at that time own a motion picture studio. Similarly, when the cable industry gathered momentum in the 70's and early 80's, only one major film company moved decisively into it on both the system and program network levels. That, of course, was Warner Communications, now Time Warner.

Both of these new media — television and cable — were missed opportunities for the film studios. The obvious question is, will history repeat itself? The less obvious question is whether this new medium requires so many non-Hollywood skills that a different paradigm is inevitable? After all, until now the electronic technologies have been one-way in character, essentially delivery systems for passive programming. The computer-based skills required for interactivity come out of Silicon Valley, not Hollywood. Is that where the action will be?

A closely related question is whether this business will be one of relatively small entrepreneurial units putting out a diversity of products (as George Gilder envisions) or be dominated by huge companies (as is today's film business) coming out of not only Southern California, but Northern California and the state of Washington too. In this regard, it is worth noting that several of our panel members have recently migrated from Southern California to other parts of the country: Straus Zelnick to Northern California, Michael Backes to Northern California part of the time, and Douglas Trumbull to Western Massachusetts. These migrations are metaphorical, perhaps, as well as physical in nature.

Michael Backes

The title, *Hollywood or Hollywon't?* is very apt. I'm more in the *Hollywon't* camp, primarily for the reasons enumerated by our moderator. Hollywood has consistently been slow to take advantage of emerging technologies. It moves with glacial speed. Innovations, whether in sound, picture, or computers, take a very long time to soak into the studio system.

The good news is that there is starting to be a shift of creative film people into interactive media because of the skill sets that are developing. The innovations taking place with a variety of interactive delivery systems — whether for the Macintosh, Pentium, or upcoming Sega hardware — show the quality of the image steadily improving. With improvements in image quality, the need for higher production value becomes apparent, requiring skill sets that are amply represented in the Hollywood community.

In trying to put together Rocket Science Games, we asked ourselves for what skill sets we could raid Hollywood. Hollywood has a very refined and mature sense of production design. My cofounder has worked as a conceptual designer in Hollywood on everything from *Star Wars* to *The Abyss* and *Aliens*. He's an idea machine who can draw his ideas. There are very few people like that in any medium. It's no accident that he is generating our first game.

The first title I'll be working on is a result of my background as a screenwriter. I couldn't do it as a film because it's more about the environment than about the characters. Screenplays tend to be about people, whereas the kind of video-game experience I want to create is about the setting. A lot of people in Hollywood have an extraordinary ability to design a setting, going back to when motion pictures were just an arcade gimmick. The biggest obstacle for them is that interactivity is still in it's infancy. It will remain like the nickelodeon until someone does the interactive equivalent of *The Great Train Robbery* or *Birth of a Nation*..

I had a meeting last week with a screenwriter who's done over fifty movies. He's been writing screenplays since the mid-1940s. He came in to pitch an idea for a video game. You're in a mental hospital. You have to discover the saw under the bed to saw your way through the bars. This would never in a million years be pitched as a movie. But adventure games have given the mistaken impression that interactive stories must be extremely simplistic: a find-something, use-it, shoot-something type of experience. The writer wasn't thinking beyond that. I told him I'd be much more interested in his figuring out how to tell a story from two totally distinct points of view, so the audience would feel a range of emotions from different emotional perspectives.

Most games don't have much emotional content. They hover in a reflex area of fight-or-flight. It would really be compelling for a video game or interactive experience to make us feel a sense of wonder, or longing, or love. I think that's how this medium will mature. A grammar will evolve to make it more than something into which to stick a quarter. It's a long road ahead, but Hollywood has a lot to offer — a level of talent that can be very beneficial to these emerging technologies.

Bran Ferren

Combining new technology and venture capital always seems to cause people to lose their minds. It's taking place now. Nowhere else in the world can someone get up at a conference and say, "It's going to be about content," and get a round of applause. If you went to a bookseller's convention and said, "We've determined that it's not the bindings, nor the packaging, nor the distribution, but the content that's going to drive this business," you'd be considered some sort of moron. But if you say it in this interactive world, you get applauded. I don't get it.

Of course, it's about story. *Of course*, it's about touching people's hearts and opening their minds, by all of the tools and techniques that we've developed to do this over thousands of years of storytelling. The embarrassment of interactivity now is that it's a solution in search of a problem. The trouble with television does not have to do with lines of horizontal scanning, but with lines of dialogue. Those are the lines we need to work on, not resolution of the image. It's the same issue with interactive entertainment.

Mostly, we need to realize that interactivity is not an emerging technology. There's been interactivity since the first creature crawled around on the surface of the earth. Human beings are born interactive. They've always been interactive. We live in a richly interactive world, except that electronic media forgot this for a few years. The notion that interactivity is a new concept is ridiculous. So is the notion that interactive movies are the solution. I go to a movie because I'm interested in the point of view of the director. I don't need to come up with a new ending. Watching the writer's ending is why I paid good money to see the movie. Concepts that are novelty-based are going to wear off very quickly — hopefully sooner rather than later.

We're living at a spectacular moment in time. But we have to understand that this is not going to be a business about television, or about PCs. It's going to be about evolving clearer ways of telling stories and communicating ideas with passion, fun, and excitement. That's what will make it work. The AT&T commercial says, "Have you ever sent a fax or done business from the beach? You will." Try reading a book on a CRT. I think the commercial should be changed to, "Have you ever gotten a $175,000 phone bill? You will." We have to be very careful that we're not driving towards unnecessary solutions. I don't need a combination word processor/food processor to do my job, even though it's technically possible to produce one.

Who's going to pay for all of this? I hope there's a lot of money available. In a society where Evian water costs more than gasoline (and it does), anything is possible. But we need to accept the importance of story, and understand that platform independence is the only way. Once the technology gets to working better, it's going to be about open formats and open platforms. Anyone who doesn't get this will be *road kill* on the information highway.

Gilman Louie

An executive at a Hollywood studio said to me recently that there would be billions of dollars lost in this industry, either your money or that of venture capitalists and institutional investors. It isn't a question of whether Hollywood will succeed. Anyone who thinks Hollywood will fail is mistaken. They will just wait for one of us to succeed, then buy us. They're very smart business people. Hollywood is about distribution, not creativity. Doug Trumbull in Massachusetts and Colossal Pictures in San Francisco are creating the real content.

A Hollywood person with a camera is as dangerous as a Silicon Valley programmer with a keyboard. The camera person wants to start filming immediately, no matter if what's being produced is to be interactive. With 72 minutes of video on a CD and a story that branches in seven directions, the result is a 10-minute game. Similarly, a programmer wants to start programming. These people don't speak the same language, and they don't understand what they're supposed to be building. If they think they're building a story, they should be working in films or books. Those are the best media for telling a story. Interactive entertainment isn't about telling a story. It's about having interactive experiences.

What I'm saying is, avoid scripts. Don't use pre-canned video. Work on creating real-time, three-dimensional playgrounds in which players make the rules and come to play. The information highway should allow people to participate together in a world of experiences. The kids who are playing Dungeons and Dragons realize that what makes the game work is the dungeon master, who concocts the story as the players are playing. We need to learn how to create a digital dungeon master, so that stories are truly interactive, not pre-written or pre-scripted. Brenda Laurel said it best. We have a dictatorship of writers and programmers who specify the only possible ways to win a game. Play it their way or they'll kill you. Then start over and try again.

The trick is being able to combine production values with creative values (properties and characters) in a compelling world where people can fantasize. It's being able to use the power of a PC, or a new Sega 64-bit system, or what SGI is trying to do with Nintendo, to create an alternate reality where people can explore and experience. The environment has to be reactive to what you're doing, rather than requiring you react to it.

Hollywood is not only about distribution. It is also (at least its creative side) about creating properties — compelling worlds and characters with which people can identify. The successful model will be a collaborative effort between technology companies and creative Hollywood to produce what real multimedia is supposed to be about — launching a property in different media. *Jurassic Park* and *Batman* are success stories where the toy line, computer game, movie, and comic books all came out at one time to cause a social phenomenon — a hit!

This business is about creating, owning, and exploiting properties in a variety of media. It's not about the video at the front of a game. Full-motion video is of no help, if creating interaction means going down three levels in quality. Ask the players who buy games. They'll tell you they're frustrated by this new multimedia that eats up their hard drives and delays the game. They dislike having to watch B movies by programmers who think they are Hollywood-ready because they bought an 8-millimeter camera and a Macintosh AV computer.

So, those of you who are going to invest in our industry, go for companies who want to create that playground, companies with the imagination and desire to create something different. If a movie or a book is what the company you're looking at wants to create, it's in the wrong business.

Douglas Trumbull
I strongly agree with what's been said. Based on my own experiences in Hollywood over the last 20 years, I believe *Hollywon't*. I vividly remember meetings with Barry Diller, Michael Eisner, Jeffrey Katzenberg and others, who insisted there was absolutely no market for the simulator ride, for Showscan, or for the interactive video games I invented in 1974. It's been an uphill battle for me on this issue.

I'm here to learn. This is a whole new bag for me. I'm not in the interactive business, never have been, yet hope to be. I'm very impressed by the intellectual horsepower here. The issues being talked about are extremely stimulating. I'm afraid I've gone down the wrong path, having just spent the last several years trying to understand hydraulics.

CD-ROMs and computerized interactivity have to do with intellectual immersion, whereas my focus has been on visual, acoustic and physical immersion at bandwidth levels completely outside the realm of real-time interactivity. The Back to the Future ride ultimately became a proof of concept for my belief in immersive simulation entertainment. I found that we could have a new relationship to a movie that crosses over the classic proscenium arch. The two-dimensional screen or tube is a framework where people love, hate, chase, and kill each other, with the viewer as a nonparticipating observer. I see the interactive business as finding a way to get the viewer inside the screen. The quality of the technology has tended to frustrate this.

I recently merged my company with IMAX, a new adventure for me, and we're now getting our feet wet. We see a tremendous future in out-of-home entertainment, directly complementing in-home entertainment. I think the home audience is much more sophisticated than Hollywood is willing to believe. It will soon be able to pick and choose in much more sophisticated ways with digital TV and stereo sound. Still, out-of-home entertainment provides a very profitable platform for some amazing things that I'm interested in doing. It's a wonderful business. The going ticket price for a simulator ride, for instance, is a "dollar a minute." The current *Wired* magazine has an article with this title that includes some rather uncomplimentary comments about my work.[3]

My company has developed a new kind of simulator at a price point that enables a version of a $60 million Universal Studios ride to be placed in shopping malls and multiplex cinemas. We have no intention of putting these hydraulically actuated, leaky, greasy simulator rides in the living room, but think there's a huge market for them worldwide in sophisticated entertainment centers. It will be like going to a multiplex cinema, but in a place that combines the cutting-edge products of companies in high-end simulation with immersive film technologies like IMAX 3D, plus simulation rides, food service, and merchandise. This self-contained envelope could be positioned in hundreds of locations around the world and become a viable and commercially profitable business, bringing together gifted people from Hollywood, people who will need massive job retraining to adapt to this new technology. We're looking for people to work with to get into this business.

Shinobu Toyoda

This is my third Roundtable. I have always been very impressed with the level of discussion here, but at times felt that it tended to be too academic for a company like Sega. So, I'm proud to be here as part of a panel which is really very well informed, with people who are right now shaping the future of interactive entertainment.

To establish a base line, the so-called video game market in the United States is today about $6 billion, about the same as the market of the film or music industry. It is growing more rapidly than other segments of entertainment, and the rental portion is growing even faster. The single biggest hit has been Sonic the Hedgehog II, which we released on November 23, 1992. We sold five million units worldwide in 60 days, grossing about $300 million. This makes for a good comparison with movies.

I experience the convergence of Hollywood and Silicon Valley every day, yet think *Hollywon't* under the current business model of the studios, although Hollywood has deep layers of talent that will certainly converge with the talents of Silicon Valley.[4]

While we are talking today mostly about in-home entertainment, we should note that theme parks have been offering a certain kind of interactive out-of-home entertainment for some time. This is also very important. A crude example is an electronic haunted house. The physical house is the same throughout the year, but the software is modified every three months, so that what is experienced inside the house changes. It is a virtual theme park. The software expertise of Hollywood and Silicon Valley can play a great role in creating a new kind of out-of-home entertainment, with much more money invested per project or program.

We need to be clear on the time frame when discussing CD-ROM, cable, telephone, and the superhighway. Virtual CDs — or whatever we call the distribution of CD-ROM-based entertainment over the network — will not happen until about 1999. That's the time required to bring this form of entertainment to the average home in America. But Hollywood must not forget what it has to do today. We'll start to see many important experiments and ventures in 1994-95. They're starting now.

David Horowitz
I might observe that so far it's a rout in favor of Silicon Valley. I'm hoping that our final panelist might help to redress the balance.

Strauss Zelnick
It's like being in grade school where the "Z"s always had to speak last and sit in the back of the room. I want to address the role Hollywood will play in interactive entertainment. I'll look at both the creative side and issues of financial involvement or ownership.

What Silicon Valley does is intrinsically different from what Hollywood does, although there are similar elements. (Incidentally, some of the biggest players in the business are outside *Silicon Valley*) In Hollywood, where I spent the better part of eleven years, the *story* is the thing. *Story* has to do with exposition, conflict, and resolution. You're trying to deliver emotional impact — the satisfaction and enjoyment that comes from a good story. In Silicon Valley, the story is a backdrop for something else altogether — a game. Games have been around for as long as stories. We can learn a lot just by recognizing that what we've been hoping to do electronically for the past fifteen years has been around since the beginning of mankind. Games are not about exposition, conflict, and resolution. Instead, they seem to be about competition, mastery, and winning or losing. The pleasure comes from winning.

What translates best from Hollywood to Silicon Valley, from movies to games? Environments and characters seem to translate well, stories poorly. But there are exceptions. One of the biggest hits recently in the video game industry was *Aladdin*, a very story-driven game.[5] Still, most video games are original and not story-driven. Of the top ten games of all time, eight are original titles, including Sonic the Hedgehog, which helped drive Sega to success, and Mario, which propelled Nintendo.

Ultimately, the key creative elements in the business are the original elements. Creative elements that fully derive from another medium don't really exist. In the movie business, somewhere around 30 to 40 percent of the movies scheduled every year are based on preexisting material, like books, television shows, and prior versions. The remaining 60 to 70 percent, which tends to be original, is always the more profitable and produces the hits, and it doesn't require paying anyone for the use of intellectual property.

We'll probably find 30 to 40 percent of game projects based on ancillary titles, with the remainder original. The biggest hits will be the original titles. What source material will be used? Not necessarily movies. It could be books, comic books, or especially characters. The game business is only fifteen years old. There will be an evolution in which multiple elements will be taken from Hollywood for interactive entertainment. We'd be foolish not to avail ourselves of the highly creative people who can write, produce, direct, and create scenarios, as Michael Backes said. Virtually every game company is trying to do this right now, including Crystal Dynamics.

I think we'll stop short of interactive stories. A story depends on the suspension of disbelief. As soon as viewers are in control of the outcome, it's very hard for them to suspend disbelief. They are now authors, not participants. Most people don't want to come home from a long day and be an author. When they pay for entertainment, they want to be entertained. Stories entertain based on someone else's creative power. Having viewers control the outcome themselves pierces the veil and drains the emotional energy from the story. I don't think interactive stories are the future of the business.

There's also a practical problem with interactive stories. After the novelty wears off and the business matures, quality becomes the thing. People are accustomed to the production values of a film or TV. The average cost of making a 90-minute motion picture is about $25 million. The average high-quality video game is played for 40 to 60 hours. If an interactive movie with enough going on to allow for interaction requires 8 hours of footage, with the same production values and actors as a motion picture, do the arithmetic. There's no way that business can work. What are being tested now are interactive low-budget movies. I learned the hard way that low-budget movies, on balance, are not remembered very well.[6]

So what's next? I think it's a professionalization of what we do: better graphics, better game play, and a use of technology and talent to create an overall better game experience. I don't think we will gain very much by changing the underlying elements of the experience. I've ridden Doug Trumbull's Back to the Future ride. It's truly extraordinary. The experience we'd like to create at home is one that has all the power and reality of that ride, but with *you* as the driver. *You* have the goal, and are trying to achieve that goal.

The second question I want to address is Hollywood's role in financial investment and ownership. We need to remember that Hollywood isn't run by Hollywood anymore. Every major movie and TV company is part of a larger organization with interests in multiple entertainment and media businesses. MCA, owned by Matsushita, has a theme park, is in television, and is part of the music business. Columbia Pictures, owned by Sony, has a television and film business, a video game business, and is also in the music business. Paramount is now owned by Viacom; Fox is owned by News Corp; Warner is owned by Time Warner; and Disney is a diverse company whose primary business, in terms of revenues and profits, has been in theme parks.

We also need to recognize that Hollywood is already in the interactive business. MCA owns a minority position in Interplay; Sony owns Imagesoft, a rather large game company; Viacom owns Viacom New Media (which includes Icon Simulations), Paramount Interactive, and a small position in Spectrum HoloByte; Time Warner has Time Warner Interactive Group and a position in Crystal Dynamics; and Fox has been making their own games. Will affiliations between Hollywood and Silicon Valley grow in the future as the business grows? Absolutely. But there is a different skill set between the two businesses — a difference in creative goals. I think we will have different creative groups running their own businesses in their own ways.

If we try to jam these creative groups together, we'll probably have the same results that some major studios had when they formed game companies in the early 1980s (which many people don't know they did). When I was at Fox thinking about forming a game company, I spoke with a number of people who still remembered that Fox had started a company called Fox Video Games in Palo Alto in 1981. I called up the ex-CEO of the company, and said, "What can you tell me about Fox Video Games?" He shot back, "I had nothing to do with that. Nothing at all." I called up some other people and learned that Fox Video Games had been sort of a marketing division whose goal was to churn out low-end video games as quickly as possible to match release dates. It failed abysmally, as we would expect.

The fact is, the video game is not an ancillary business. It's a stand-alone business. If we run it like an ancillary business, it becomes market-driven, and if we focus too much on synergy, it won't do very much at all. It has to be run with its own rules. Synergy is great for *Jurassic Park*. Investing in twelve different things that all pay off is wonderful. Synergy is not great for *Last Action Hero*. Investing in a $100 million movie that fails can produce a domino-effect with other investments also tending to fail. It's tricky to invest in many different lines of business simultaneously.

When people ask me why I'm not making games based on movies, given my background, I tell them that the hit ratio in the game business for a good company is around 50 percent. (That's better than most entertainment businesses.) The hit ratio in the movie business is around 25 percent. As near as I can tell, we have to multiply the two together to get the hit ratio for a game based on a simultaneously released movie. That's 12 1/2 percent. Then I pay $1 million for a license. I think I'll stay out of that business.

I believe game companies will be developed and run largely by independent entities, perhaps co-owned or owned by the studios. They will have to focus on getting the job done, which is making the highest quality games and distributing them in the most appropriate ways.

David Horowitz

Apart from a unanimity that different skill sets are required for interactive entertainment than for film, I did not get a sense of the varieties of forms possible. I heard games and more games. What else does the panel see in this new world? Let me pair that with a related question on the extent to which you see interactive entertainment displacing part of the film marketplace?

Douglas Trumbull

I don't see it displacing, but adding to. With the evolution of new ideas and technologies that enable different ways of doing things, there's always room to add to the repetoire of what we do, as with videotape and motion pictures. We asked if the theater would be replaced by film. Would motion pictures be replaced by television? The answers were no. There's a ripple effect with a new form, but if it has validity and adds value to people's lives, it will expand and take on a life of it's own. It does not necessarily impact other forms near-term, unless it renders them obsolete. I don't see that happening with the new interactive forms.

Gilman Louie

I would agree, except to say that there will be an impact on other media. You can see it today. The big complaint when I was growing up was that we watched too much TV. We would sit and look at all the shows after school. Now the criticism is that kids play too much Sega and Nintendo. There is substitution taking place. It will not be limiting to the art form. This is a new art form that requires a new way of thinking. Kids who were fifteen-year olds four years ago will soon be adults wanting higher quality, deeper interaction than available today. They will drive the marketplace when the industry matures by the end of the decade and they start having families.

David Horowitz
What about my other question? Are there any new forms besides games?

Doulas Trumbull
I don't know exactly what it will be, but I have some ideas now that I've joined with IMAX. IMAX has made a very sucessful business of its theaters in science museums, showing films with strong educational content. Its movie, *The Venus Alive*, a wonderful documentary about the space shuttle, grossed over a $100 million (and it's only in 106 theaters). There's something going on here that I'm very pleased to be aligned with — a huge and growing market of parents and children going out together to science museums or big theaters for educational experiences very different from the crap on TV or in the movies. We're building more theaters every year. We want to create educational simulator rides through the body and the mind, through DNA and particle physics. I think people learn by experience. We can deliver a profound experience that they're going to remember like nothing we can achieve any other way. I'm all for using this medium to make education fun.

Bran Ferren
Incidentally, we *did* watch too much TV, and video games are a plague.

Shinobu Toyoda

Based on conventional wisdom, the so-called video game market currently consists of one-third of U.S. households. About 30 percent of Sega's audience is 6 to 12 years old, 30 percent is 12 to 18, 40 percent is over 18, and 80 percent is male. This is where games now work. When it comes to new content, educational entertainment is very promising, and by the year 2000, we expect interactive advertising to provide important entertainment for the home. Our view is that video games can be made to capture the emerging market. That's where new content comes to play a very significant role. It's where we'll need to work with Hollywood. For the existing market, we don't need Hollywood, except for licensing. Also, electronic distribution of interactive content may change the requirements. Sega has started testing cable distribution of video games in Japan. We found that people play games after the kids go to school. So we asked, who's playing the game? It's the mom.[7] But moms want different kinds of games. So there will be new content requirements.

David Horowitz

Strauss, let me put the question a little differently to you. Do you see interactive entertainment as a new art form, or simply more and better kinds of "shoot-'em-ups?"

Strauss Zelnick

I think it can be both. One person's art is another person's "shoot-'em-up." Art movies, for example, represent only a tiny portion of the movie business. But many movies with artistic elements do very well.

David Horowitz

And one of them, *Schindler's List*, just won the Academy Award!

Strauss Zelnick
Exactly, and actually made money, though that's unusual. As for whether new forms of entertainment will replace old, new media tend to expand, not cannibalize what's available. Having said this, the fact is that those of us in the video game business are also in the TV business. Our games are played on TV — generally the TV in the family room, often 8:30 at night in households with a 14-year-old boy. Video games are cannibalizing television distribution in such households right now.

I'd like to beg the question of whether this is just about games. New electronic media do not create new human activities. They support existing activities, allowing people to do things more easily and conveniently. The telephone allowed people to communicate over long distances. The word processor made it easier for people to write. (Before that, the typewriter made it easier to write) A video game platform allows people to play games conveniently, at home, in their living room, electronically, without regard to the weather outside or the availability of people with whom to play. A boy does not have to get drafted to play major league football; he can have that athletic experience vicariously at home.

I don't think there's anything wrong with the fact that games dominate. It's very likely that, in time, our definition of games will expand to other things that take advantage of the new media but are not exactly games, or stories, or anything we've ever heard of. Unfortunately, the fact that we have a technology desperately in search of an application that we have not yet heard of is the biggest pitfall for investment. Not understanding where we are heading makes it hard to set course. Still, we can continue to create better, more interesting, more intricate forms of video game entertainment. That's the upside.

Thomas Stockham
On this tantalizing question about *Hollywood or Hollywon't?* would the panelists clarify their answers? Who is *wood* and who is *won't*?

Bran Ferren
The entertainment industry in Hollywood represents a lot of smart people with access to a lot of money. Generally speaking, if there's a good idea, they'll be players. So, to that extent, I'd say, *Hollywood*.

Gilman Louie
It's a very hard question. *Hollywood* will buy what it needs and learn from people like ourselves. *Hollywon't* in its current form and in its ability to dictate the future of content.

Douglas Trumbull
My experience is that all of the major studios are looking at this very seriously, but with a lot of trepidation. So, *Holly-maybe*.

Shinobu Toyoda
As I mentioned, *Hollywon't* under the current business model, but a new *Hollywood* will emerge.

Jac Holzman
Hollywood or Hollywon't? It doesn't really matter. From my own personal experience, I think Gilman Louie had it 90 percent right. Hollywood is about distribution. Hollywood is about finance. Hollywood is ultimately and forever about control. My question to the panel would be, what is it that Hollywood offers that you need and can't go out and get for yourselves? A Hollywood production hires writers, cameramen, and directors, all of which you can do yourselves — without taking on their additional overhead.

Strauss Zelnick

That's what Michael Backes is doing at Rocket Science in picking the members of his team. If you're asking why we need the big companies in Hollywood, the honest answer is that many of us have gone to them for financing. They're an excellent source, because we're in the entertainment business, and so are they. Some of us have gone to them for distribution. For example, a major record company is now distributing Crystal Dynamics' products overseas.[8] Some of us have found it very useful to work with these companies for generating expertise we don't yet have, although I've been working in this business long enough to know where to go and how to hire actors, and I can work with agencies. Other companies don't have that experience. Over the long haul, it's not going to be a matter of whether we need Hollywood or Hollywood needs us. The fact is, there's going to be continued consolidation in the entertainment business. We're part of that consolidation.

Gilman Louie

I totally agree. We should realize that even if we get a property, it only provides us with the use of the name. We're the licensee of *Star Trek: The Next Generation*. Paramount is one of our investors and sits on our board. We have a terrific relationship with them. But so far as *Star Trek* is concerned, all we get is the name and use of the likenesses of the characters. If we want to use their voices, we have to negotiate with the actors themselves. If we want to use the theme music, we have to buy the sheet music from the group who originally composed the song. A relationship may not provide us with anything more than the name of an existing property in the marketplace. The rest we have to do ourselves.

Strauss is doing it the right way by going out and hiring new talent. We don't need that. But down the road, Hollywood is going to play an important role in distribution. Make no mistake about it. Distribution is going to be part of the game. Content is the premium item, but it has to be sold. The best distribution companies right now are the studios, especially overseas. They have the ability to access the record and video stores. That's where the battle's will be fought — not in the computer specialty stores. Distribution will not be done through the Eggheads and Computiques of the world, but via the Blockbusters, Tower Records, and Musiclands. We have to have access to them. It's not important right now, but it will be down the road.

Bran Ferren

Aladdin is an exception. It was not just a matter of transfering a name. Walt Disney's animation skills, storytelling expertise, and marketing and cross-marketing abilities were brought to bear in the *Aladdin* project. It's the first of a line that will acquire more than a name from Hollywood. The Hollywood skill set shouldn't be dismissed.

Jac Holzman

The point I wanted to make is that the record companies are your natural allies, more than the Hollywood studios. They are the ones with the distribution.

Gilman Louie

I agree. I also believe that the television studios are going to start moving very quickly to the ownership and creation of content, rather than simply being distributors of content as in the past.

David Niguidula

Mr. Toyoda mentioned that about 80 percent of Sega's video game market is male. I'm sure you're thinking about expanding your market demographics. How do you envision that happening, and how might it relate to the way the television and film industries have marketed to different demographic groups? Is there overlap between their approach and developing entertainment products?

Shinobu Toyoda
This is a very important issue. There's a gold mine if we can find a way to embrace the rest of the demographic spectrum. It's a huge potential market, one we have not been able to tap so far. Males like challenge. Females like a sense of accomplishment. Current video games use 16-bit, sprite-based technology. They are not story-oriented. Advanced technologies will allow a new 3-D form of entertainment. If we can find the answer, we would instantly double our business. It's the big challenge.

Gilman Louie
The hardware just can't do it. We've tried a number of approaches. Sometimes we do it by mistake. When Tetris came out, we found that 40 percent of the users were women, and they outscored men in the game.[9] It's one of two categories that appeal to women. Television studios asked us if we could do something based on the soaps. Well, maybe on the PC, but not on the existing video game platform. I think this will change as performance improves and we try out new ideas. We'll fail, but we'll also find forms that succeed. Then everyone will do it.

Bran Ferren
It might help to have more women in this industry producing the software. Most little girls I know don't want to rip the hearts out of people. At some point, you'll realize that you need to get the audience you're designing for to be the designer.

Gilman Louie
All of our female programmers are doing either Tetris or Star Trek simulations.

Bran Ferren
Maybe they can put the hearts back in. Design a nurse/doctor game as an antidote to *Street Fighter*.

Matthew Miller
I have two separate but related questions. The first has to do with the timing of electronic as opposed to physical distribution. I think this touches on the issue of *Hollywood or Hollywon't*? The second has to do with the importance of multiplayer network games that incorporate genuine competition, as opposed to just displacement over the network. I'd like to hear some points of view on when these two elements will have an impact on the business.

Shinobu Toyoda
As I mentioned, this year Time Warner is undertaking a joint venture with Sega for commercial distribution on the Sega channel. In fact, we have a listing this month for a commercial program. This is the real thing. It's actually happening. It will be based on current 16-bit technology, but this can change. I think wide distribution of CD-ROM will come in the very late part of this decade. However, we will start seeing experiments in 1994-95 by Time Warner in Orlando, Viacom and AT&T in Castro Valley, and so forth. The program direction observed in the next three years will be very important.

Strauss Zelnick
Looking at what human beings like to do, solitaire is fun, but gin is more fun, and poker's even more fun. Multiplayer games represent

the top-selling video games of all time. All of us are going to do multiplayer games, whether that means games that are multiplayer-capable on one screen or multiple screens. The problem is that some of the most exciting video games involve a player flying or driving into a 3-D environment. It's very hard to get a multiplayer capability on a single screen, but it is possible on multiple screens. Since most households don't have multiple screens side-by-side, one household must be made interactive with another in real time. This can produce a pretty trippy environment. The great example is virtual racing in an arcade, where there are four screens, four chairs, and an overall screen. A variety of products now coming out will achieve this effect using modems on personal computers and dedicated game platforms. The next step is network games. Ten years down the road, that's where it will be.

Gilman Louie
It's already here. In fact, our best-selling simulation game, *Falcon*, is as popular as it is because of its modem feature. Players have national leagues where they hook up to modems and home line services without having met. They even have tournaments and conventions. Two hundred people who only know each other from bulletin boards dress up in flight suits and spend a whole weekend together in Las Vegas having fly-offs. This is not something our company sponsored. The players just started doing it themselves. Group play is so much more compelling than solitary play. People interact not with machines, but with people through machines. They want a personal experience. The greatest games in the world — chess, monopoly, Go — are just vehicles to understand the other person. Ultimately, games will do that in an interactive world.

Strauss Zelnick
Wouldn't it be great if you received the income for that added use?

Gilman Louie
We're working on it.

Strauss Zelnick
That's what the studios manage to do. Every time something gets distributed and used, they get a piece of it. You're not getting any of that money yet. In the future, you'll be able to keep it.

Shinobu Toyoda
When we did a psychological analysis of game players, 40 percent were what we call social players who like to play together, 40 percent were serious players who like to play by themselves, and 20 percent were mature player who just play occasionally and don't care too much. The significance of this is that the future is definitely in networking, with companies like AT&T playing a great role.

Martin Harris
I hate games but love immersion. What's the chance for people like me to have a more personal immersive experience at home? Where is that addressed, and how will it appear in the marketplace?

Shinobu Toyoda
For that, the electronic distribution and networking of video games will be very important. Just think about playing interactive mahjong with real players in New York, San Francisco, Los Angeles, and Tokyo — watching their faces on TV. We'll have digital TV all over the world. You call the host, with the faces of the other players already on the screen. AT&T links you in and puts up your face. You can move around to any side. At that time, I think you will participate.

Gilman Louie

The immersive experience is a hard one to plan for, but Sega and the hardware manufacturers are working on new display technologies, like virtual reality. It will come in a few years.

Strauss Zelnick

You said you don't like games. Do you like Ferris wheels or roller coasters?

Martin Harris

I can take them or leave them.

Strauss Zelnick

Well, that's better than saying you don't like games. I don't know if we'll ever convince you to play games, but if we don't catch you, Doug Trumbull will.

Martin Harris

The reality of the experience Doug Trumbull has produced is very attractive to me. People and games on a computer screen are less so. I can't get the Doug Trumbull experience at home. That's what I'm saying.

Doug Trumbull

IMAX has started an aggressive program to remain dominant in the extremely immersive, extremely high-bandwith, large-image medium, knowing full well that sooner or later silver-halide, emulsion-based, sprocketed plastic will disappear. We see a big future for very highly immersive, extremely high-bandwith display systems. Our general philosophy is that as the bandwith goes up, and as the immersiveness of the environment and the field of view that can be filled with the screen image increases, the experience changes in nature, becoming more of direct adventure than a game experience per se. There's a balancing between the value of intellectual game playing versus the stimulation of physical, acoustic, and visual immersion. They are different things.

Ralph Derrickson

I have a question about game playing on a network. How do people who want to play find each other? What is the ultimate experience enabled by mutual game play? Are the fast twitch or intra-game aspects the most intriguing in the long term?

Gilman Louie

There's a range of experiences. People typically meet each other now by getting onto America Online, or one of the other on-line services, and posting their desire to play at a certain time. In the future, there should be much more effective ways of dialing into, say a flight simulation that's always happening.

The kinds of experiences that people are beginning to plug into suprised us. They are not competitive games. Even in flight simulators, the most popular category right now is people flying together against the computer. Players dial in to be in the same squadron going out after a computer-generated target. They find that learning how to cooperate is more fun than simply flying against each other. There's a whole group of noncompetitive cooperative games appearing on the market that take advantage of the modem. It's getting exciting. It's going to change our thinking of games as an antisocial to a very social activity.

Stewart Alsop

I watched television four hours a day throughout all of my childhood and, in fact, kept right on going. I'm now a happy and productive member of society. I'd like to challenge the notion that by watching television four hours a day ...

Bran Ferren
But you should have seen yourself if you hadn't watched so much!

Stewart Alsop
I wonder about that sometimes, Bran. But the whole time I was growing up, I was made to feel guilty about watching television four hours a day, as though I would turn out to be a drooling idiot. I suspect that the shoot-em-ups and fast-twitch games I keep hearing about are actually not that bad. They may be encouraging the children of our society to be interactive, compared to children in other societies.

I was trying to set up a panel very similar to this one for the Software Publishers Association a while ago, and had to talk to both Silicon Valley and Hollywood people. I noticed a difference. The Silicon Valley people tended to listen to their own voice mail, or pick up the telephone if they were there when it rang. The Hollywood people generally did not pick up the telephone and talk. Their secretaries listened to their voice mail for them, and told them who called. Then they might call back. There's a cultural difference. I want to ask Strauss, now that you've both physically and metaphorically moved to Silicon Valley, what are the personal differences between Hollywood and Silicon Valley?

Strauss Zelnick
I'm amazed that some Hollywood people actually called you back.

Stewart Alsop
They didn't.

Strauss Zelnick

There are a couple of differences and a similarity. What's the same is that, at their very best, the people in Hollywood are highly creative, energetic people who are working to perfect their art. That was one of the most exciting things about the movie business, and it's one of the most exciting things about the video game business. I think we've assembled an extraordinarily strong team at Crystal Dynamics, people who are in this for the art. We provide them with financial incentives, but they do it for creative passion.

What's different is that making video games is still a very difficult technical exercise. My biggest surprise in Silicon Valley was to learn how technically difficult it is to make a leading-edge high-quality video game on a new platform. It hasn't been technically difficult to make a movie for a long time, unless you're Jim Cameron stretching the envelope with effects. Telling a story is technically rather easy. If I picked four people at random here, gave them $10 million, and said, make a movie, they'd come back in a year with a movie. It might be a terrible movie, but it would be a movie. You could show it on a screen. You could conceivably make some money. But if I gave four people picked at random from the audience a million dollars, plus some SGI equipment and related software, and told them to make a 32-bit video game, they would likely come back in a year with nothing but code salad.

The kind of people who can create in Silicon Valley often have to be highly educated and almost always very intelligent in the work they do. It's the first time in my career that I've had Ph.D.s on my payroll. Many of my creative executives speak Japanese and other languages. I'll never forget the day at Fox when one of the creative executives responsible for spending tens of millions of dollars of Fox's capital came into my office and said, "I keep on hearing about a distribution fee. What's a distribution fee?" I compare that to the executives at Crystal Dynamics who come into my office wanting to know the most intricate details of every transaction, whether it pertains to what they do or not.

But the primary and most pleasing difference is the absence of cynicism in Silicon Valley. Entertainment — whether games, movies, or TV — is a tough business. The hit ratios decline as the business matures. The ratios have fallen to such an extent in movies, and the underlying economics have gotten so bad, that it almost looks arbitrary. It isn't, but it looks that way. This creates an element of cynicism among many people in movies. What's great about the video game business is there's no cynicism at all. Everyone believes they will make the next Sonic the Hedgehog. Everyone believes they are contributing and on the cutting edge. They're really excited and passionate.

Bruce Polichar
One of the threads running through this Roundtable and its predecessors has to do with creativity and involvement with new media by the next generation. Have Sega and Spectrum HoloByte been looking at software products and hardware for the younger audience, including the pre-school age group? What do you see as the marketplace for this audience?

Shinobu Toyoda
At Sega, we certainly believe in the kid's market. To make it a mass market, we feel the machine must be under $200 — ideally under $100. We want to cultivate a significant new mass market to compete with the Apples and IBMs, and would like to use the video game technique to attract kids to use the technology for educational content.

Gilman Louie

There's a huge opportunity for a company like Sega to work on machines already in use. A generation of kids now know how to use a computer before they have the ability to write, or even put together a grammatically correct sentence. Their mothers and fathers teach them to use a mouse before they learn to ride a bike. There's a real opportunity with this technology to allow kids to explore — not structured drill and practice, but trying things out to see what happens on the screen, as with *Grandma and Me*. What we're waiting for is a machine that's kid-proof, where mom and dad can leave the room without having the PC destroyed. That's just around the corner. The fact that Sega is going after this market is good from a social as well as a business standpoint.

Notes

[1] C.P. Snow, *The Two Cultures and the Scientific Revolution*, London, Cambridge Univ. Press, 1959.
[2] Martin Greenberger, ed., *On Multimedia*, Voyager, 1990, pp. 3-5.
[3] Michael Krantz, "Dollar a Minute," *Wired*, May 1994, pp. 104, 142.
[4] Later that month, Sega and MGM announced an agreement to produce jointly a lineup of interactive video games, as well as to collaborate on movies and television programs. This was seen as an attempt to meld the technical know-how of Sega with the creative talent and film expertise of MGM. *Wall Street Journal*, April 27, 1994.
[5] "Aladdin," developed with Walt Disney and Virgin Games, was Sega's biggest hit in the Christmas of 1993.
[6] Zelnick headed the division at 20th Century Fox that was unable to emulate the success of low-budget movie producers using a major-studio format.
[7] Tetris is reported to be a special favorite of moms, even addictive to some. "Game Makers Study How Tetris Hooks Women," *Wall Street Journal*, May 10, 1994, p. B1.
[8] Five months later, it was announced that Strauss Zelnick would become president and CEO of BMG Entertainment North America effective January 2, 1995. BMG (Bertelsmann Music Group), a major record and electronic media company, is the international distributor of the products of Crystal Dynamics.
[9] This compares with 99 percent male users for most of its other games. Echoing the experience of Spectrum HoloByte, Nintendo reports that women account for 40 percent of the 27 million buyers worldwide of Game Boy, its hand-held video-game player that comes bundled with Tetris, twice the percentage of women purchasing its other machines. "Game Makers Study How Tetris Hooks Women," above.

The lineup is great, says moderator John Doerr. Ravenel is calm, thoughful, strategic, and candid. Mundie adds a sense of power and drama. Ruth Otte is spectacular. Bob Lucky wins extra points for humor. The session is a turning point, according to Doerr, providing balance for the George Gilder sentiment that the PC is it, and TV is dead, or a dead end. A straw poll reveals that participants are not representative. The average household has TV on 6 hours a day, true for few participants. But an amazing 60 percent claim they watch The Discovery Channel.

The panelists are sober, but confident. Ravenel stresses the rapid rework of physical backbone with fiber, not for new services, but to lower maintenance and personnel costs for today's businesses — a good thing, he reminds us. Ravenel is conservative about how soon new technologies will be mass deployed; maybe 1996, maybe 1997 or 1998. Mundie says Microsoft views the PC and TV as co-equals in the home. He describes his efforts to design a new lightweight operating environment, optimized for set-top boxes, that will accommodate both PCs and TVs. Otte says the Discovery Channel's experiments show how simple interaction can be compelling. She describes the complexity in today's programming environment, where schedulers have to decide now what should air next February. Lucky is a healthy skeptic. He suspects most trials successfully prove what their designers believe. He feels we underestimate the momentum of the Internet and its importance to interactive media.

Panelists come up with key questions for the Roundtable.[1] *Additional questions come from the group at large in a brisk cadence called by Doerr. The Roundtable has fun responding to a challenge that it be more visionary, producing a stream of both light and serious suggestions for new services. Ruth Otte, definitely upbeat, insists that the world of advertising will undergo fundamental change. Advertisers will not be a hindrance to progress. "It's bigger than they are," she says, "and they will see the opportunities."*

John Doerr

This is going to be a singular panel on two dimensions. First, it's a little smaller than any of the others, so there will be more dialogue and interaction. Second, the organizations represented account for about $40 billion in market value. We have some of the most powerful, aggressive, and successful organizations in our industry to converse with for the next 90 minutes.

Let's begin by surveying the group at large. How many of you have the home TV on 12 hours a day? (No hands) The average household has TV on 6 hours a day. How many of you have it on 6 hours a day? One, two, three — four people now. You're coming clean. How many have TV on less than one hour a day? (Many hands) How many don't watch TV at all — and are proud of it? (Still a significant number of hands) How many are served by TCI? (20 percent of the group) TCI serves 18 percent of America. Now, who watches the Discovery Channel? (60 percent of the group raise their hands) So, most of us watch TV less than an hour a day and most of us watch the Discovery Channel.

I'll say a little about each of the panelists before turning it over to them. Bruce Ravenel of TCI has been a friend for 15 years. It's a little known fact that he is co-architect of Intel's 8086. He might tell us later how he was publicly and anonymously fired by John Malone. Craig Mundie heads up advanced consumer technology at Microsoft. He, too, is a computer architect, dating back to the days of Data General. Neither Craig nor Bill Gates watch any of today's television (and they're proud of it) yet they'll be helping to bring the new interactive systems of the future to us.

Ruth Otte used to be part of David Horowitz's MTV operation. She runs the Discovery Channel, apparently the most watched network among people here. TCI owns roughly a 50 percent stake in the Discovery Channel. It's one of the few boards on which John Malone sits. He loves the Discovery Channel, as does panelist Bob Lucky of Bellcore, who is a skeptic on trials and their value.

For my own part, I'm a partner in a venture capital group that has been interested in interactivity for a long time. Two of my partners here today — Roger McNamee and Vinod Khosla — would suggest to us that for every question there are several right answers. The trick is to ask the right question. The panelists have all agreed to what we call the Martin Greenberger Modified Protocol (not the Judge Green Modified Proposal). That is, everyone has the obligation to come forward with a compelling question about users and the new environment.

Bruce Ravenel

When I first met John, we had both just joined Intel and were working on this new microprocessor. It was a very exciting period in my life, and a very exciting period in the computer industry. There was an electricity in the air. We could tell that something big was about to happen. We couldn't tell exactly what it was, although John, to his credit, thought it was something called a personal computer. No one believed him. It was the Model-T era in computers and microprocessors. We knew that in very short order — five or ten years — we'd have the equivalent of superhighways, but we certainly didn't know how it would play out. Looking back, I think our sense of what was going to happen was correct.

With broadband interactive networks, I believe we are today approaching a similar historical threshold, even though we're more at the horse-and-buggy than the Model-T stage. The networks are going to come quickly, but, again, we don't know exactly how it will happen. It will mean a big change in society, culture, and technology — bigger than the PC. No one grasps the full implications, although the press seems to think it does. I find that a little disquieting.

At TCI, we know pretty well what our customers like today, but we're not sure why they like what they do. We want to understand better. The only way to do this is give them new things and watch what happens. We've put a lot of energy into testing over the last few years, including: (1) a test started a couple of years ago in Denver on digital video on-demand; (2) an upcoming market test of the Sega Channel, which Shinobu Toyoda mentioned; (3) a test of utility load-management services just announced with Microsoft and Pacific Gas & Electric; (4) a test of our being in the telephone business in the UK; (5) an upcoming test of a 120-channel cable system in Illinois that prototypes digital compression; and (5) some recently announced tests with Microsoft in Seattle and Denver for full interactive TV, which we hope to have going next year.

From TCI's perspective, all of these tests are attempts to learn what customers do with real services. In the meantime, we're rapidly deploying fibre optics for the networks of the future. We'll have about half of our networks upgraded to a fibre node design this year — 100 percent by the end of 1996. We announced today the opening of the National Digital Television Center in Denver, which is compressing digital TV, playing it back, and uplinking it. Compressed digital TV is now real. I think we'll see 150 to 200 channels of digital programming within a year. MPEG2 compression is just around the corner. Compression will roll out in the cable industry with a vengeance next year.

The central questions have to do with what services and business models will prevail? Will the cable industry become a common carrier? Will the telephone industry become an entertainment provider? Are marriages between telcos and cable companies over? Are they going to be head-to-head competitors? These are the key questions of industry structure. Yet the most compelling question is, what do customers really want? Does anyone know? How can we find out?

Craig Mundie

I'll mention some issues we've thought about at Microsoft in the process of planning for broadband networks, interactive television, and their relationship to the evolution of the personal computer. Because of the high media attention to trials, many people in the content community feel they have to get on board with something, or be left out. Our message would be not to get on the train too early. We've tried to avoid that ourselves. Our work with TCI and others is to design a system we believe will be robust enough to go into volume deployment. We are waiting to begin testing until the architecture is well-defined, in contrast to a more common focus on market testing, or the testing of a concept, without a technical basis for going full scale.

I thought it would be interesting to create a taxonomy based on the reasons people are conducting trials:

1. Telcos and cable companies are basically going to have new physical plants when all is done. There's work to do in trying to put these plants in place and characterize them.

2. Computers are suddenly arriving on the scene, especially in the cable industry which has not had a computerized network.

How do the people who work in these environments install all of the necessary computer equipment? How do they maintain it? What do they do when it breaks? How can they be sure the right software is installed? This is a skill set they don't currently have. Trials help them develop it.

3. There's much concern about the user interface. The interface for traditional computer applications doesn't work for television. The focus on interactive TV has to do not only with the right application, but the right setting for the application, including the most primal TV watching we do today. Trials can be used to gain the information and insight needed to design the proper interface for the technologically naive user.

4. Some trials are intended to seduce the content community into participation, in hopes of acquiring needed content. Indeed, content availability is a critical question in trials. Without suitable content, there's a high likelihood that no matter how technologically good the service, consumers may reject it. It has to add enough value to make a difference.

5. A new computer network will underlie all of this. The architecture of the application will have to adjust to a whole new concept of computing.

6. For some companies, trials are a vehicle for new financing. The high level of media attention and merger mania can help companies get the financial strength to go off and compete in these networks of the future.

7. Finally, as Bruce mentioned, testing can be valuable in determining market elasticity. That's critical, since broadband

networks are not now seen as a public works effort, despite comparisons to the interstate highway system, for which Al Gore's father helped pass legislation in the Senate years ago. Although much of the work on the Internet was federally funded through DARPA, we now believe there are applications that are going to allow the private sector to pay for the infrastructure change-out on a worldwide basis. We need to identify these winning applications.

At Microsoft, we tend to view many of the trial activities posited for 1994 as tests of quick prototypes that may contribute to learning, but not to product engineering. The need for product engineering is a very large problem.

Five kinds of bootstrap applications could make the systems financially viable at the beginning: (1) movies or television on-demand; (2) catalogue shopping; (3) advertising; (4) games; and (5) directory services that provide geographic localization and value-added content not available today.

I don't believe the installation and initial operation of these systems will increase GNP, at least not in the short-term. What is more likely in the early years is a shifting of market share from one distribution form to another. We will not be able to get consumers to pay significantly more every month. The money must come from somewhere else.

Microsoft has a different slant than others on how interactive services will be received. We view the PC and its evolution, and the TV and its evolution, as ultimately co-equal partners in the future home or office. We think broadband networks will bring these services to both PCs and TVs, not because the PC and TV are technologically dissimilar, but because interacting with the PC at two feet is fundamentally different from interacting with the TV at ten feet, particularly in a shared experience. In either form, having the computer become a vehicle for delivering "social computing" will produce a profound change.

I have three questions. First, if we assume wide-area broadband networks are an impending technology discontinuity, how are they different from all the other technological discontinuities we've experienced — electricity, the gasoline engine, radio, the telephone, television, the computer, and the microprocessor? Each of these have brought sociological change within a few decades. I don't think there is anything substantively different about this latest discontinuity, except for the amount of media hype it is attracting. But I'd be interested to know if others think there is something more fundamental about to happen.

Second, given effective worldwide communication and competition, and the efficient markets for systems and content, why is there such a tendency for pre-regulation and pre-standardization of this technology? We did not do this to other technologies.

Third, I was very intrigued with Pavel Curtis's idea that personal communication would be the application for the nineties, and also the view expressed on the education panel that the positive new way for the computer to play a role in education is by what may be called computer-mediated learning, where the computer is essentially a mediator between teacher and student. Is CD-ROM-based multimedia just a single-user warm-up version of a consumer-oriented computerized platform that goes beyond video games? Is it the platform that induces person-to-person interactivity? Is this what interactive computing is going to be?

Ruth Otte
We reach 60 million homes every night on the Discovery Channel and 30 million on the Learning Channel. We consider that an awesome privilege and responsibility. It might make Alan Kay feel better to hear that we were told, "No one will watch" and "we couldn't build a business." It isn't truc. We are among the most-watched networks in cable. You may be surprised to know that 65 percent of our viewers, and 80 percent of our heaviest viewers have not finished college. Extensive dialogue with them over the years indicates that we provide something they consider enriching and empowering. They can enter a world of Pharaohs, pirates, or cheetahs — a world they can't enter in their daily life. I think this bodes extraordinarily well for the interactivity many are doing and we hope to do with the information superhighway.

At some risk, given what's been said about television this morning, I'd like to share with you the ways we think interactivity can make television a more satisfying experience. The testing we have done tells us that the number one feature that people want is control. The opportunity of seeing good things they missed is important to people. When they sit down at 8:00 o'clock, all they can see is what the schedulers think they might want. It's a game of chance, especially with as many channels as there are. Believe it or not, my schedulers are right now deciding how many men age 25 to 54 are going to watch *Safari* next February. When people can exercise more control over what they watch and when, they will probably be much more satisfied with the television viewing experience.

One thing we think will be truly exciting is near-video on-demand. When you finish a program, the new technology will allow us to tell you when future programs like it will be on, or how to get one like it right then. We did some tests of simple things like being able to click on a globe at the bottom of a TV screen to learn which part of Africa a certain nation is in, or being able to see the name of the program being played when cruising across the channels. These features were very seductive to consumers.

We just finished 25 new episodes of *Connections*, a program that draws connections between science and history, We would like to put James Burke, the host of the series, on-line and make him available to our viewers. We've never had a chance to have a dialogue with viewers who are excited about something, providing them with the opportunity to see more video or speak with a master teacher. We think they'll appreciate that. When we hit a nerve, people get very passionate. *Beyond 2000,* a program about scientific innovations, gadgets, and how they affect our lives, can result in several thousand phone calls to find out more. We were deluged with calls from a back operation we had on a few weeks ago. We're not equipped to handle that level of consumer response, and think television would benefit enormously by being made interactive.

In terms of key questions, we have concerns about the kind of access we'll have to the information superhighway, and how much we'll be charged to make our programming available. What does *open access* mean? How will my content be promoted and distinguished? How will the navigator enable our viewers to know what's available? Are we going to have to configure content in expensive ways to provide some of it for the telcos and differently for the cable companies?

Robert Lucky

I'm one of those people that Danny Hillis characterized this morning as having a "telephone mentality." (I don't think he meant it as a compliment) But one of the highlights of my life occurred during the antitrust trials when Judge Greene referred to me as the only witness who didn't have a bell-shaped head.

This is an unusual meeting for a telephone person. It's really neat, Martin, to bring such disparate groups together. It doesn't happen very often. At a meeting some months ago at the National Academy, we had a CEO of a telephone company sitting next to a Hollywood person. Someone from the audience asked, "Well, now that content's important, don't you people deal with each other?" The telephone executive replied, "Well, uh, not really, but it's very good to meet you. Oops. I've got to go. My corporate jet's waiting for me." That's the way the corporate world works. Indeed, my quick sample at lunchtime showed that the unclaimed name tags were predominantly those of telephone executives.[2] Anyway, it's good to have this mix.

My experience makes me a skeptic on trials. Even though, by accident, good and surprising things occasionally emerge from trials, I'd have to be convinced of their value. Let me give an example.

A decade ago, home information systems were the thing. Many people were running trials. AT&T set one up with Knight-Ridder newspapers in Coral Gables, Florida. The executive running it told me that the homes in the trial would be given an extra telephone line without charge, and a free television set to connect to that line, so they wouldn't have to use their regular telephone or TV. They would also be given free service. By this means, he would determine if this was promising. When I expressed incredulity, he pointed his finger in my face and said, "You don't understand, Lucky. The objective of this trial is not to fail." Suitably chastised, I shut up. In fact, the trial met all of its objectives. It didn't fail, and showed that this was a wonderful service for which people were perfectly willing to pay $10 a month (it's always $10 a month). The first customer actually charged asked to have the thing ripped out of his house. AT&T lost a lot of money, as did many other companies, all of whom had "successful trials." The operation was a success, but the patient died.

It's hard to run a fair trial and get an unbiased answer, particularly when the people running the trial believe in it. I learned this during another highlight of my life. As an editor of a respected technical journal trusting in freedom of the press, I elected to publish a paper on ESP, which put me on the front page of *The National Enquirer*. I discovered that the outcome of experiments in ESP depend simply on whether the experimenters believe in them or not.

The worst way to find out about a new service is to ask people. They don't have a clue. The information simply isn't there. For example, if the people who started ARPANET in the mid-seventies had asked potential customers how they would like to use network access to supercomputers, would the reply have been, "I think I want e-mail?" No, e-mail just arose.

The social knowledge isn't there. We don't know what we want, even when told what we might have. We have to wait until the whole sociology is established, until everyone has decided whether this is a good thing. When I see all my neighbors doing it, then I know I want to do it. We have to reach this threshold.

In the early '70s, AT&T conducted extensive, expensive trials of PicturePhone. People loved it, until they got their first real service.

Again, a total failure. Economists and mathematicians used the plague phenomenon to model the projected adoption. They concluded that it would start slowly, then take off. They were half right. AT&T repeated the mistake two years ago with the consumer videophone 2500. Marketing studies again showed a big market which just failed to develop.[3] So, I'm skeptical.

What would I like to know from these trials? I'm an architect and a builder. I want to build the information superhighway. What I want to know is how should I build that highway to facilitate the services to come that I don't know about yet? There is a real dichotomy between the entertainment infrastructure that we've been mostly talking about, versus an information infrastructure. A system that delivers mass market entertainment may not be a good system for delivering information. They are quite different with respect to issues of symmetry, bandwidth, latency, and whether they should be packet switched.

Nicholas Negroponte said this morning that "bits are bits." It's one of his favorite expressions. But I've argued with him that bits have different properties. There's nothing more anonymous in the world than a simple bit — a 1 or a 0. Yet some bits are more urgent than others. Some have different latencies. People in the content business tell me that only a network-centrist telephone fanatic could believe that a bit is a bit.

I believe Internet is the best trial going. It has a huge audience doing great things. *Mosaic* is a wonderful hypermedia tool that has been made available to everyone. Its usage is growing at the rate of 11 percent a week (a week!), with a couple of million users already. People create their own things. There's a tremendous trial going on out there.

My question is, how will we get an open-access architecture, what does that mean, and how will we ensure it is open despite the fact that companies like the ones I'm associated with don't want to make it open? Everyone wants a competitive advantage. My two sub-questions are, how will we define *universal access*, and how will we handle intellectual property on the information highway?

Stewart Alsop
What's the difference between a trial and a rollout? When do we know we've stopped the trial and started operating the system?

Craig Mundie
For the system we announced with TCI in Seattle and Denver, we specifically said we'd start rolling out an architecture in a staged way that we think will grow to full scale. We'll start with 200 homes, then do 5,000, then 50,000. Nothing other than scale will change as we go forward. As a result, we'll have the ability with each step to do the market and content testing necessary to reach the next level of evaluation of the whole product. We're not lashing together computer systems as soon as we can to simulate a broadband network. We're not doing that phase.

Max Hopper
In current TV, advertising is broadband and not well segmented or measured. In the new world, it could be segmented and measured. What implications does this have for the existing framework?

Ruth Otte
Advertisers tend to buy advertising in broad demographic groups — 25 to 54 is a standard; 18 to 49 is a standard. In fact, concerns are very different across those ages. What we look for is different, what we can afford is different. There is an illusion that we can

target advertising by having different networks, like Discovery versus MTV. That's not very targeted. I think you're right when you suggest that all of the standards and practices associated with the way media is analyzed and bought today are going to change dramatically in the future digital world.

Although there are times when we consider advertising a pain, and want to be rid of it as fast as possible, the right kind of information from a provider can be extraordinarily valuable when we're in the market to buy something. Advertisers are beginning to recognize that they will be able to target much more directly when they have knowledge of what homes are doing and who, for example, is looking for a car. There could be a database that a car buyer accesses to look at videos on auto models, to order up brochures, or to request a dealer to bring a car to test drive. It could be wonderful for both the advertiser and the consumer. At first, advertisers were in shock about the prospect of 500 channels. Now there is an openness to the idea of reinventing advertising.

Bruce Ravenel

I don't know — Charmin ads on-demand? It's an interesting dilemma. If video goes truly on-demand, and we think it ultimately will, what happens to the advertising which broadcast television thrusts upon us, whether we want it or not? Ruth is talking about information-oriented advertising, which clearly can become much more important, especially for people ready to buy.

Robert Lucky

There are deep questions of privacy and security. Some people may want to be targeted. Others will prefer to remain anonymous, as when using cash in a store. The information infrastructure must provide for anonymity too. It's a tradeoff.

Mark Stahlman

Bob Lucky is being far too kind and generous. I was director of new business development at General Instrument ten years ago. I've stayed fairly close to the cable business. Trials don't all work. Cerritos didn't work. Quantum in Queens didn't work. There has been more than a decade of failed trials designed by people who wanted the trials to succeed. Why should we believe any of the current plans will materialize as described?

For a regulated monopoly, today's press release is just the latest negotiating position. The telephone business is very different from the computer business. Why believe that investment in fiber optic plant has any purpose other than to replace linemen or reduce maintenance costs? Why believe it is justified by new services? Has any significant business ever been built on such totally untested technology? What's being proposed is barely out of the laboratory? ATM switches? Give me a break. Brand new Microsoft operating systems? That's ten years away from even being plausible. None of this is likely to happen very soon.

Bruce Ravenel

I agree that the prodigous fiber upgrade in the cable industry isn't justified or motivated by revenues projected for new interactive services; but that's good news. We can make the investment based on our existing core business. This will provide us with an infrastructure capable of offering a range of new services, even though we can't be certain of the revenues they will generate.

I empathize with the point you're making. I almost got fired for making a similar point last Fall when I was called on to give a keynote speech in Washington, D.C. in place of John Malone. It was not a fun assignment. The other keynote speaker was Ray

Smith, CEO of Bell Atlantic. The event took place shortly before announcement of the TCI/Bell Atlantic merger on October 13, 1993. Someone asked me when I thought video on-demand would be as broadly available as basic cable. My answer was, "Maybe around the end of the decade."

Then the merger was announced. There was a big press conference. Ray Smith said that video on-demand would be available next year. A reporter stood up during the question-and-answer period and pointed out to John Malone that some TCI executive had recently been quoted as saying that video on-demand wouldn't be real before the end of the decade. Malone shot back, "As soon as I find out who it was, I'll fire him."

These things are evolutionary, not revolutionary. Consumers will pay for movies on-demand. They already spend $16 billion a year going to Blockbuster. We started our test in Denver knowing they would spend something, but we didn't know what. We were able to determine that they would spend money month-in and month-out. We didn't create a false success. They really did spend money month-in and month-out. So, a lot of this will evolve, and a lot is fairly obvious. But the claims of the press about an idyllic universe with broadband video and everybody interacting are not real.

Stuart Alsop
Max Hopper brought out the Sabre reservation system for American Airlines. Max, how fully tested was that system? Did you do trials before you introduced it?

Max Hopper
Yes, but a trial never catches all the bugs. Sabre failed when it was brought up live for the first time; then it came back two years later.

John Doerr
Did ten years elapse between Sabre's trial and its being functional?

Max Hopper
No. It was a much shorter time; months as opposed to years.

Marc Canter
I'm struck by how little vision this panel and the last one have shown about future content. I can't believe there isn't something besides on-demand shopping, games, pornography, and gambling. We're at the pre-Griffith stage of placing the camera four rows back, center aisle.[4] We're mapping old stuff onto new technology. Please, everyone, give me one good content idea — your favorite whatchamacallit.

Bruce Ravenel
Bingo!

Marc Canter
That's gambling.

Bruce Ravenel
As the last panel commented, human behavior doesn't change very quickly. We tend to to do the same things over and over. Craig Mundie referred to the discontinuity in technology. Things happen in such discontinuities, but we can't see around the corner. I don't know the answer to your question, but it's a good one.

Ruth Otte
I have an idea. Your child has to do a paper on the Pharaohs of Egypt. You go into a section of the database and pull excerpts from shows on ancient Egypt from our library, or the BBC's library. The

same for a paper on whales, or lions. Thousands of consumers over the last ten years have told us how frustrating it is with 57 channels not to be able to find something at the moment they have time. If you missed it, it could be exciting simply to have access to last Sunday's *60 Minutes*. It may not be revolutionary, but it would be useful, and could be worth 50 cents of your money.

John Doerr
Let's keep it going. Your single best idea?

Robert Lucky
It's a helluva question. I used to keep a list of a hundred things, and scratched them off one by one. I was left with video on-demand. The people working on broadband access at Bell Labs have a box next to the customer on their Vu-Graphs labeled "Mystery Services." Nobody quite knows what they are. That's the grand question from the sky: "What else is there?" I often argue with myself internally. Would I like it? That's how I determine what the world will be. I was dramatically wrong about home shopping. I thought it wouldn't catch on. I was wrong.

Craig Mundie
My best idea for a way to create applications involving people is what I'll call the *virtual community* — essentially the hybridization of two-way video, telephony, and computer programming.

John Doerr
Let's put Marc Canter's question to the group at large. Do you have a blow-away idea that ought to be tried? We'll take as many ideas as we can in two minutes. Marc, you can't answer your own question.

Max Whitby
Intelligent television. Interactive networks have the potential to overcome the passive, superficial, and ephemeral limitations of present-day broadcasting.

Stuart Alsop
Interactive archeology.

Mark Stahlman
The videophone as a peripheral to the PC.

Skip Porter
Interactive foreign languages.

Gilman Louie
Interactive history.

David Nimmer
Confession and prayer.

John Doerr
And penance.

David Bunnell
Interactive government.

Ann McCormick
Interactive simulation.

Carol Peters
(hearing "interactive stimulation") Why hasn't anyone suggested broadband porn?

John Doerr
Who would go for broadband porn? Someone in the very back.

Philip Zimmermann
Porn has played an important role in getting video stores off the ground. They took porn out of the slimy theaters and put it in the hands of yuppies. Couples buy one movie for themselves and the kids, then after the kids are in bed, curl up for their own movie.

John Doerr
I'm passionate about education. My favorite would be an interactive cancer channel. People get some very life-threatening diseases. In an economy where the costs of health care must go down, we need better informed consumers. Right now, one percent of the population goes to the medical school library. Dialing into the breast cancer channel would enable people to learn as much as they can about the disease, and get some consultation. The channel could be subsidized by the people providing the therapy.

Ann Marion
We can structure conversations to construct knowledge from electronic mail. A small example is a project in Toronto where keywords are attached to electronic mail messages, so students in the classroom can construct knowledge together. Otherwise, the information is ephemeral. It goes away, which is especially unfortunate in something as important, for example, as a cancer colloquium.

Craig Mundie
First, we need more tools. We think there are tools that can do for the community what they did for the average person, such as

taking a letter and making it look pretty. Second, the next generation of standard computer products and operating systems should move away from the spatial metaphor toward content addressability. Instead of having to know the location of lists of things, any word or sequence of words should enable us to find whatever we archive. The technology will make it affordable. A huge investment is being made. The combination of tools, forms, and content addressability should go a long way toward making information more shareable.

Roger McNamee
One more idea I believe will be important: *karaoke,* the equivalent of singing in the shower, another application requiring privacy.

Laurin Herr
Craig Mundie mentioned that he hopes we'll have more desktop services and tools. How will the network and new delivery methods change authoring and the production process? When the Discovery Channel produces for the interactive network, will it produce an hour-long NTSC television program, and download it? Or will parts of the program be nonlinearly produced and nonlinearly consumed? Also, what about the VCR? Except for the television and the telephone, it has the hightest penetration into the home. Nonlinear authoring and editing is a big trend in video production. Will we have nonlinear watching and using as well? The trend in consumer electronics has been to reduce the cost of professional-quality production tools so that everyone can be an author. What will happen on the superhighway in that regard?

Craig Mundie
In our view, the form of transmission is going to change production in fundamental ways. This is not a computer networking problem,

but a distributed computing problem. To develop nontraditional content, people must be given a set of tools and a programming paradigm that allows them to think in terms of a distributed computing environment. It's a different way to think.

Authoring tools of the future will probably assist the content creator target multiple run-time environments, allowing material to be authored and played back either simultaneously or synergistically on both PC and TV platforms. We don't think these platforms will converge. NTSC and the resolution and interlacing issues are likely to be with us for decades. Given this duality, content creators will want authoring tools that enable them to create for both playback environments.

John Doerr
I have a question for Steve Case, who has an interactive service with 700,000 subscribers interacting on the PC part of the equation. What are we missing, Steve? What about the users is really important? What questions should we be asking?

Steve Case
Craig Mundie said it. We've always asserted that it's as much about the community and the people as about the content. The most interesting applications will involve marrying content with interactivity to get people really involved. Pure community is interesting, but lacks a certain depth. Pure content lacks a certain humanity. If we mix them together in the correct way, it can be very interesting.

Craig Mundie
Isn't chat the most popular service?

Steve Case
It depends on how you classify services. But, overall, communications is most popular.

John Kernan
We keep talking essentially about consumer applications: video on-demand, home shopping, and so on. Do you see any solid institutional applications in health care, government, education, or business that might turn out to be just as important?

Craig Mundie
Absolutely!

Bruce Ravenel
The genre of health application that John Doerr mentioned will become very important in an era in which spending on health care must be lowered. Increasing the ability of people to undertake self-care at home can reduce the enormous number of unnecessary visits to clinics and emergency rooms. Extending education outside the classroom into the home is equally important. It's an area we are going to be testing in Seattle and Denver.

Robert Lucky
I'd like to mention two good applications. One, standing between the home and the workplace, is telecommuting. People may not all be working from home, but they will be using their home as an adjunct to the office. All of us do this. Facilitating telecommuting will become very important, particularly as states pass clean air bills putting pressure on business to support employees at home.

The other application I like is computer-mediated cooperative work, where we share a video space and can work together with others geographically separated from us. I think we can achieve real efficiencies this way, although, the many demos I've seen so far always seem to have a script played by actors. Real people don't work that way. We may have to change the way we work, as well as having the technology adjust to us.

Craig Mundie
I agree. Workgroup video applications haven't yet been created. Someone out there may do it. These killer apps are still to come, but the technology is there to support them.

David Horowitz
What's *your* concept of the killer app? As I see it, it comes down to video on-demand, and I'm a real skeptic on that. Yet, if video on-demand is not significant, I'm not sure the other applications will be affordable.

I was involved in 1977 in the Qube trial in Columbus. We had a genuine two-way system, including the impulse ordering of films. It didn't work. Pay-per-view has subsequently been tremendously disappointing to those who believed in it. Mark Stahlman is correct that Quantum's experience with near-VOD in Brooklyn/Queens has not been a raging success. In an interview in the *New Yorker*[5], Dick Aurclio, head of the operation, acknowledged as much between the lines, but said they think VOD is going to work in the full service network because people now will have the ability to stop, rewind, fast-forward, and so on. I doubt this will make a difference. We can do this when we rent a video.

So, I have great reservations. The home shopping application on which the cable companies are relying heavily is the one which could work, based on the HSN and QVC experience. Home shopping brings in transactional revenues, which is a whole new ball game.

Bruce Polichar

You indicated that TCI is testing to find out what the customer actually wants. I find it surprising that there's been so little information distributed about the Littleton test. Apropos David Horowitz's comments and the discussion in general, what can you tell us of substance about what you learned from the Littleton test so far?

Bruce Ravenel

I disagree with David Horowitz a little. What constitutes success? Pay-per-view has been a disappointment based on the early expectations for it; but from our experience in Littleton, I think the right measure should be what it takes to support the business and technology infrastructure for delivering services.

The Littleton test has been true video on-demand: 2,000 titles ordered by remote control, selling for $3.95 each, with the ability to pause. Literally, it's a rack of VCR's into which a tape is inserted. It's not a technology test; it's a marketing test: 24 channels side-by-side (expanding to 32) of pay-per-view with frequent start times. Pay-per-view in the cable industry has historically been a two- to three-channel offering at $2.95 per show, heavily promoted, with a hit movie starting every half hour (now every fifteen minutes). It's a very different environment.

What we've discovered is that video on-demand is slightly more popular than pay-per-view, but not wildly so, and the buy rates are four to five times higher than the industry's historic buy rates for pay-per-view. We consider that to be a tremendous success.

Consistent with Lucky's magic $10, we've been realizing close to a steady-state $10 of incremental revenue in those households. Is it enough to support the switched broadband network infrastructure? We think it is, but not until the prices of servers and set-top boxes are lower. We are confident that they will fall to the necessary levels as semiconductor and memory costs continue to decline. We know what the costs have to be. It's just a question of whether it will be 1996 or 1997.

The demand is there. These are not stellar deals, but they are enough to put in place a basic infrastructure. Once the infrastructure is installed, the much more speculative services can be brought to market with marginal capital investment. It then becomes more compelling. Small niche markets might evolve.

Bruce Polichar
How long will you run the test in order to see whether or not that buy rate can be sustained?

Bruce Ravenel
The test has been going on for about 18 months. Our philosophy has been to run the test until we achieve steady state behavior. We're monitoring it very closely. We didn't know how long steady state would take. We planned on nine months, but reached it in about six months. We're pretty confident the numbers are valid.

Danny Hillis
To what level do the costs of the server and set-top box have to fall?

Bruce Ravenel
The set-top costs have got to be $300 or less. The server cost has got to be on the order of $100 to $150 per simultaneous video screen.

Jonathan Seybold
Craig Mundie identified several transitional bootstrap applications, reflecting a standard presumption that such services will be sufficient to pay for the broadband network. I want to ask Bob Lucky whether he thinks we have enough credible evidence to support this presumption.

Robert Lucky
It costs about $500 more for switchable broadband into the home than for a normal telephone line. Whether or not this can be supported is an article of faith, yet businesses are rushing to do it. The house may be wired three times, by the telcos, the cable companies, and even the electric utility people, all in the hope that they can capture those dollars in the broadband. It is exacerbated by the feeling that the telephone business is a bad business. It's only growing at 3-5 percent a year. The unknown looks better.

Jim Long
If I've produced my own little movie, would I be able to allow a hundred users to see it at the same time? Could I get it on the superhighway without negotiating with ten corporations?

Robert Lucky
That depends on whether the architecture is going to be two-way or not. It's going to cost a lot more to do it two-way, and no one knows what that's worth. But I don't think there's any video you can make as an amateur that I will want to see.

Bruce Ravenel
I don't think it's a question of technical feasibility. It's probably not a viable business. Our belief is that these things require large-scale economics and large promotional budgets to be successful.

Peter Forman

I know the studies have gone to a great deal of effort to look at consumer motivations. I'm wondering if any studies are looking at the "demotivators" or fears that individuals might have about privacy issues and participating in what is a fundamentally new way of interacting and experiencing.

Bruce Ravenel

We've done a lot of focus group work both before and during testing. The people in the pre-test focus group were very negative. They did not want interactive television. That's the quickest way to summarize it. They liked Blockbuster. They liked the way they were doing things just fine, thank you. They didn't feel the need for a fancy hoohah. But 18 months later, attitudes have flipped 180 degrees. They now like it. They want it. They don't want to see it go away. They can't think of going back to the old ways of doing things. We're not sure exactly why this occurred, but yes, there definitely is a resistance to new services. Behaviors have to change.

Craig Mundie

On the privacy issue, some years ago people did not carry around credit cards. They did not trust them. They were worried about the banks. Convenience ultimately won out in a dramatic way over whatever loss of privacy occurred. The same phenomenon will be true here. In the end, it will be like credit cards.

Philip Zimmermann

I find it troubling that the public will accept this loss of privacy.[6]

Bruce Ravenel

It's unlikely that this will evolve in a way that diminishes consumer privacy. There's no history of this being the case, at least in the cable industry. Congress has been on top of privacy issues, as when videotapes first came out, and with the Clipper chip.[7]

Philip Zimmermann
The Congress is not responding very quickly to the Clipper chip. I think we're about to lose more of our privacy on the information highway. I think we have to do something as an industry to try to resist the government pressure to take away our privacy.

Marc Canter
One approach to interactivity is to make linear programming randomly accesssible, creating environments in which to roam. Another approach is to change the media fundamentally, so that a viewer of CNN can ask for more information, or someone watching a show can branch to a new thing. When will the traditional media — Hollywood and the television industry — go from the piggybacking of existing material to true interactive programming?

Ruth Otte
I can't speak for my colleagues, but from where we sit, it has to be now. We need to learn how to create interactive programming. We are publishing CD-ROMs to get our production people out of the mode of thinking exclusively about television air dates and into a mode of thinking about both the air date and the interactive experience. If we're in Africa, we must put the added filming sequences on the production schedule and do them then. This is the direction in which we're beginning to head. We need to change our culture to be ready to go interactive in the near future.

Mark Gorenberg
Will the advertisers who financially support the current system slow down industry timetables for moving quickly from trials to

full implementation of interactive TV? Are there certain ways we are going to have to work with advertisers to bring this along, or will they turn out to be a hindrance?

Ruth Otte

I think it's bigger than they are, and they will see the opportunities. I agree with Bruce that the people who sell everyday kinds of products are *extremely* concerned. I'm also thinking about the broad-based corporate-image kind of advertising, which is not targeted for an immediate response. But things just *have* to change.

Bruce Ravenel

The advertising community with whom we speak is very excited about the prospects. Change is threatening, but there are also tremendous opportunities.

Roger McNamee

It seems to me that an Internet-like model to facilitate narrowcasting might be appropriate here. Bruce Ravenel is suggesting that, no, we really need to have a big monopolist in control. Can we get a little comment on the opportunities for an Internet-like operation?

John Doerr

How much will these systems be in control, and how much will the people have to say about the programming? How much of a role will there be for entrepreneurs?

Craig Mundie

I'll comment on how it looks from the computer side. Historically, the regulated monopoly was based on managing scarcity. A cable system has x number of channels, and only so many prime time hours. To maximize revenue, the business model has to pick the single best thing to put in every slot every hour of the day. There was not an unlimited number of slots. But the situation is changing. The broadband network with two-way switch capability now allows an individual television to have its own stream of programming at any point. The scarcity model no longer applies. With almost unlimited capacity, the goal should be, as with Prodigy and the Internet, to fill up the capacity in a way that provides something interesting for the maximum number of people.

Bruce Ravenel

My comment was not meant to suggest monopolistic control. That's not realistic. Its enevitable that there will be opportunity for access from anywhere for anyone. My comment was more directed to marketing realities. Internet is great, but I don't know if money can be made with it. It's not a path for economic growth. TCI and the cable industry are not trying to throttle entrepreneurs. On the contrary, we'd like to see a thousand flowers of creativity bloom. That's the way for things to happen.

Robert Lucky

I wouldn't count anyone out. The Internet is a very interesting model. The protocol could change in the next year or two to permit television and voice to be broadcast, thus opening up the use of the Internet with a whole new paradigm.

Alfred Sikes

I'm interested in having a reality check on what we're doing. We're partners with Le Groupe Videotron in Quebec. Videotron has put together a consortium which includes: the National Bank of Canada, which will download money onto a Smart Card;

HydroQuebec, which can use the network for electric load management; Canada Post, to set up the obvious; and Lotto-Quebec, which will provide games. As a consortium, we will buy all of the in-home equipment, including a set-top box that IBM will make, and a transaction box with a printer and Smart Card port, and a PIN for security. The consortium will underwrite the investment in in-home equipment. Videotron will make the investment in the infrastructure, adding the fibre and the nodes. There's been an interactive television network in Montreal for five years under André Chagnon, founder and chairman of Videotron, who's a serious man. These are serious people. I'm confident it's going to work, yet no one in the United States seems to be talking about it. Why not?

Bruce Ravenel
We think André Chagnon is a pioneer in this area. He's been very successful. The services have proven that there's an opportunity that far exceeds $10 a household. His results are incredible. U.S. industry has been slow to pick up on it. The Canadians are ahead. It's as simple as that.

Philip Abram
Three of the companies represented on the panel have felt the sting of Federal regulators. I'd like to hear some discussion of the possible implications of open public access. What is the downside of federal regulation?

Bruce Ravenel
Coming from the industry that has just been hit the hardest, the least I can say is that rate regulation has an obvious chilling effect. The cable industry has had a huge amount of capital availability removed from its business horizons. Clearly, that slows down the

necessary investment to make this happen. We're sad to see the government intervening in this way. We don't think it's appropriate, but we're going to get on with life. We're glad there is an arena for unregulated business growth which the government is encouraging us to pursue. I don't think the open-access and common-carrier regulatory concerns are material issues. Its the financial impact that's important.

Roger McNamee
What concerns us about the regulatory environment is the desire to encourage as many providers as possible and use this as a way of helping to balance the federal deficit. Given the very high cost of the visual network, and the marketing dollars that will have to be spent to push competing standards like direct broadcast satellite, cable, and alternatives to cable, no one is likely to reach critical mass for a while. There will be a long and enduring shakeout without any significant economic return. Is that something people worry about?

Craig Mundie
It's the level of investment required to play. It's why I asked whether this technological discontinuity is any different from preceding ones? It seems different in the amount of pre-regulation of the environment. Every other technology-driven change in society since the turn of the century has created a situation where the marketplace rapidly winnows out losers, leaving a small handful of winners. I personally think that will happen again here. But is it a level playing field?

Roger McNamee
Because of the scarcity of allocated bandwidth, the only skill set necessary for success in the past has been the ability to gain access

to the frequency spectrum. As available bandwidth proliferates, we'll get competition of a totally different sort, with a different set of skills and a major increase in the amount of capital required to be successful. People looking backwards underestimate the true cost of competing. The result is a relatively low starting cost, followed by a geometrically escalating cost to continue to participate. It worries me that the early birds, the people willing to put up the first two billion dollars, are going to have a bloodbath.

Steve Case
I have a question about the video on-demand trials of TCI. How much of the additional $10 a month is really incremental cable revenue? I've been spending $10 a month for HBO and never watch it. If you gave me pay-per-view for less money, or true video on-demand, I'd cancel HBO. You'd still get about $10 a month from me, but your costs would be higher. What's your experience? Have you been cannibalizing pay-per-view, or just Blockbuster?

Bruce Ravenel
There's been surprisingly little cannibalization of pay-per-view in our experience thus far. I don't know if it's long enough to be indicative of ultimate behavior. We heavily wired these homes with Nielsen and have a good bit of knowledge of what they've done in buying tapes and so on. We think most of the cannibalization has been of tape rental, not conventional pay-per-view.

Steve Case
Are the people who pay typically not the ones who subscribe to HBO? Or are they subscribing to it as well?

Bruce Ravenel
Thirty percent of the new viewers were not cable customers. Non-cable homes that do not want regular cable but will subscribe to video on-demand represent a big net revenue gain for us.

Louise Velázquez
We have a film and television company with a top-five show on NBC. I find it hard to believe that what has happened in network television will not also happen on the information superhighway. Structure eventually places limits on the amount of access, except for public-access television on cable. NBC is our partner, not because we started out with them, but because it decided it would be a partner in a certain number of shows it would do with us. We could not, for example, just pay an access fee to be on the air. How can a thousand flowers bloom under these circumstances? I do not think the model is changing. It's more likely that all of a sudden everyone will be our partner, whether we like it or not.

Bruce Ravenel
Partnering is not the issue. The largest cable operators often invest in networks. Black Entertainment Television and the Discovery Channel are two that prospered. They were not quid pro quo deals where partnering was the only way to get into distribution. They were entrepreneurial risk investments. David Horowitz and MTV are other examples of very successful endeavors where that wasn't the case. The issue is more one of availability of capital and promotion. It's not in the interest of the cable industry to limit good programming. We're happy to see people with good ideas.

John Kernan
I'd like to have universal access discussed from both cable and telco perspectives, apropos of the information-haves and have-nots.

Robert Lucky
That's a deep and difficult question. It's not only access to the communication facility that's at issue, but also the terminal cost and even the cost of the information. I don't think universal access is something we should rush into and have the government proclaim tomorrow. It's very delicate. Personally, I shudder at all the special interest groups that have a cause to advance.

Bruce Ravenel
I agree wholeheartedly. It's a very complicated subject. If you look back at the universal service obligations of the telephone industry, they arose after the creation of the telephone network. It took 30 to 40 years. TCI owns many small rural systems. The average size of our 1,600 systems may be 6,000 to 7,000 subscribers. So we have a great deal of interest in the access issue. It isn't very different for us to bring these services to smaller communities than to Chicago. But the economic reality says that services get launched in big markets.

Notes

[1] These are some of the questions offered by panelists:

Bruce Ravenel. What services and business models will prevail? Will cable become a common carrier? Will the telephone industry become an entertainment provider? Are marriages between telcos and cable companies over? Will they now be head-to-head competitors? What do customers really want?

Craig Mundie. Are wide-area broadband networks an impending technology discontinuity that is different from others that have brought sociological change this century? In a hotly competitive environment, why is there so much pre-regulation and pre-standardization of the technology? Is CD-ROM just a single-user, warm-up version of the interactive media communities that are the end-game?

Ruth Otte. What kind of access will content programmers have, and how will they be charged? What does "open" mean? How will content be promoted and distinguished? Will it have to be configured in expensive ways to provide it for both telcos and cable companies?

Robert Lucky. Are we building a highway for entertainment or information services? Are bits really bits? How will we get to open access? What does it mean? What impact will the the Internet have? How will we define "universal access" and how will we handle intellectual property on the information highway?

[2] The telephone executives Lucky refers to came later to participate in the session on *The Telco Cable Dance.* When told of the allusion to his absence, one executive expressed sincere remorse. His frenetic schedule had not allowed him to be at the previous sessions, he said, as much as he would like to have been there. "It's a circus out there. "But it would be the same with Bill Gates. It's not peculiar to the telephone industry."

[3] See Lucky's remarks at the Third Roundtable. *Multimedia in Review*, pp. 181-2.

[4] D. W. Griffith, 1875-1948, was a pioneering American filmmaker who developed the cinematic techniques of fade-in, fade-out, close-up, moving-camera shots, and flashbacks. *The Birth of a Nation* (1915) is his most famous film.

[5] Ken Auletta, "The Magic Box," *New Yorker*, 4/11/94, p. 40.

[6] Zimmermann and his encryption program PGP, widely used on the Internet, were the subjects of a feature article in the *Wall Street Journal*. See, William M. Bulkeley, "Popularity Overseas of Encryption Code Has the U.S. Worried," *Wall Street Journal*, April 28, 1994.

[7] The Administration has been promoting the Clipper chip to allow the FBI and other law enforcement agencies to tap into digital communications networks. Senator Patrick Leahy expresses serious questions about whether a sophisticated criminal or terrorist organization would use a code endorsed by the U.S. government, for which U.S. government agents hold the decoding keys. Leahy also doubts that foreign buyers would want U.S. high-tech equipment that includes this controversial computer chip. *Wall Street Journal*, May 4, 1994, p. B9.

Librarian of Congress

Electronic Content and Civilization's Discontent

James Billington is a recognized Russian scholar, in addition to being Librarian of Congress. He has made many trips to the former Soviet Union. On one of these trips, in August 1991, he became a living witness while inside the Russian White House to the startling coup attempt. Dr. Billington draws two lessons from that harrowing episode. The first has to do with the inherent perishability of electronic media. Much of the electronic information was quickly destroyed after the collapse of communism , including a great deal of the most important information. The second observation is how, in that secret system, everyone stockpiled documents for self-preservation. There were multiple copies — presumably paper copies — of practically everything. The ability of the regime to destroy documents really did not exist.

Of the many differences between the United States and the former Soviet Union, one of the most striking is the overwhelming number of computers and networks in the U.S. We cannot begin to imagine the multiple copies of programs and endless data that we store electronically. Does this make our information less perishable — or just less private? Does it contribute to American society's being more secure — or just more litigious? Dr. Billington wonders whether the new media will be more successful than television in reinforcing the values of society and its dynamism . It could be, he believes, by reinvigorating the active mind and human interaction in the assimilation of information. He gets a strong dose of human interaction himself in the question and comment period following his address. Some of the darts respectfully thrown may have surprised this distinguished and seasoned veteran of untold academic and political skirmishes. The give and take makes for a lively session.

Martin Greenberger

It was not until James Billington came to the Library of Congress six years ago as the 13th Librarian of Congress that interest officially came alive there in the role electronic media could and should play. Dr. Billington set out on a special mission to turn the esteemed institution into a first-class facility for scholars, and to make its priceless contents more accessible to the public at large. An essential part of the goal he set for himself was to bring the Library technologically up-to-date. This commitment sets the tone for his address.

James Billington

Far more than we have ever understood, human civilization is shaped and limited by the way people communicate. Take the invention of the alphabet in Korea in the second millennium BC. It enabled a small nation to establish its own cultural identity and sustain to this day an independence from Imperial China, with its inaccessible and elitist language of ideograms. The introduction of vowels by the Greeks in the second millennium BC turned words from sound events into symbolic vehicles for abstract, analytical thought. The invention of the printed book at the dawn of the modern age opened the way for humanism and individual critical thinking on a wide scale. It helped bring into being in the new world of North America something that no one previously had ever thought possible: democracy in a multicultural context on a continental scale.

The United States is the first great world power whose entire history has unfolded in the age of print and whose modern destiny has been to incorporate into its population significant numbers of people from all over the world: East and West Europe; East and West Africa; East, West and South Asia; Hispanic and Lusitanian

America. Our nation has been unified not by an established religion or ethnicity, as have most nations, but by shared laws and institutions, and more than we realize, by a common language and a print culture made democratically accessible through relatively inexpensive systems of education and publication.

Libraries were temples of pluralism in which warring books stood peacefully alongside each other, just as conflicting groups were expected to coexist in society — seeking as books do to convince rather than coerce — yet maintaining their own internal integrity. Enlightened capitalism and an enlightened Congress had combined by the early years of the 20th century to make knowledge more accessible than it had ever been in any human civilization. Industrialist Andrew Carnegie's benefaction created public libraries in most major cities of America; Senator Justin Morrill's legislation created new systems of state universities built around research libraries; and at the dawn of this century, the Library of Congress began producing catalog cards for all libraries large and small across the nation, thus absorbing at the federal level most of a cost far greater to libraries than the cost of books themselves.

All of this has been dramatically changed in ways we still find difficult to describe, let alone understand, by the latest revolution in the way people communicate: the new electronic culture of audio-visual media and instantaneous data transmission. Sigmund Freud in his last major treatise on human culture, *Civilization and Its Discontents*, suggested in 1930 that enlightenment was incurably threatened by irrational forces beneath the surface. He was writing in Europe at the end of the age of print. He would live to see a fellow Austrian, Adolph Hitler, use radio and cinema to destroy the leading book culture of Europe and drive Freud to exile in England, his papers being sent on to America.

As the custodians of these papers — among so many other treasures of civilization — we at the Library of Congress are preparing an exhibition of Freud's works. And as we approach a new century — indeed, another millennium — reflecting on Freud's dark prognosis 65 years ago for a Europe that was seemingly enlightened but actually on the verge of a cultural nightmare, I fear that we may not be *discontent* enough in our somewhat complacent society, and that the technological changes to which we often unconsciously look for deliverance may, if present trends continue, make the problems worse rather than better. In short, I fear we are today a little too con*tent* about a civilization with too little *con*tent.

Whether in foreign, national, or local policy we often seem interested in pursuing a line of action that makes us *feel* good rather than *do* good. For our financial, physical, or even spiritual needs, we increasingly look for instant returns today rather than the savings, sacrifice, and discipline required to build for tomorrow. We have separated our cherished ideal of freedom from its Siamese twin of responsibility. Those great temples that brought a measure of unity through enlightenment out of all our diversity — our public schools and libraries, including the Library of Congress — are in many ways dying through a slow budgetary suffocation that no one seems to notice much or mention. I am told it is now easier in this state to get access to libraries in prison than in the public school system.

Overall literacy is declining in America. Most important for our deliberations here, the new electronic modes of communication, despite all their glorious potential for the enhancement of our troubled civilization, may in actuality be hastening our decline, even preparing our fall. U.S. society, perhaps more than any other, has taken an aggressively optimistic view of impending technological change. So it was with television almost fifty years ago: the picture tube would improve education, bring culture and the arts to everyone, and create a better informed, more engaged citizenry. The reality, as measured by voter registration, social statistics, and student test scores has been less impressive. Television, except as a marketing device and a family babysitter, has not been widely touted lately as a major engine of American progress, even by its practitioners.

Our kind of democracy depends on the active mind that the print culture produces and television spectatorship does not. Television increasingly derails any serious train of thought with its emotional bumper-car violence, sex, wise-guy chatter, and sheer manic activity. It has in many ways replaced the church, the school, even the family as the norm setter for our society. Yet, as cable moves it ever more into narrow-casting rather than broadcasting, television is less and less able to provide even a minimal common language (let alone articulate any shared values) for our increasingly atomized society. If you listen to the commercials, the soundscape tends to revert to animal forms of communication. When man uses well the gift of language, he moves forward to law and rationality; when he drifts into incantation, he reverts back to pack behavior and is ready for irrational allegiance to arbitrary authority.

Societies that do not affirm common values from within eventually have them imposed from without. Indeed, a culture controlled by television could in the long run favor the more disciplined and authoritarian Confucian-based social structures of East Asia over our kind of pluralistic and open democracy. Perhaps we, like Freud's German-speaking world, might react more passively to an autocratic drift of our own than anyone thinks possible in a civilized country. Perhaps, as electronic technology accelerates the trend in the American media to replace moral values with aesthetic ones, we are already morally anesthetized. We tend to talk now more about lifestyles than life's substance, about the game of power and the choreography of political manipulation rather than about governance and public service as inherently moral activities.

A key question today is whether the new Information Superhighway, variously envisaged, will reinforce the values and dynamism of our society more fully than television has proven able to do. At first glance, the answer would seem to be a confident *yes*. This new interactive, multimedia world that you all know so much about does, after all, engage the active mind in intellectual calisthenics and in creative interplay with useful information. But the answer is less clear when we move beyond technical questions about what the highway will look like and whose trucks will travel on it, and ask: What is it bringing and to whom?

Do we want this new technology simply to provide movies on demand, video games, home shopping, telephone services, telebanking, teleconferencing, virtual reality, and databases for individual consumers? If the superhighway provides just entertainment and high-priced information on demand, the gap will widen between the information haves and have-nots in our society. Many Americans will lack inexpensive access to the knowledge they need to learn and prosper in an ever changing economy, and we may all forfeit this technology's great potential for genuine national renewal.

Let me address the quintessential human question of to whom what information should go on the electronic superhighway? I will deal with this question only partially, of course, but I hope very concretely by discussing the special role that can and should be played in this emerging Brave New Multimedia World by libraries, in general, and by the Library of Congress — an institution that you all support as taxpayers.

I'll begin by saying that I see a long life ahead for books, not just because we still find them user friendly and familiar, but also because, as a matter of historical fact, new technologies rarely replace old ones entirely. Television, after all, did not wipe out radio. Nevertheless, we expect that the Library of Congress will relatively soon be receiving and organizing vast amounts of new material in already digitized form: films, music, encyclopedias, legal records, maps, scientific papers, government documents — all kinds of data. It's beginning to happen already. For preservation purposes, we will get periodicals and books in digital as well as paper formats. At the same time, the Library, alone or in joint ventures with the private sector, will be digitizing some of its most useful already existing paper and film collections for dissemination via the electronic highway (while duly preserving intellectual property rights) to local libraries and schools where people, rich or poor, will have access to on-line services either free or at reduced fees negotiated collectively with the providers.

This material will be supplemented by other material digitized by the Library itself. Properly organized and made accessible, this material can have results as positive as Andrew Carnegie's public library movement had a century ago in giving the general public unprecedented access to knowledge and self-improvement. People forget that the late 19th century had the most violent ethnic and labor wars of the entire civilized world. Carnegie provided access into the stream of upward mobility that was not then available in the educational system. Today, the effort to set high national education standards, newly approved by Congress, and to come out of the educational slump that began during the 1960's will necessitate and increase the demand for more access to knowledge at the local level — access that local libraries can provide using the new technology.

The Library of Congress is moving to help meet this challenge in four important ways:

(1) by enriching and energizing the existing network;
(2) by creating core content for a National Digital Library;
(3) by defining the Library's own strategic digital plan; and
(4) by helping lay the groundwork for the network of the future: the National Information Infrastructure.

I'll discuss each briefly. First, the Library of Congress is enriching the existing network by becoming in recent months a major (even massive) presence on the Internet. We now provide free into the Internet more than 26 million records including: the entire Library of Congress card catalog; summaries and status of federal legislation; copyright registration records; and abstracts and citations from foreign laws.

The Library of Congress also makes available electronically over the Internet the images and accompanying texts from its major exhibitions including: Secrets of the Russian Archives, Columbus 1492 Quincentennial — Meeting of Old and New Worlds, Treasures of the Vatican Library, Dead Sea Scrolls, and African-American Mosaic. There are 7,000 log ons to the Library of Congress files over the Internet each day. Something like 400,000 on-line visits have been made one way or another to the oldest of our on-line exhibits, Secrets of the Russian Archives. Much of this is participatory discussion, not merely the downloading or scanning of materials. The Library's staff has designed an easy—to-use menu system, called LC MARVEL, for accessing Library of Congress information and connecting to other resources on the Internet. The staff is continuing to build new tools to improve access to our resources over the Internet and to make additional materials available.

Second, and even more important for the long run, may be the core content we are creating for a new National Digital Library. We are nearing completion of a five-year pilot of our American Memory program, which now includes 210,000 digitized items from our Americana collections, including prints and photographs, manuscripts, sound recordings, and motion pictures — a true multimedia database, although still only a very small fraction of the 104 million items we have in our collections. American Memory has been tested in 44 schools and libraries around the country, and is being further tested this year in several different delivery modes. The Library's goal is to assemble an Americana collection of 5 million digitized items by the end of this century.

American Memory is designed explicitly to bring the values of our older book culture into new electronic media. We want it to offer true substantive content for whatever form the superhighway takes -- a vitamin enrichment for hard-pressed schools and libraries. Teachers and librarians will mediate the material. Young people will be motivated to delve back into books to answer questions prompted by multimedia material interactively called up on the screen — the electronic equivalent of browsing and making choices.

In delivering our unique collections by electronic means primarily to libraries and schools, our goal is to reinforce local communities of learning, not enhance or supplement the home entertainment center. We seek not to be an acquisitive retailer, but a benevolent wholesaler for the local institutions who will be the most efficient retailers of knowledge and information to students, teachers, and the general public. When the digital delivery system is in a library close to books, people will be drawn back to books rather than pulled away from them. We want to stimulate the active mind, not the passive emotions.

We have found that American Memory works well with children even in the 4th and 5th grades, activating their intellects by stimulating the kinds of open questioning that the hitherto inaccessible primary materials of our history and culture inevitably raise. Almost everything we put on the system exists only in one copy in the Library, usually in some fragile, impermanent form. American Memory exposes young people simultaneously to new technology and old materials (implicitly, to old values), feeding both their memory and imagination. It exposes them to historical rather than political correctness, to the good as well as the bad in our history, and thus to a mature but heightened sense of our complex yet common culture.

The recent acquisition of the massive archives of Leonard Bernstein is another example of our commitment to creating digital multimedia content and making it available to the American people. We hope to make this almost entirely televised record of one of the great teachers of music for young people available, at least in partial form, as part of this project.

American Memory is primarily an electronic archival transfer of our existing collections, based largely on the copyright deposit. This will make it, in many ways, truly America's memory of its copyrighted creativity. Core material will be taken from Library of Congress collections that include most papers of most Presidents up to Hoover, cartoons, photographs, posters, television tapes, almanacs, recorded sound, sheet music, 250,000 unpublished American plays, and the largest book and periodical, map, and movie collections in the world. To make at least a small part of this store of knowledge available digitally is not only an opportunity, but an obligation as the Library of Congress nears its own 200th birthday in the year 2000.

The effort to build the National Digital Library is in collaboration with the private sector and other major depositories. The National Digital Library will not merely be an extension of the Library of Congress, but something to which other great depositories will contribute. It will benefit people in the most remote parts of the country and the most disadvantaged parts of the cities — segments of the economy that have produced some of the best responses to the pilot tests conducted so far.

We are well aware that part of the genius of the new networked world lies in its decentralization. But even in the distributed world of computer networks, the National Digital Library linked to the Library of Congress will have a critical function to perform. It will be the permanent home for files of digital research data that would otherwise disappear. In time, most files mounted by commercial services will lose their money-making value. Those files having permanent research importance must find a safe home accessible to all. The National Digital Library will offer such a home. Scholarly institutions may shift interest or lose resources and need to remove valuable files from their networked computers. These files, too, would find a place in the National Digital Library, along with the accumulating electronic files derived from the Library's traditional collections. This archival function fits well the mission of the Library of Congress as the American library of record.

The third way the Library of Congress is moving into the digital age is by defining a strategic plan covering future as well as current collections. The Library, accordingly, is attempting to build its capacity to acquire, catalog, preserve, and provide access to a future collection that will be increasingly digital in format, as well as to convert parts of the current core collection besides our Americana into digital formats, and effectively integrate both digital and non-digital materials. The Library intends to play a useful leadership role by doing those things it is uniquely equipped to do; namely develop new approaches to organizing, managing, and preserving digital materials, and create necessary procedures for protection of intellectual property (our statutory obligation, since the copyright office is part of the Library of Congress). The most difficult and essential task of all will be to acquire the resources to convert current collections to digital formats.

Several projects already underway are building the foundation for doing this. Let me mention three. First is the Electronic Copyright Management System, jointly supported by the Library of Congress and the Advanced Research Projects Agency (ARPA, formerly DARPA). This will serve as a testbed to evaluate electronic copyright deposit, registration, and recordation concepts and issues. Second, the Electronic Cataloguing in Publication (CIP) project is testing on-line transmission of galleys from several publishers over the Internet to facilitate the preparation of cataloguing information and establish the foundation for an electronic library of machine-readable books. Third, the Library of Congress is establishing partnerships with the private sector in the last stage of our American Memory test to disseminate more broadly its digital materials. This includes specific agreements for pilots with Jones Intercable and Bell Atlantic.

Finally, the Library of Congress wants to contribute to the electronic future by being an exemplary catalyst for the library community in building the National Information Infrastructure. Vice President Gore in Buenos Aires recently called libraries "the key to American success in fully exploiting the information superhighways of the future." The Library of Congress' collections are part of the nation's *strategic information reserve* that will provide much of the intellectual cargo on the information superhighways.

We want the National Digital Library to serve as an inspiration, perhaps a *de facto* standards-making model, for the many libraries that will begin making their collections available electronically. Our experience with American Memory and other projects over more than five years should provide useful lessons and help establish common techniques and standards for the much larger community that is only now beginning the burdensome and expensive task of becoming a community of electronic libraries.

My assumption is that there's a critical need for non-entertainment material to be easily accessible and inexpensive for the American public, and that libraries will be important dispensers of that material on the network. An early draft of one Congressional bill called for creation of local information nodes for the distribution of such material. I pointed out to the people who had done the drafting that they could save money on that particular aspect of the bill. The information nodes already exist. They are called *libraries.*

Libraries will be important information nodes where users can access a vast variety of information services not profitable enough for homes, but desired sufficiently to be located in communities. Librarians, increasingly freed from traditional repetitive tasks, will serve as knowledge navigators, guiding users to the information they are seeking, working as European *archivists* or *scriptores* have long worked in the great medieval libraries. In a sense, these older institutions have never accepted modern cataloguing, relying instead on human navigators. They have some of the greatest scholars serving as knowledge navigators for their colleagues.

This critical role of libraries has been recognized in the Administration's "NII: Agenda for Action," which calls for linking all schools and libraries to the National Information Infrastructure (NII) by the year 2000. The Library of Congress is and will be playing an active role in the development of this strategy, working with the Administration and other government agencies to insure that the needs of libraries are addressed. The Library will contribute answers to critical public policy questions, such as protecting intellectual property rights and developing bibliographical standards for the electronic age.

There is one other area we have explored, without yet having done anything decisive about it. It has to do with the possibility of creating an electronic index for the private sector to databases of scientific and technical information. This would not be a giant service of our own, but rather a central switchboard that could direct people to the many directory and database services of this kind that are coming into being.

There is a desperate need for support to realize these goals. The tragic fact is that just as the nation's Library is getting ready to develop real *con*tent in new electronic forms, it is being overwhelmed by society's continuing *dis*contents, not the least of which is discontent with the legislative branch of government. The cuts to Congress end up impacting us very heavily at the Library of Congress, confronting us with a shrinking budget at the very time of unprecedented new opportunities to serve better both the Congress and the Nation. The lack of appropriated resources, and the unlikelihood that they will be made available despite the high rhetoric that abounds on this subject, requires that we seek private donations. To pursue its leadership role, the Library will also need to redirect its internal resources and get Congressional support for this. In addition, it must have access to executive branch resources for funding the NII initiatives, if the digital library is to become a reality.

Finally, there is a momentous opportunity for creative approaches — and this is the most important point — involving partnerships with the private sector. We've only begun to discuss this at the Library of Congress. It makes my presence here all the more welcome. I hope we can open up a dialogue on this critical subject. It is the private sector that will distribute the products. We are not going to get into that business. Our job, first and foremost, will be to provide basic access to digital materials that serve the public interest.

We think it centrally important that the new digitized knowledge be mixed in with the old books. Few believe that even this most prosperous of nations will find the resources or the interest to undertake a comprehensive conversion of the existing human record to machine readable form. So long as there is a substantial portion of the human record residing only in traditional books, books will play a vital role in human culture. Humanity must not suffer unintended memory loss in the world of instant information. For, beyond all the data, the information, and even the knowledge that we can accumulate and disseminate electronically lie the twin peaks of human accomplishment on which the future of our civilization depends: wisdom and creativity.

Wisdom is a practical quality that has historically grown up among those who live with books. (It's not accidental that humanism arose in a print culture.) And creativity is that special breakthrough quality given to a small number of us who add new ideas to our store of old ones, keeping the creative process going. But that creative process is always fed by memory, which we are in perpetual danger of losing in an instantaneous electronic universe, just as we are in danger of erasing the memory of our computers.

One commentator has said that exile is caused by forgetfulness and the beginning of redemption is memory. A Native American, whom I met not long ago, likened the libraries of today to the ancient tribal guardians of the oral culture of Indian tribes in the past. They were not just seen in those days as the *gatekeepers* to knowledge, he said, but as the *dreamkeepers* of the tribe.

Surely books, those mute witnesses from the past, are often better guides to the future than talking heads in the present. In dialogue with other living people, there are always games going on — politics, psychodrama, showmanship, who can talk the fastest, the loudest. But alone with a book, we are in Keats' world of silence and slow time where the only limit is one's own imagination. One is not bound by someone else's picture on a television screen. The train of thought is not broken by a bumper car of emotion.

Unlike the teacher who explains or the librarian who labels, the book itself gives no answers. It only gives rise to questions. It beckons us to both mastery and mystery — master enough of the material you've read to understand the created object; yet at the same time, sense something of the mystery of the other person who created it, and ultimately, perhaps, of our common Creator.

Libraries are a link in the human chain that connects what happened yesterday with what might take place tomorrow. We need living connections with the past the way mountain climbers need a lifeline; and the golden link is memory, which, as the commentator stated, keeps us from exile and points to redemption.

The business of libraries, and the business of all dissemination and communication of stored human knowledge, is the continued pursuit of truth. This is the highest form of Jefferson's pursuit of happiness. It is the surest way to protect us from the pursuit of one another. It is the only pursuit in a time of growing physical and economic limitations where the horizons for our cherished ideal of freedom can still safely remain infinite.

Libraries can and should be the base camps for this pursuit of truth and for the discovery of the new truths we will need to be making in all kinds of ways in the Information Age. Digital multimedia materials can provide both an educational hook to attract people into libraries and a line of self-generated questioning that pulls people back into books rather than away from them as television generally does.

Libraries need electronic additions but not electrocution. For librarians are the guardians of an institution central to the American dream, where knowledge can slowly ripen into wisdom and occasionally break through to new creativity. A better life will come in our America, not just from more data and a modem, but from the better understanding of one another that comes from books and from seeking access to *con*tent from others rather than just indulging in con*tent*ment with ourselves.

The Jesuit Order left China in the early 18th century after the most scholarly, book-intensive and most nearly politically successful effort in history to build a real bridge between the ancient Eastern culture and the Christian West. They left behind as their last legacy to that valiant effort a haunting written epitaph: *Abi viator / congratulare mortuis / condole vivis / ora pro omnibus / mirare e tace.* "Go away now voyager / congratulate the dead / console the living / pray for everyone / wonder and be silent." Wonder and silence. That's easier for readers than for TV viewers, for adventurers than for spectators, for dreamkeepers than for image-makers.

Let us hope that we can keep alive the values of The Book in the new multimedia age into which we are now entering, favoring active minds over spectator passivity, putting things together rather than just taking them apart. Whatever the confusion of our own minds and the profusion of information that will be gushing out of all this, things can still come together in a book, just as the left and right halves of the brain come together in one human mind, and the hemispheres — East and West, North and South — coexist in a single fragile planet.

Martin Greenberger
Thank you. We can now take questions and comments.

Donald Norman
That was a beautiful talk, but I think you fell prey to the hype to which this business so easily lends itself. I also feel that the history is somewhat flawed. For example, the statement that new

technologies never replace old ones is wrong. We've only had TV for 50 years, so it hasn't yet replaced radio, but come back in 200 years. Take note that we don't have the art of memory anymore; it was replaced by the printed book. And we don't have the village storyteller anymore, either. So, in fact, if you allow enough time, the new technologies do make a major difference in life.

You talk about the digitization of libraries and the fact that the librarian's task will be transformed. I've heard similar words from some of the people here — that education is transformed through technology. But it's more than that. It's a social and cultural issue. It can be very complex.

Finally, there are the dreams that we will have crossroads of self-indexing. But the real problem is standards. We have to develop standards so that all the libraries of the world can communicate to all the peoples of the world — standards that will maintain the kinds of materials we've had for decades and centuries, and maintain itself for further decades and centuries. We don't know how to do that. We don't know how to preserve digital records in such a form. The medium we use to preserve digital records does not survive more than decades. Libraries must survive for centuries. Not only do the materials like magnetic tapes or even laserdiscs die, but the technology required to read invisible information dissipates with time. We can't read wire recorders today, let alone older technology. NASA has thousands of buildings filled with magnetic tapes of records from satellites that are no longer readable because the technology does not exist to read the tapes.

The point is, what you're trying to do is exactly what you must do, but I think what you've missed is an examination of the huge difficulties. History is full of ironies. Socrates,[1] you remember, complained about the book because you couldn't argue with it. It would replace people's reasoning and imagination with a simple act of reading.

James Billington

Well, you've raised quite a number of questions. I wrestle with the difficulties every day. If you want me to talk about difficulties, I'd be glad to do that.

I think the words I used were that a new technology rarely replaces an old one entirely. I would stand by that. If you take a long enough time frame, *nothing* survives. But what's surprising is the extent to which technologies overlap and former technologies continue to survive. The only example you mentioned where there really isn't any significant survival is the old storyteller. He may be disappearing, although the Indian I mentioned is having a bit of a comeback.

Maybe I exaggerated somewhat what will really be able to happen, but I was describing in American Memory something that is actually being done and will be done. It's just a question of what scale and how large? I am not engaging in hype when I describe the reaction of very young people to it, and I'm not being overly romantic about the possibilities of the new technologies. They will not replace reading, but they can be an interesting supplement. I do think they can largely replace television, which would be a great relief, it seems to me. I'm in the process of trying to make a little television myself, so I'm conscious of the possibilities, as well as the limitations. But even good television is basically someone else's flow of images and ideas. Because it's audiovisual, it gets much more directly to the emotions than do books.

By being mediated through words, books are somewhat more respectful of the individual. You quote selectively from Socrates on the subject of books. He said that books are the basic form of immortality. This is the more important quote from Socrates.

All forms of knowledge require human mediation. If information does not flow into some kind of direct human mediation, it's not going to be as rich as it could be. A book is great, but continuation of the issues raised in the book with real people — with some of the mystery and insight of the book flowing into people's lives and into the way they behave with others — is what books are all about. Books are not just there to sit on the shelves.

The weakness of television is in its inherent passivity and the fact that we're getting someone else's flow of images and music. We have very little choice but to respond. It's a medium for which people sit. Even when there are five people in the room, they're all watching the television. It denudes them of the human interaction which ought to be a part of the transmission of creativity. You could say a play does the same thing, but a play is still real people interacting with real people. There's a back-and-forth between how the audience reacts and how the play is performed.

I once played in one of those wonderfully ambiguous plays of Chekov[2] where the audience doesn't really know if it's sad or happy. It was fascinating to watch the different reaction every night. It became a different production. But television is not that way. There isn't the same kind of human interaction. Increasingly, there's an evisceration of the normal human reactions that would take place in a family or in another human community. We are in a sense made mute by the television screen in our midst. I think that's a big difference.

Louise Velázquez

Although I work for an entertainment company, I spend a great deal of time reading and only a little watching TV. What you're saying about books and the American Memory program is interesting, but neglects to mention that every author has a point of view. Every work, including your own, has a point of view that is political as well as historical. It cannot help but be influenced by the politics of the time; authors select what they feel is important, and those doing the choosing are the ones in a position to do the choosing. A learned and well-read person cannot discount the political element and social context. You said that the American Memory program exposes young people to historical rather than political correctness. Historical correctness according to whom?

I would raise the same question about books, television, or someone talking. I'm just as likely to fall asleep at a play as listening to someone at a conference, or watching television, or reading a book. I make the choice of how I choose to interact with the medium myself. Television doesn't pretend to be a book.

For me, the biggest problem in what you said was not recognizing that reading gives the point of view of the author, whether the book is an encyclopedia or a treatise on scientific research. I was taught to regard books critically as being in a context. I look at everything that way. So, I find it amazing to hear you suggest that the collection in the Library of Congress that's being digitized is historically correct. This makes huge assumptions about the version of history someone had at a particular time ...

James Billington

Well, you touch on an important point. There's no question that what ends up in the Library of Congress is to some extent a product of political and social forces. Thurgood Marshall[3] was chosen for the Supreme Court. So we have his papers, not someone else's.

Louise Velázquez
That's trivializing what I said. Justice Thurgood Marshall and all that aside, in our culture ...

James Billington
You haven't permitted me, of course, to make my point yet. But that's all right. Go ahead.

Louise Velázquez
By virtue of what was not published or allowed to be voiced at a given time, a statement has been made. So, I think that's trivializing it. I can see where you were going, but if there's some other place you were going that I wasn't aware of, please go on.

James Billington
We won't know until I get there, will we? The point is that if we were just digitizing a small amount, we'd have to make a choice. The people who'd make the choice are people of today with their various limitations. But the basic choice has largely already been made by writers who decided to pay $1 for copyright, or later $2 and then $5, because they thought they had created something important and were afraid others might take their idea. The copyright deposit is the great bulk of what we're dealing with. The act of copyright was the basis for that choice. Then perhaps a political or social choice is made.

A library as comprehensive as ours not only has the official papers of Presidents, but the largest civil rights collection in the country, the files of the NAACP, an enormous anarchist file, and countless papers of the Legal Defense Fund, women's organizations, and protest groups. Many different parts of the American perspective are included. The beauty of the American Memory program is that if one feels something important has been left out, we can add a new segment if we have it. We're trying to be reasonably honest brokers in transfering a representative cross segment of our collections to electronic form.

With all due respect, I think it is the thrust of your comments that trivializes the issue. It relativizes everything. Social, political, economic, religious, and ideological forces act on all of us, but there is a distinction which your deconstructivist[4] type of criticism obliterates in regarding books and works of art as nothing more than the sum total of the pressures and elements making them up, with no integrative individualized statement. It is the essence of a library to have many different books contradicting one another together on the shelves. They all may be opinionated, but you have the opportunity to thread your way through, finding your own path and your own perspectives. You do it by confronting a series of relative coherences, which is what books are, witnessing works that at their best represent an additive element of human creativity which can never be explained in their entirety by those forces.

I think you express the deconstructionist approach, which seems to be the basis for your criticism, by asserting that a novel is basically no different than a political tract. I think they're very different.

Louise Velázquez
That's not what I said. I think the picture you were painting is a picture of a neutral mediator. You're a mediator for sure, but with a point of view. That's what I was saying. I wasn't saying that everything is a consequence of social and political forces.

James Billington
We all have points of view, but some mediators may be more faithful to the totality of the collections they are dealing with than others. We're in a world of grays, but there's a big difference between dark gray and light gray.

Someone asks about the issues in building a vast multimedia collection.

It's not too vast yet, but it's significant. There are large problems in preparing the materials. Most of what has been digitized for American Memory are special collections. Books and printed works are relatively straightforward, but not pictures. We have a wonderful map and almanac collection, for instance, that gives a concrete feel for historical developments; but the definition isn't good enough for us to digitize the maps. Paper-based and film-based materials are often too fragile, and must be re-photographed before they can be digitized. We haven't been digitizing films much yet. With the early Edison films, I think we are still doing our tests with an analog version. Many of the materials are in different formats, different thicknesses, and so on. Many have to be reconstituted in a more permanent form before they can be reused. Interestingly, sometimes we get better definition in the digital surrogate than we had in the original, so there are compensations.

Anonymous
Donald Norman noted the NASA buildings filled with 16-track magnetic tapes that are not easily read. You refer to the difficulty of working with the fragile old Edison films. Although digitizing these films will expand their consumption, since electronic distribution will be much easier than replicating the film, the ability of digital media to be archived over long periods of time is still unproven. No one knows if CD-ROM will last 30 years.

Furthermore, formats in this business go through enormous turnover. Eight-track tape is not popular anymore; experiments in quadraphonic sound never went anywhere. Norman's allusion to this turnover in formats got a little lost in the Socrates debate. Has the Library recognized its responsibility to assure the archivability of what comes to it? When material arrives in digital form, it won't be a matter of converting to digital, but protecting the digital.

James Billington
We do not use CD-ROM as a preservation device. We still use microfilm basically, because it has a proven life span. We use a safety base film, which lasts a long time, though also not forever, and we are working on a gas diffusion process that will de-acidify paper. Preservation is our fundamental responsibility. We don't confuse that with the American Memory program.

We have no illusion that digital media are permanent forms of preservation, and we recognize the unproven nature of different formats. We do not know and are not going to determine the best format. We think that private firms will have to distribute this material if they want it. All we can do is try to do a fair mediation in selecting an interesting and representative segment of our collections to get out, inviting others to add to it and welcoming critiques of what we do. We're testing this year with American Memory, trying different delivery systems with several partners.

There may be a fragility in the digitized formats, but we do not discard the old. My first decision as Librarian was to keep the old card catalog. We do not destroy books when digitizing them.

Someone asks if the Library expects to be receiving books in digital form rather than paper in the future.

We haven't crossed that bridge yet. We may do some kinds. We're talking about it. What we are getting now are advanced galleys that speed up the cataloguing/publication process. One point Dr. Norman made that I forgot to address has to do with standards. The Library does work with cataloguing standards, word authority, and so on. Standards become important. Our cataloguing people are addressing new emerging problems, but we can't do it alone. There may have to be large committees set up, as always. This is the kind of problem that falls between stools and that we usually pick up if no one else does. We're looking into that right now. Maybe we can make a contribution.

Ching-chih Chen
I am from one of the few educational institutions that was selected early on to be a beta test site for American Memory. Isn't it true that the original purpose of the program was to enhance information access? You have images, prints, and so much information that simply is not accessible to anyone. Putting it in an electronic format makes it much easier to distribute and bring out into the open. As end users, that's what we felt your purpose was. Also, I thought American Memory up to now was on analog videodiscs. Are you contemplating digitizing the works? Have you started digitization?

James Billington
The movies are in analog form so far, but there may be some digitization going on. In other areas, early tests were predominantly with videodiscs, but the balance has now swung rather heavily in favor of digitization. You're right. The original purpose of the program was just to broaden access so more people could use the material. As we began testing, however, we found that younger and younger children were asking different kinds of

questions and taking a lively interest. We were impressed with the educational value, both at lower levels and for research and teaching at the college and advanced high school levels. When you see the immensity of these collections and how little they can be used because of their fragility, you have a feeling that the nation is being deprived of an awful lot of its memory. It's as simple as that.

When I came to the Library of Congress, I took an inventory and found that we had nearly 40 million uncatalogued items. (Sometimes it's better not to ask questions.) A lot of the material we're now working with no one knew about at all. We're taking it directly from being uncatalogued to being available very widely. Whole aspects of American (and world) history still haven't been touched. There are 250,000 American plays that have never been published, let alone read, but they've been copyrighted.

A summer intern last year who studied early silent films of Native Americans found that the image of the American Indian in these films was very different from the standard stereotype in later Hollywood melodrama. The inventive early movie culture generally gave a much more positive image of the American Indian. This factual discovery came from looking at a body of material that no one had examined before. I'm sure many more facts — bad as well as good — will be unearthed.

I may have been carried away by talk of the *Super-hype-way* — the idea that we can take this material, make it available to everyone, and people will love it. That's probably not true, nor do I know we can do it. It's a tremendous effort. We've got to put an awful lot of things together. But the American people did pay for the accumulation and storage of this material over nearly 200 years. It seems to me that they are entitled to see more of it.

Philip Zimmermann
Something we should look out for in digitizing our historical archives is the possibility of history's being revised without detection. In George Orwell's book, *1984*[5], the main character's job is to go to work every day and revise history, which he accomplishes on paper and film. The Winston Smith of 2084 may go to work to revise history in ways that will never be detected. Each succeeding government could revise the history handed down to it from the preceeding government, which revised it from the previous one, with no government ever knowing the lies it's revising. The digital archives could turn out to be more volatile and shifting than the crumbling paper archives they replace.

James Billington
You people really are suspicious, aren't you?

Philip Zimmermann
Nothing against you personally. It's intrinsic to digital information.

James Billington
It's intrinsic if you throw away the old. I'm an incurable pack rat.

Philip Zimmermann
Your successors a century hence may not be.

James Billington
Well, I can't control that, but I hope my precedent creates at least a measure of embarrassment that we're able to sustain. Let me be clear. American Memory is a selective archival transfer. We're not putting interpretations on it. Someone has to make the selection, but we're not trying to rewrite American history.

Philip Zimmermann
I didn't mean to imply that at all. My comment wasn't a criticism of your current program, but rather a longer-range observation of a danger inherent to this kind of technology shift. Please don't interpret it as a criticism of your policies.

James Billington
No, you're entitled to criticism. You pay your taxes, and I'm a servant of the taxpayer. People don't want anyone in Washington writing American history. We're not even writing educational manuals for the program. We want to give the materials to the people and let people use them locally on their own, without guidance from *Big Brother*. But, yes, technologically there is a risk.

Philip Zimmermann
There is also a solution — digital signatures.

James Billington
I gather that's something you know a bit about. The beauty of the paper-based culture, and of our somewhat messy pluralistic system, is that it's very hard to control the agenda. There's always plenty of variety. Books are affordable and portable. There's definitely a risk, but in a way, we're almost overwhelmed by the proliferation. The greater risk is that the real history may not be recorded at all. People I talk to who work in the archives feel that the closer we get to the present, the less the paper and even the tapes (if recorded) tell us. The important decisions are made orally in meetings, then people often paper the record. Or the paper record is of secondary items, and the really important matters are decided in small groups out of the public eye. That's got to be more of a problem for the future than people destroying records.

There is an inherent perishability to the electronic media. I helped to advise on some of the protocols in opening up the archives of the former Soviet Union after it collapsed. It was interesting to see how in that secret system everyone stockpiled documents for their self-preservation, so there were multiple copies of practically everything. The ability to destroy documents didn't really exist. On the other hand, much of the electronic information was apparently destroyed very rapidly afterwards, and that seems to have been much of the important information.

Martin Greenberger
One subject of great interest to this group is intellectual property. At the Library of Congress, you play a dual role. On the one hand, you issue and enforce copyright protection; on the other hand, you seek to make copyrighted works widely available to the general public. Does this put you in a position of conflict?

James Billington
Well, it's a tension. We have the statutory obligation to enforce the intellectual property laws, and a special need to help define how these laws will be enforced in the new electronic universe. We've put together a national committee, the so-called Accord Committee, to provide top legal and technical advice on these matters, and we've also recently acquired the Copyright Royalty Tribunal, a mediation board which was formerly independent. We don't run the Tribunal, but we do administer it. So, we have these added responsibilities to protect intellectual property.

Up to now, the American Memory has been done almost entirely with older materials in the public domain. If it gets more comprehensive, it will include more materials for which intellectual property rights are still maintained. This does lead to conflicting impulses that move in opposite directions, but I don't think they're necessarily contradictory. We are obliged by the Constitution to keep a record of the creativity of people so there can be a spurt of fresh creativity. The implication has always been that the same Library that is available to Congress for legislation is freely available to all citizens for their use. We should get this material out, and in an electronic universe, out *there*. The public should not have to come to Washington. We have to reconcile these two responsibilities: the statutory responsibility to exercise intellectual property rights and the moral responsibility to get the material out.

But, frankly, not everyone thinks as I do on this. Many people in the Library would rather not push to get the material out. Many would rather not have too many people in the reading rooms either. There's a certain proprietary nesting instinct that's inherent to libraries — a seeming contradiction. Yet most people in the library business are in it because of idealism and a desire to see more people get more benefit from more knowledge. With that goal, I don't understand how we can run a national library in a democracy and not try to get the material out. Sure, it's a conflict — something we have to live with — but I don't resent either side of the obligation. It makes the job more interesting.

Martin Greenberger

That's a good note on which to bring this session to a close. You've given us a fascinating panorama of the responsibilities, obligations, challenges, problems, and awesome opportunities that exist at the Library of Congress. It's reassuring to know that our National Librarian is committed to using advanced technology to make America's information resources more accessible to the people. These resources can be the true treasures of the 21st century. We wish you well. Your success will be our collective gain.

Notes

[1] Greek philosopher Socrates used a question-and-answer approach to teaching as a way of achieving self-knowledge. His theories of virtue and justice survived through the writings of his famous pupil Plato. Socrates was executed in 399 B.C. for allegedly corrupting the minds of Athenian youth.

[2] Anton Pavlovich Chekhov, 1860-1904, the Russian writer whose dramas have to do with the inability of human beings to communicate with one another.

[3] Thurgood Marshall, born in1908, served as an associate justice of the U.S. Supreme Court from 1967 to 1991.

[4] Deconstruction or deconstructionism is a philosophical movement and theory of literary criticism that questions traditional assumptions about certainty, identity, and truth. It asserts that words can only refer to other words, while attempting to demonstrate how statements about any text subvert their own meanings. The deconstructionist critic claims there is no meaning to be found in the actual text, but only in the various, often mutually irreconcilable, virtual texts constructed by readers in their search for meaning.

[5] George Orwell, *1984*, Harcourt Brace Jovanovich, New York, 1949.

The Telco Cable Dance
Scenario for an Information Superhighway

Five hundred years after Columbus' voyage to America, another historic exploration was underway. Like the Nina, the Pinta, and the Santa Maria, the Network, the Digital, and the Interactive were pushing ahead to awaken and galvanize public consciousness. It was late in 1992. Al Gore and Bill Clinton were preparing to move to Pennsylvania Avenue. Part of their grand vision was to bring to pass the information superhighway, a bold idea dating back to the days of time sharing and the ARPANET. As in the journey 500 years earlier, the superhighway initiative was intended to open up a territory of enormous opportunity — a New World seen previously as the domain of "wild" people.[1]

At the First Roundtable in Multimedia in the Spring of 1990, Jonathan Seybold was a panelist/adviser. Later that year, he initiated his own much larger conference that aptly captured the essence of the times, naming it Digital World. A seasoned visionary, Jonathan has a pragmatic sense of the significance of what's happening.[2] *As moderator of this session, he orchestrates the Telco Cable Dance like a maestro.*

There's more to building the information superhighway than providing the physical lines. Jim Cullen of Bell Atlantic feels success will come to full-service providers who offer a wide range of services, both local and long-distance. He wants competition opened at all levels, with two or more wires into every home. Bob Kavner[3] *calls first for demonstrated competition in the local exchange. John Cooke of Disney Channel, a major potential user of the infrastructure, says entertainment companies want to join in too, with partners who help them create and distribute new product. Mark Stahlman provides spice to the discussion by asserting that none of the touted new technologies will be ready for broad deployment within a decade. Near term, his faith lies in ISDN and the personal computer. Robert Pepper of the FCC breathes a sigh of relief at the return to fundamentals now that the torrent of unrealistic expectations has subsided. Yo ho! The hot wind has died down and LAN's ahead!*

The Telco Cable Dance

Martin Greenberger
References these days to the information superhighway abound — an exercise of the imagination which the press has not ignored. This panel, including some of the major players, is one of two that will look in earnest at the prospects for what has been a much publicized vision. Panelists in this session will consider scenarios, roles, intentions, and perspectives. Panelists in the concluding session will look at the practical side of the infoway[4]: the politics, problems, and public interest issues surrounding it.

I asked Jonathan Seybold to moderate this session a long time back, before we had a title for it. The name subsequently agreed upon is deliberately fanciful, which gives it a chance of fitting the discussion of a still uncertain and amorphous subject. Jonathan, it's all yours.

Jonathan Seybold
Thank you, Martin. I would like to do a couple of minutes of scene setting in which I'm going to grossly oversimplify in the interests of time and as a way of drawing out the issues more sharply. I'll then ask each of the panel members to present a brief opening set of comments. We'll have a little dialogue to follow up on this, then open it up to everyone.

It's been clear from the beginning that high-bandwidth communications is the missing foundation for the digital world. It's what we need to make everything else work. The question for some number of years has been, what sort of infrastructure will we build and how will we build it? The focus has been (as it will be in this session) primarily on wired communications, because of its higher bandwidth potential. Wireless offers a whole other spectrum of considerations that play into future possibilities as well.

The assumption right through the 1980's was that wired communications would be provided by the telephone companies. The phone companies would replace twisted-pair copper wiring with fiber optics into the home at a cost of billions of dollars, and it would take until 2015 (a typical magic date) to reach critical mass. The phone companies weren't at all clear what the payoff was for doing this.

Things started to shift fairly rapidly around 1990 when the cable companies and the industry at large woke up to the fact that coax was passing 90 percent of American homes, entering 60 percent of them, and was a high bandwidth connector. Since the last mile to the home was the expensive part of the whole proposition, cable emerged as an interesting alternative. A fierce competitive battle erupted between the cable operators and the telephone industry. I think it has been marvelous for us. It has pushed things forward much more rapidly than would otherwise have happened.

The initial focus for cable was 500 channels, and that's where most of the popular press got stuck. But we've had some interesting turns in the road over the last couple of years. The cable industry concept has moved from 500 channels to a full-service network. This means shifting from a broadcast mentality — with switching among lots of channels — to a fully-switched two-way network, which is very different from what the cable companies originally envisaged. This shift took place in less than a year — probably a nine-month period. Not all that well articulated, it was nevertheless a fundamental change in thinking. The change was clear by early 1993. The phone companies were then still talking about a configuration in which they ran fiber into a neighborhood, and then used twisted-pair phone lines from that point on to bring video into the home.

Last fall, we had two very significant changes in the marketplace. One was the Bell Atlantic/TCI merger (now unmerger), a quintessential alliance between the leading cable company and a leading telco. The other, at about the same time, was the filing by Pacific Telesis with the PUC in California of a plan calling for the company to replace all of the existing twisted-pair phone lines with a fiber optic cable configuration that looks exactly like the configurations for prototypic cable companies.[5] The filing states that most of this will be paid for by money that would otherwise have been spent in replacing existing copper plant, and by savings in operation. Under the filing (not yet approved), the incremental cost per household of creating this broadband network would be $139, rather than $1,000. This altered the economics of the picture completely.

Since that time, as we are all well aware, some major cable/telco alliances or mergers have broken down (Bell Atlantic/TCI, Southwest Bell/Cox), in part, I believe, because the economics have changed. The telephone companies realize that they don't need the cable companies as much as they thought they did, and are in a better position than they had known to put in the new infrastructure.

Two other points before we get to the panel. First, the focus up until now has been on installing the wiring. That will probably turn out to be the easy part. The hard part has to do with the fact that these really aren't highways, but giant interactive open-network computer systems, in which a large part of the population will be on-line. The interesting issues will have to do with network protocols, servers, and set-top boxes. How do they talk to each other? How do we get standards? How do we make this huge network system open? We've just begun to nibble at the edges of these issues.

Second, there have been people right along who ask why we need this new wiring. Why are we focusing on television sets? What we should be talking about, they say, is interacting through computers, and we can use the Internet for that. If we really care about improving phone service, we can have video telephony using ISDN. Why do we want to put in all this wiring?

That's a hurried tour through some of the issues leading up to this discussion. We have a very interesting panel, covering the entire landscape except for cable operators.[6] Let's go first to Jim Cullen.

James Cullen

Thanks, Jonathan. I will be very brief, leaving a few place setters that we can return to during the dialogue. Three-quarters of what I say will probably not be new, because we've had so many opportunities recently to make news. For us, the dance of the telcos and cable companies goes on, but with the crash of the TCI deal, the beat has changed a bit, shifting from rock-and-roll to the Tennessee waltz. Yet the strategy remains the same. Our view is that there will be continued consolidation in the industry, but the kind of big-bang merger opportunities that Southwest Bell/Cox and Bell Atlantic/TCI have pursued are probably not doable for the near term.

Quickly, a few general observations on the marketplace. First, our assumption is that success will come to full-service providers using primarily what we are calling full-service networks. Ultimately, these are broadband and interactive digital networks offering a full set of services, both local exchange and long distance — voice, data, video, and interactive video. We do not believe that success will come to those who wish to remain just a local exchange company, a long distance company, or a cable company.

Second, barriers to entry are dropping very rapidly, but not rapidly enough. Barriers to entry have had to do with technology, regulation, the legal situation, and in some cases, market and branding considerations. These barriers are collapsing. In fact, this is a big part of what we had hoped to accomplish with the TCI transaction, bringing accelerated competition with other RBOCs across the country.

Third, competition will result in at least two wires into every home, supplemented by probably two wireless connections, and perhaps more. The competitors will include existing cellular carriers, PCS providers, DBS broadcasters, and, of course, telco/cable. The current ground rules make little sense. They need to be revamped as soon as possible, as effectively as possible, and as fairly as possible. This means state regulation, federal regulation, and the kind of legislation that is moving now through both House and Senate.[7]

If we expect companies such as the ones represented here to invest significant amounts of capital in the future, we need to have a reasonably reliable future. We need to know what the ground rules are. From an RBOC perspective, we cannot be participating in markets in which we're absolutely precluded from entering certain segments. We do not see this as a successful competitive scenario long-term. Frankly, as we look at our options for resource allocation, investing outside the country or in other businesses starts to look more attractive than investing here. What we seek, simply, are normal business incentives to invest in our territory, where we have a reputation, a customer base, and, we think, great opportunities to improve what is there today.

Bell Atlantic is currently the only RBOC authorized to provide what we call cable service (video programming in its region) by virtue of a court case and challenge that we have pursued successfully to this point (one appeal remaining). We intend to proceed very rapidly to offer cable service ourselves "in-region" in competition with existing providers in overbuilds. We will begin that process with some rudimentary delivery of video on-demand in Northern Virginia this summer. It will be over ADSL, a technology and capability we think still has use. The quality is high and the software is effective for the early application. We may expand that.

Furthermore, we are hoping to provide cable service to a company called FutureVision of America in Dover Township, New Jersey in competition with Adelphia Cable Communications, and as a cooperative underbuild with Sammons Communications in Northern Jersey under the video dial tone ground rules. Unfortunately, we are totally bogged down in the process. Approvals have been languishing for well over a year.[8] That is becoming very frustrating to us. Finally, we intend to begin building as soon as possible in Alexandria, Virginia, where we won the court challenge.

To answer the big question, we are looking at a variety of technologies for delivery. We are not pushing all our chips one way or another. We continue to look at ADSL; we look at the hybrid fiber/coax to which Pacific Telesis is committed (as Jonathan mentioned); and we continue to look at the full broadband digital that BroadBand Technologies is offering.

In conclusion, I want to dispel any rumors that may still remain (I saw one repeated again in today's *Wall Street Journal* piece[9]) that the collapse of the TCI/Bell Atlantic deal had anything to do with personalities, cultures, or clashes. It had to do with money and a sudden dramatic change in value, creating a gap that could not be made up by either party. I'll stop at this point and allow the discussion to proceed.

Jonathan Seybold
You do believe strongly in a two-wire scenario, plus wireless? You believe there's enough revenue to support both wires, and make a profit?

James Cullen
I do. If there's a market for interactive video services, there's enough revenue. I think there will be strong competition. There are opportunities in some secondary and tertiary markets for a telco to build a common carrier network and offer it to all providers. In Morris County, New Jersey, where we're underbuilding with Sammons, we're committed to 384 channels. Sammons wants 60 channels. That leaves 324 channels for other providers. There will only be one literal wire in Morris County, but it will have a huge capability for all video information providers to ride.

Robert Kavner
It may be useful as an opener to give a perspective on AT&T's different businesses and where we are spending our time in

multimedia. We are focused on four different areas. First is the largest part of AT&T, providing a substantial portion of our cash flow — our communication service business. That business is a global digital network, encompassing the United States and connecting almost every country in the world. It carries voice, data, image, and video, so it is a multimedia network. We are looking to position it as a global network of choice for the transport of all forms of media requiring variable bandwidth.

The network in the United States comes down to Bell Atlantic's network and into the local exchange. One of our concerns, which is the inverse of what Jim Cullen talked about, is that there be plenty of competition in the local exchange to give customers choice. If there were demonstrated competition in the local exchange (not just an intention of competition), we would be very supportive of Jim's desire that we all be allowed to enter long distance over the exchange with a full service network. An important criterion for us is demonstration that the bottleneck has been eliminated. Although it may seem somewhat esoteric to many people here, it affects how quickly things can evolve.

AT&T's second strategic area in multimedia is a plan to put services on top of our network, so that customers can use the network not just for voice, visual, and data communications, but also for entertainment, productivity, gaming, and other environments. The on-line service industry is creating such environments on top of networks like ours. We're looking to see what role to play. We took a step in this direction by announcing a relationship with Lotus that establishes Lotus Notes as an adjunct to our network. Customers with Lotus Notes in their office environment can enhance productivity by having collaborative sessions over a wide-area network. We are exploring many different ways to participate in the value of information services that ride the network. We accept this as another level of the food chain above the transport layer.

The third strategic area in multimedia for AT&T is providing network systems integration and technology for those who operate or who would like to operate networks. It does not get a lot of public attention, but it is a core part of our capability set. We do about $11 billion a year selling software and hardware systems to PTTs and RBOCs. Bell Atlantic is a good customer. We're beginning to do business with the cable industry and other service providers. Bell Laboratories provides us with the necessary technology and engineering systems capability. A great deal of attention in the computer software industry is understandably on the video server, but from a systems standpoint, the video server is just one element. The requirements for network management may be more important than how the video is brought in on demand. We happen to have those skills. We are doing a number of trials, one here in California with Viacom in Castro Valley, not primarily to prepare software for market, but to test market sensitivity and understand how this affects the customer.

The fourth area is providing communications systems for businesses, the home, and mobile environments. The most robust part of multimedia today is probably in the office. Most of us think of consumer multimedia first, yet the broadband capability is in the office. The innovation and learning some corporations are doing should be transferrable back into consumer markets. We created a venture capital firm a couple of years ago, with an $80 million fund initially, mostly to force ourselves to understand parts of the market that are a step ahead of our core businesses. It's been very useful. A number of people here have dealt with our venture firm.

Jonathan Seybold
James Cullen emphasized the desire for open competition. I believe that if he could wave a magic wand and say everything is open to competition on Monday morning, he would. Everything is lifted and communication firms can do anything they wanted. Is that a fair assessment of your position, Jim?

James Cullen
Absolutely. We spent twenty years trying to micro-manage and regulate competition in the industry. As you suggested, Jonathan, in the last year the pace of change has accelerated. If I could wave a magic wand, I'd do two things. I'd say, one, let's figure out how to deal with universal telephone service, and preserve that; two, stop screwing around with the rules. Let everybody into everything — period! We'd be very happy with that.

Jonathan Seybold
Now, Bob, you have said that you want to see demonstrated competition before that happens. I'm curious as to what represents demonstrated competition, and how we get there from here, before you're willing to see things opened up in the fashion Jim has suggested?

Robert Kavner
It's an awkward position we're in here. All of us would like to stand on the side of the gods and have open competition and a competitive marketplace in every area today. That's our general attitude. But there are some real problems. Those who own the monopoly bottlenecks will have an advantage that will be highly distorting to the open environment we dream of. We need a mechanism for the local exchange to have demonstrated competition. Without it, we're going to get a very large tilt in

deployment. With demonstrated competition in the local exchange (everyone would agree there is already demonstrated competition in long distance) competition could be free and we'd all benefit. But opening it up before the monopoly is broken would cause some very serious problems.

Jonathan Seybold
Wasn't part of the idea for the McCaw purchase to bypass local service?

Robert Kavner
No. That is not our intention at all. The reason we are trying to merge with McCaw Cellular is that the customer is more and more mobile. Mobility is an important part of life, and we feel that AT&T needs to provide mobile services. It is not an intention to bypass. Today, almost all cellular service goes in to the local exchange.

James Cullen
I don't want to jump into a full debate before every panelist has been heard, but let me just make three brief comments. First, the only place a monopoly exists is where there are no profit opportunities. If anyone thinks there is a bottleneck monopoly that could not be bypassed on Monday, I'd be very surprised. Second, we're just asking to do what one of Bob's friends and colleagues, Sprint, does — offer both local and long distance service. Third, there's no way a local exchange carrier can influence in any way selection of a long distance carrier. This was the remedy to the problems of the 1960s that resulted in the antitrust suit in the 1970s, and divestiture in 1984. We're now ten years past that. It's like your parents pled guilty to a pending antitrust charge, dodged the

charge, and have you serving the ten year sentence. We're simply looking for a possibility of parole, or a halfway house.

John Cooke

Why is it I always have to follow the great line? I want to echo what Jim Cullen said. His points coincide with what I've heard from other RBOCs. There's no doubt that we are going to have competition in major markets. From our conversations with all the players, it's clear there will be more consolidation along lines Jim suggests, different in pace and other ways from TCI/Bell Atlantic. There are operators out there who desperately need to find a way to form alliances and make new equity arrangements. One of our good friends in the industry who happens to be in Denver and owns the largest MSO in the country, told me the other day that virtually all the cable operators beyond the top six have their operations up for sale. I think that's substantiated by looking at the number of investment banking firms now trying to peddle the cable companies. Some of the consolidation may be on a piecemeal basis by locality according to what makes sense. I would also agree with having some kind of common carrier arrangement in small markets between cable operators and telcos.

Entertainment companies and major players like AT&T and the RBOCs are clearly seeking a way to be in alliances and joint ventures to make things work for consumers. There's no doubt that entertainment companies in Hollywood and elsewhere feel there is a play somehow with these marvelous companies that have access to the home and to business. That waltz is going on just like the waltzes with cable and telco and other software creators.

There are some interesting public policy issues that need to be sorted out. Universal service has been alluded to. How does it work? What does it mean? How universal is it? Also, privacy and the protection of intellectual properties are important issues. I know these are topics for the next panel. For programmers, access to distribution is critical as well. This is one of the reasons why entertainment companies are interested in forming alliances as they build further programming for the new interactive services.

Jonathan Seybold
Let me follow up on that. The old model is that the John Malones of the world are gatekeepers because of the limited bandwidth in the cable systems. The squeeze on what gets bundled in the basic cable package, as opposed to what is premium service, will get worse with the current reductions in cable rates. So I can understand why a company like Disney feels it needs to do deals to ensure access to the consumer. But if the market truly opens up, as we've been discussing, why do you need these deals? Isn't it in your interest to have more direct access to the consumer when bottlenecks are removed?

John Cooke
I mentioned access, but there is a bigger point. All entertainment companies, not just Disney, have a great interest in developing interactive programming together with partners. The idea of an entertainment company marrying the distribution and the technology company makes an enormous amount of sense. The marriage would not just be to deliver the existing programming now being offered by cable companies, but to expand these offerings.

Mark Stahlman
Let's see, what spice shall I be today? We have Bob Pepper at the other end of the table. I'll be salt. Then we'll have salt and pepper.

Jonathan asked me last night what I was going to say. He remarked, "I think I understand your position. You're a skeptic on the information highway." I told him, I'm more than that. I'm absolutely confident that the information highway as currently described will never happen. The services and mergers that we read about in the headlines will not come about. The notion (by John Sculley and others which started this whole thing) of a convergence of industries into a $3 trillion mother of all industries is nonsense. It's a con job. What we are observing is really quite straightforwardly explained by the business self-interests of the various parties involved. I've written a lot about this recently.[10]

What I'm not skeptical at all about are the sweeping changes that our culture is going through, and the absolutely crucial role technology will play. There is something happening of enormous proportions, but it is not the convergence of existing businesses. It is, in fact, the emergence and invention of a brand new industry or collection of industries, which I call the *new media*. The reasons for what is happening relate partly to questions being posed and discussed at the Roundtable. Incidentally, I want to thank Martin and everyone involved in organizing this conference. It's one of the very few places where we can have conversations among businessmen, academics, and others about a core of central ideas underlying these changes.

Alan Kay told us yesterday that he read Moore's Law many years ago and was able to think ahead about its implications. We've incorporated the inevitability of Moore's Law into our lives. We know that the performance/price ratio of digital economics is doubling every 18 months to two years. What we don't know is what it will mean when we replace telephones with videophones, when the obscene phone call takes on a different character, when we have enough processing power to morph ourselves on the screen of the videophone, when it's our words but someone else's body (a different gender), when we have digital Visa cards that allow us to adopt a dozen different digital personas, none traceable back to us, when suddenly two-thirds of the population of the United States dies, Social Security numbers are retired, and then, overnight, five times as many Social Security numbers arise with all sorts of aliases. We don't know what it means when we are able voluntarily to participate in communities — with leaders, fools, cops, robbers — where we can come and go, adopting and dropping personas along the way. Our lives could change profoundly.

What I would like to call for today is a massive effort with government and corporate funding to revitalize research on the relationship between technologies that we create and our society and culture. This was a very active subject of investigation thirty years ago. Marshall McLuhan[11] and many others worked at a time when every sociology, anthropology, and psychology department had funds to do research on these questions — much of it federal and military funds. This ended with the Vietnam War and the transition from ARPA to DARPA. A Dark Ages crept into the social sciences. We now have a unique opportunity. Thirty years after McLuhan's work, we understand far more about the technology and have far better research tools. It is time for us to begin to explore our future scientifically, rather than just stumbling into it.

Jonathan Seybold

Mark, let me bring you back from the future into the focus of this panel. You said it isn't going to happen. We're not going to be installing what everyone else here says we will be installing. I don't want you to be so wishy-washy about it. In thirty seconds, why isn't it going to happen? What makes you so sure?

Mark Stahlman
It takes at least ten years for technologies in the laboratory to go from initial commercial deployment to the point where they make sense on a broad scale. Video servers, ATM switches, ADSL networks — none of these technologies will be ready for broad deployment for at least another ten years. The only infrastructure that makes any sense for digital interactive services is ISDN. It is installed. It will be widely deployed and tariffed at residential rates. With compression, it will provide 500 to 800 kilobits of throughput. We'll telecommute, we'll have videophones, and we'll do it on our PCs. We don't need the rest of it. The market will gravitate towards the straightforward solutions. Nothing we see in the headlines will happen the way it's described.

Jonathan Seybold
Bob Kavner and Jim Cullen, do you agree with this?

Robert Kavner
I generally agree with the second sentence of each paragraph. That first sentence is so condemning, I don't know how to think about it. Mark's important message worth contemplating is that none of us know how this will roll out. The amount of change, and the simultaneous nature of the change, means there will be many wild cards. I completely agree with that. I also agree that ISDN is a sleeper. Shame on us in the communications industry. ISDN should be widely deployed in this country, fully tariffed, and the customer should have access to it. We could do wonderful things with it. This country is behind a number of other countries in ISDN conformity.

Jonathan Seybold
But you think that in the end ISDN will not be sufficient?

Robert Kavner
My life is an interim life. ISDN is an interim technology. In contradiction to Mark's point, everything is interim. Everything is changing. But ISDN has a role. Following ISDN, or overlapping ISDN, will be technologies like ADSL, full-fiber deployment, and digital wireless carrying broadcast. There's going to be a lot of overlap. The wonderful thing about the world we live in is that there is a lot coming.

James Cullen
Let me just tip-toe through interim life in a dozen digital personas and get to an important point Mark made. We, in fact, plead guilty to having our investments driven by business interests. We found in the last hundred years or so that this works fairly well. I would just say three things.

First, we should not lose sight of the fact that fiber optic deployment, per se, is not the be-all and end-all. But it does offer substantial benefits to the average telecommunications customer who's never going to get on the superhighway, and doesn't care. It can reduce operational costs and increase service reliability. It has many benefits, and the tradeoff with copper is now very close. If you believe copper will last forever, you never need fiber. If you believe rehab will continue and copper must be upgraded, you do need fiber. The questions are cost, pace, and timing.

Second, we are not likely to be deploying full-service networks everywhere in the next three, five, or seven years. I think Mark is right. This is going to take a long time just by virtue of how much is required.

Finally, in my mind, what will set the pace are the cost, development, and user-friendliness of the set-top box, particularly for digital services. We have not made a commitment to do anything in particular for the next fifteen years. We have made a commitment to get on with it, and see what the market is and what the costs are, so that we can determine our future investments.

Jonathan Seybold
If you were guessing on the time schedule, would you say that we are talking ten to twenty years to complete this transition?

James Cullen
I think Bell Atlantic will be up to sixty percent of our customers — the attractive markets — by the end of the decade. Or it could be forty, fifty, or seventy-five percent, depending on how the technology and the marketplace evolve. The remaining customers may take us to the year 2015. On the other hand, ISDN could meet everyone's needs, as Mark suggested, and wireless, satellite, or other technologies could carry these services.

Jonathan Seybold
Putting this into an historical perspective, a decade or two is actually a very short period of time for a change of this depth and impact. Let's move on now to Bob Pepper, who is sitting in a position of trying to make sense of all this from a policy standpoint in order to set the ground rules for development. You've been getting a lot of unease from the troops here about the nature of these ground rules, Bob, and how long it's taking to put them in place. We're eager to hear from you.

Robert Pepper

It's interesting. When the highway metaphor reaches the covers of *Time* and *Newsweek*, everyone begins to adopt it, and extend it. So now we have the article in yesterday's *New York Times*, "Ruts on the Data Highway." The National Association of Broadcasters is concerned about "road kill on the information superhighway." A Cox Cable official claims the Administration wants to build the information superhighway, but "the FCC is blowing up the bridges" on it.

One of the best headlines, explaining things going on right now, is in yesterday's *Washington Post*: "Hurdles Slow Information Superhypeway." I think that hurdles slowing hype are not bad things. What we are now seeing, after an explosion of unrealistic expectations, is a return to fundamentals -- the underlying trends that are going to result in increased investments to convert the information infrastructure in this country and globally from narrowband to broadband, and from one-way to two-way. Let me outline what I think these fundamentals are.

First, I disagree with Mark Stahlman when he says there is no technological convergence. I think there is technological convergence. Technologies used by traditional industries that were once separate and identifiable are beginning to merge. I've never quite known what convergence meant in the broad *Time* magazine sense, but the underlying technologies and architectures of previously distinct industries are beginning to blur.

Second, the fact that people are using similar technologies implies a new set of realities in technology and markets. Previously distinct industries that had segmented users and segmented services are finding that customers don't really care where they get their services. They just want high quality services, on demand, when and where they want them, at a price that is commensurate with the level of quality. Not everyone wants bells and whistles. Some people want Volkswagens, others want Mercedes. The problem is that the old rules try to keep the industries and technologies distinct. We still regulate based on technology when we should be regulating on a technology-neutral basis.

A third fundamental is that investments in the new technologies are, in fact, going forward. I agree with John Cooke that alliances are moving ahead. Companies are seeking new alliances. People are developing software for entertainment and other applications. Five years ago at the First Roundtable in Multimedia that Martin pulled together, participants had some idea of what the future might look like, but nobody else really did. We're now beginning to see some of these products rolled out.

Another fundamental is that the rewards for these investments are not immediate. The media love to create myths and then very quickly destroy them. Time Magazine wrote a cover story in April 1993, almost exactly a year ago. I quote: "Suddenly the brave new world that futurists have been predicting for decades is not years away, but months. By this time next year, vast new video services will be available at a price to millions of Americans in all fifty states." *Time* created this myth on which everyone is now dumping. We can get back to fundamentals. The fact is that reaching critical mass with new technology and new services takes time. It's evolutionary, not revolutionary. It will take six to eight years.

All analogies are imperfect, but the cellular industry provides a good one. The FCC in 1983 (again, after delaying too long) finally authorized cellular service. At that time, the best thinkers about mobile communications thought cellular would be a wild success. The few thousand radio common carriers had insufficient frequencies, resulting in blockage. To use the car phone in Los Angeles involved a wait. Predictions were that by the year 2000, cellular would explode the market and there would be 900,000 customers. In fact, by the end of 1994 there will be 16 million customers at a minimum.

I agree with Mark that we totally underestimated demand, misunderstood how people would integrate mobile communications in their lives, and missed how it would change the way they communicate. But that's not bad. The fact is we created opportunities, and it took off. It was not until about 1990 that the industry and the regulators figured out what cellular was going to be, and the impact it would have. It takes six to eight years to reach critical mass.

I would expect the same to be true here. We will not know for six to eight years what this will look like, and rewards will not flow during this period of time. What we do know is that unless investments are made in these next two years, there will be no rewards in six to eight years. That's the reason for all the positioning, jockeying, and dealmaking. Some of the dealmaking is to cover the rear ends of people not sure where to invest. Much of the activity will continue, but instead of a big bang approach, the strategy will be more of a piece-by-piece approach. Investments are occurring. We do not know precisely what the rewards will be, but we should begin to find out by the end of the century.

Another underlying fundamental that has not changed is that there will be lots of players. I would not discount wireless. I think it will be terribly important. It is not going to be a wired world; it's going to be a wired and wireless world. It's not going to be fiber; it's going to be fiber and copper. It's not going to be just broadband; it's going to be broadband, narrowband, and ISDN. I agree with Bob Kavner's point that ISDN is a very good interim technology. We can see the coexistence of ISDN with narrowband and broadband.

So, I do not see the reassessments of the last several months as a problem. A little debunking of some of the hype is very healthy. Getting back to fundamentals is a very good idea, and a more realistic assessment by people making investments is very good business.

Jonathan Seybold
Bob, if it's going to take six to eight years for this to happen, we have to lay the foundation in no more than two or three years. Isn't that right?

Robert Pepper
That's right.

Jonathan Seybold
So, this means the window for the policy issues to be resolved is actually quite short, so far as you're concerned?

Robert Pepper
That's correct. That's why I think today's B-1 page in the *Wall Street Journal* is interesting and reaches the right conclusion. The article, titled "Washington Slows Speed on Information Superhighway,"[12] recounts Judge Greene's throwing cold water, at least for the time being, on the McCaw-AT&T wireless deal; the

FCC's regulation of cable rates and the rate cuts it recently imposed; the breakup of the Bell Atlantic-TCI and Southwestern Bell-Cox deals; the protracted and very difficult process of granting waivers to the RBOCs; FCC delays on the approval of video dial tone and more than a dozen requests for interactive network tests; local government's clogging up the works — New York City, for example, balking on an FCC request by NYNEX to wire up three buildings in Manhattan for video services.

Taken together, these problems constitute very strong reasons for legislation. We need to clear up use of the regulatory process for game playing by all players. I find it wonderfully ironic for AT&T to be complaining about Judge Greene, when it is constantly making accusations about the RBOCs before Judge Greene. I find it wonderfully ironic for the cable companies to be complaining about the FCC's rate regulation, when one reason it is taking so long to work through the approval process is that every time a telephone company files for approval, the cable companies rush in to file oppositions. The administrative process, in trying to be fair and allow everyone to participate, is totally elastic. The next two years are very important for the regulatory framework. The conclusion of the article is correct. We need legislation to reconcile these troublesome issues.[13]

James Cullen

I agree on the need for legislation, but after having slogged through 400 pages of it, I find the bottom line is to give more, not less authority to both the FCC and the Department of Justice. Like Bob Kavner, I agree with the second sentence. There are some benefits. I also agree that this presents a discouraging picture of what it takes to make an investment with some level of assurance. If we're going to move forward to clear it up, whether through a state, FCC, or legislative solution, I will vote for it. I will support it and urge anyone interested in seeing real investments made to do the same.

Robert Pepper

A large part of the debate on legislation has to do with whether the RBOCs should be permitted into the long-distance business. AT&T insists on a test demonstrating local competition to ensure that there is no bottleneck. The RBOCs say this is not needed. The fact is that there are more important issues than long distance, such as whether the local telephone networks will be able to grow as common carriers from narrowband to broadband, and carry all kinds of communications — not just one-way, but two-way. This gets lost in the long-distance debate. I scratch my head and wonder why it's necessary to have local competition in voice before we allow phone companies to provide competition in broadband. We already have a broadband provider; it's one-way; it's not a common carrier; it's called the cable company. At the Consumer Electronics Show, Bob Kavner alluded to these issues. They have nothing to do with long distance.

Jonathan Seybold

If I'm sitting here listening to this, I'm by now getting extremely frustrated at what I'm hearing. The promise of the infrastructure upon which I want to build a digital world is getting all tangled up with politics, regulation, and special interests. Is there some way of cutting the Gordian knot[14]? Is there some way of doing something significant to cut through the messiness and go forward?

Mark Stahlman

Or, if I could just add, what's it going to take to get a $13 flat-rate, residential ISDN tariff? Who's standing in the way? The technology's already there.

Robert Pepper
I think the companies have very different strategies. Bell Atlantic announced a couple of weeks ago that they will make ISDN available virtually anywhere in their territory, although I'm not sure that it's for $13 a month.

Mark Stahlman
It's business plus. It's charged by the minute. The tariffs are all wrong. It should be cheaper than plain old telephone service (POTS).

Jonathan Seybold
Okay. To get back to the question earlier, is there a *deus ex machina* here? Is there a simple solution? Or is this going to drag out for the next few years?

Robert Kavner
I don't think there is a simple solution. I think it's going to take a couple of years to work out. But I also think we're looking at only a segment of the set of opportunities; namely, how the transport networks line up in order to carry all forms of media? Other issues need to be addressed with equal vigor. What is the home and office environment? How open will it be? Will the one who has carriage also have the responsibility to provide, in its future evolution, what is now the set-top box? Who owns the video server? How do we get on it? Do we use the model of the cable industry, where a deal is cut to share revenues or equity to get content up on the server? Or will there be open access? I'm concerned that we're narrowing in on one segment of the overall set of opportunities, albeit an important one, and neglecting other important elements that need to be addressed.

Christopher Herot
Why isn't ISDN cheaper than POTS?

James Cullen
The pricing of ISDN, like every other service, reflects the cost of providing the service. While it may not necessarily be usage-based pricing, it is certainly pricing based on usage and on the cost of providing it. If you look at the patchwork across the country, you'll find a variety of pricing. At Bell Atlantic, the pricing in total is a little over $20 for a residential line. You can ask me why it isn't $10 or $5 or $15, and I'll say it's based on cost and anticipated usage. Pretty straightforward — reviewed and approved by 62 levels of regulators.

Stewart Alsop
I want to ask Jim Cullen a question. Following up on the last question, if you're talking about installing multiple fibers to the home with a fully-switched broadband network, and if you expect that 60 percent of your customers will have access to a full-service network in approximately five years, why has it taken so long to roll out ISDN? You just said that the pricing of ISDN was based on the cost of providing the service, but ISDN is a fundamentally cheaper service than the fully-switched network. What's the difference?

James Cullen
I honestly don't know why it took so long. It's a function of marketing, our engineers, and the fact that benefits were purely one-dimensional. A lot of the fault lies with us in not promoting ISDN — and now we may have overly promoted the information superhighway. But the benefits with fiber optics are clearer, more

direct, and more immediate. It will be an enabling technology for much of what we think is coming.

Robert Kavner

I want to comment on ISDN. I've been around it for awhile. It is a screw up from which all of us connected with it have learned. My view is that it was a convergence that was not leveraged. ISDN was invented at a time when the relationship between the communications industry and the computer/software industry was inadequate. We couldn't show sufficient value for ISDN to get the terminals and software applications built to use it. It was chicken-and-egg. You build the applications, then we'll build the networks. No, you build the networks, then we'll build the applications. The healthy development of the 90's is that we now have groups of people from different industries, as at this Roundtable, discussing how we can work together for mutual gain.

Stewart Alsop

I have a second question, this one for Bob Kavner. You mention the need for demonstrated competition in local access as a precondition for opening up long distance. But did MCI have demonstrated competition when long-distance service was deregulated? You have enough money to build a system that would provide competition for local access. You're complaining that Bell Atlantic has billions of dollars invested in an infrastructure that gives them an unfair de facto advantage. Why can't you go in there and build your own infrastructure?

Robert Kavner

Putting aside regulatory environments, we can do that. It's an expensive thing to do, but if it were required, we would do it. We much prefer having Bell Atlantic treat us like a customer. We pay

$16 billion a year for that access loop. If there were competition, so the person at home had a choice of using Bell Atlantic or someone else, Bell Atlantic would not have a market-preference position over what the customer buys on a full-service network. It is somewhat parallel to what we've gone through, but I wouldn't wish upon the local exchange business the pain we've had to endure to allow MCI, Sprint, and others to enter the long-distance market. They put an arm behind our back. We're still in regulation, whereas our competitors operate with minimum levels of regulation.

Stewart Alsop
But you still have 80 percent of the long-distance market.

Robert Kavner
Oh, no, no! In some market segments we're at 25 and 30 percent. Long distance is not one market, any more than local exchange is. It's a highly segmented market. AT&T considers how to deal with each market segment and its pricing separately. In some market segments we are at 80 percent, but not most.

James Cullen
Bob is a great businessman, and he's just told us that there's no great future in building local exchange facilities. If AT&T does not do it, who will? And if no one does it for 80 percent of our customers, when do we get into long distance?[15]

Matthew Miller
Everyone wants price competition for the other guy. That's the definition of open architecture. It's a matter of business principle. But there really are some fundamental issues in the regulatory environment. One was alluded to yesterday by producer Louise

Velázquez from Quincy Jones Productions. Bandwidth isn't infinite or free. If we allow people providing the bandwidth to have interest in the content, don't we run the risk of discrimination at some point, in some way? Isn't the ultimate objective to separate content from transport?

James Cullen

Bandwidth may not be infinite, but using a telephone-switching paradigm for delivery rather than a cable-broadcast paradigm could mean access to an effectively infinite number of channels. (Many here know more about this than I do.) Given the proper separations, there is no reason why a Bell Atlantic should not have some interest in content. This question has been reviewed thoroughly by the courts and a final exhaustive opinion was issued last year. From a practical business point of view, Bell Atlantic does not have the incentive to make the investments needed if it is just going to be a plain-vanilla carrier. There's not enough opportunity for profit if all we are is a commodity provider.

Jonathan Seybold

Bob Pepper and I had a conversation on this very topic three years ago. Do you agree, Bob, that it is necessary to give companies like Jim's the opportunity to participate in content and services to provide incentives to build the networks?

Robert Pepper

First, I think it's important to ask what is meant by open access? It means that all content providers have access to all customers, and all customers have access to all content providers. Traditional one-way media like broadcast television and cable have not been designed this way. One of the differences between these traditional distribution media and a common-carrier approach, like video dial tone or a fully interactive two-way network, is that in common carriage the transmission provider cannot block access to the content provider.

The issue of economic incentives is very important. We're looking at significant investments, and start-ups have a chicken-and-egg problem. Given that a large portion of existing programming over networks is controlled by incumbents who don't want to see competition in transmission, what kind of incentives will encourage the very significant capital investments necessary to put a network in place? If the network company provides its customers on an equal basis through an arms-length arrangement, and if it happens to be financing or backing a customer in some way, as long as there are equal access provisions, then it seems to me the risk is reduced significantly. We can provide an economic incentive to invest in networks, with all content providers receiving equal access.

Jonathan Seybold
Isn't it true, however, that Bell Atlantic Video Services, which is set up as a separate subsidiary of Bell Atlantic, will set the de facto protocol standards on the network as things stand now?

James Cullen
No, it's not true. I urge you to look at the opposite issue. Should Bell Atlantic make this size investment in the network and then try to find someone to come and compete with the existing cable company? How many do you think we'd get? Essentially zero. We've done this across the territory. We've looked for people who want to compete with existing cable providers. So far we have FutureVision in Dover Township, New Jersey for 38,000 customers. It would be ludicrous for us to build a network and hope someone

will want to ride it. If we're going to meet the needs of our customers, Bob Pepper is absolutely right. This is a two-part issue. They have to be totally separate; and they are not, Jonathan, going to set de facto standards. This is going to meet all the FCC level one and two gateway requirements. Bob will be able to get on the network; John Cooke will be able to get on it. It will be open to all — 60 channels in northern New Jersey used by Sammons, 324 still available for anyone else.

Matthew Miller

I don't know the answer. I think we're running into a Goedel's Theorem, which says that if we want completeness and consistency, we've got a problem. In the cable industry (where frankly access has been more open than many want to believe), it has been our experience that if we expand the means of production and distribution, we get more producers than can adequately be serviced. That's very positive, although ultimately we run into issues regarding discrimination against a producer. Twenty years ago, people thought three channels of television were all anyone would want. Twelve-channel cable seemed excessive. Now 150 channels are not enough. Okay, there will be latencies. In a switched environment, you say we theoretically have infinite bandwidth; but we don't have infinite switching capacity. The fact is that a successful system is one that is constantly being taxed to its limits.

Robert Pepper

You're absolutely correct. There's a shift. There's a transitional question as we move from limited capacity networks toward switched networks. But the reason telephone networks don't crash all the time is that people work out the statistics.

Matthew Miller
But they don't have two-hour connect times, as in watching television.

Robert Pepper
So you design a network system.

Ralph Derrickson
I'm curious about how Disney in creating content can get access to various interactive systems. I think software compatibility is at the center of the issue. How will a strategic deal between any one content provider and any one network system advance your ability to get to a number of systems, given different software architectures? Do you plan on playing any sort of driving role in getting access to various markets?

John Cooke
If I understand your question correctly, any alliance we make with a technology company and distributor company would be for the purpose of jointly building new programming and software that we would want to distribute, and also offer to other distributors. It would not be intended as an exclusive arrangement. That would not be in the best interests of our partner or ourselves. We would both want wide distribution and a licensing of the product elsewhere. Everyone who creates programming wants wide distribution. I don't see alliances resulting in programming having limited access to only certain markets.

Ralph Derrickson
I think you see my question exactly backwards. You want to get on multiple systems. Several different people are talking about software architectures for providing content. Some are big names,

and there'll be at least two winners, like the Macintosh and PC platforms today for building CD-ROMs. The problem gets worse the more complex the architecture and the more things we have to deal with. I was asking if you have any plans to try to drive some standards and make it easier on all of us?

John Cooke
Now I understand. We do have concerns about architecture standards, although I don't know that we'll be able to drive them. We have people at Disney right now who are worried, and they are working with a lot of players to see if we can in any way ensure some commonalty to help us get access everywhere. But we're unlikely to be the driving force. We have to be lobbyists.

Denny Hylton
Some of the Hollywood and computer people here expressed concern yesterday about having enough channels to bring their products to market. I asked at dinner last night, "If Bell Atlantic made available four channels on its video dial tone platform free of charge to everyone in this room to transmit their content, could we fill up the channels?" The answer was, "No." The real problem is not channel capacity, but distribution and marketing-reach. John Cooke is right on point about how to distribute products across the open network. The creative talent represented here has to come together to create the environment. Bell Atlantic will build a network open to all. It's not in our interest to close that network. We need the revenue to pay for it.

Robert Kavner
If Bell Atlantic builds an open network on a set of APIs (Application Programming Interfaces) that are class A, and if Pacific Telesis does APIs on another architecture, AT&T on a third,

and Ameritec on a fourth, we're going to create a big problem for the Disneys. That's the concern I hear. We need an API layer that's constant for sixty to eighty percent of the market, one that people can write to with the assurance that there is a large enough addressable market in which to make money. We need to avoid locking up creative people from writing because they don't know what platform to write to. That's going to be an issue for us in 1994-95.

Jonathan Seybold
This is precisely the problem we're going to be facing. It affects both the creative people who want to produce interactive content, and anyone who wants to be in the server business. If the people at L.L. Bean want to put up a server accessible to their customers nationwide, they do not want to have to deal with different network protocols for every geographic region. That would drive them crazy. We don't know how to resolve this issue yet.

Denny Hylton
This is at the heart of what Danny Hillis and I were talking about at breakfast this morning (along with what a Bell-shaped mentality really meant). We strongly agree with Mr. Kavner that this was one of the underlying failures of ISDN. We face the same issue today.

Jonathan Seybold
But it's much worse.

Denny Hylton
It's much worse, and it reaches not only into the computer and communications industry, but the entertainment industry as well, with a much wider variety of content. I am suggesting this topic to

Martin Greenberger for next year's Roundtable. We have tried to address these issues in seminars at Bell Atlantic with content providers about what they can send across our network. It is very important to have a well-defined operating environment that accommodates the vast majority of content providers, and still leaves room in architectural design to permit innovation and the introduction of specialty products.

John Walsh
People are obviously not going to use these services if they're too complex. It's hard enough to devise a mechanism for linear services, like movies, no less interactive services. What do you think the human interface at home should be today, and what does it need to be tomorrow? Standards are a big issue.

Robert Kavner
We are looking very carefully at whether there is any merit in having a marriage of the technology of server software with client software in the home. We would prefer to have a defined interface in the home, and let innovation occur in the set-top-box environment. Others believe that, technically, the handoff from the server to the home environment is critically important, so whoever provides the server software should be responsible for the home environment. The best I can tell you at this point is that we want to solve the problem so there is lots of innovation. One possibility we're exploring at great length is to use the human voice as a natural language interface for dialogue with the interactive world.

Jonathan Seybold
Bob, we are at the very beginning of exploring what this interface should be, what services should be provided, and how one should

relate to these services. Yet we said we need standards. How do we reconcile the need for innovation and the need for standards?

Robert Kavner
Again, it's a technical issue. We want a set of protocol standards against which the consumer electronics industry can innovate. We should not set standards on what processor, what operating system, or who is involved. These should be open to full competition. But there need to be technical protocols that deal with such things as compression, decompression, encryption, decryption, and conditional access. Once these standards have been set, innovation can occur on the other end.

Jonathan Seybold
They also have to include commands to make inquiries of the server, get information from it, define the language and vocabulary for talking with others on the network, and deal with a world in which there are a thousand servers and transparency. These are not trivial issues. How do we set those standards?

Robert Kavner
... With as little government intervention as possible.

James Cullen
... I agree totally with all the questions that have been asked.

Mark Stahlman
The personal computer is the only programmable platform with any chance of penetrating fifty percent of U.S. households by the end of the century. There's no chance of even ten percent penetration for any alternative offered. Interfaces like Magic Cap, which Pavel Curtis compares to an empty city after a neutron

bomb, assume people are naive. They don't make any sense. By the year 2000, the marketplace will produce three generations of Power PC and Intel microprocessors past today's, with enough processing power to develop new interfaces with a great deal of speech recognition built into them. It will all happen on the personal computer. That's likely to be the mechanism that gets us there.

I remember going to a communications conference almost twelve years ago in North Carolina, where I met with a group of very smart people from Bell Labs. They said that the interface to the telephone system — tip and ring wiring, with 48 volts DC and an AC ring battery — has been the same for all these years. Their job was to try to figure out the data equivalent — the one interface that would do it all. I was flabbergasted. There is no such thing. Standards like that don't and never will exist. The right place to think about standards is exactly where Bob Kavner said, somewhere in the protocol stack, as far down as possible.

Robert Kavner
You just contradicted yourself. You said that the personal computer would be the interface, which means the standards are going to be set in Redmond.

Mark Stahlman
Absolutely not.

Carol Peters
I would like to throw out a small challenge to Bell Atlantic, AT&T, Time Warner, and a couple of the other players. If you would take the bold step of making public to us independent producers the APIs that you have, to the degree that you can describe them today,

we would reward you with an enormous amount of input about how those things are useful and not useful. The difficulty we face as independent producers is that we spend almost full time trying to figure out what you're doing, as though it were a 5,000-piece jigsaw puzzle. Is it at all possible, given where we are today, for you to be generally more open about the twenty or so key API elements?

Robert Kavner
Listen, I have a similar dream, but I'm not sure it's the right time to deliver the consolidation you're suggesting. We're in a period of heavy innovation on these APIs. There's still a lot of work to be done in the video server area. It would be premature for us to lock in on one solution.

Carol Peters
Bob, I'm not asking you to lock in. I totally agree that we need this innovation for another two to five years. I'm only requesting more openness to the independent producer community. This would allow us to speak more freely about the elements we most value. For example, if all the people building interfaces said, "We guarantee that you will have real-time voice capability house-to-house through the television set-top box," I would shout with delight. It's one of the most important things you could possibly offer. There are only about seven such things, but without some of them, I can't do what I want to do. I don't want consolidation. I just want a little more participation in the innovation.

Tim Conroy
I'd like to address a question to John Cooke. You are a producer and distributor of programming, which is what the information superhighway is being designed to deliver. If you could form joint

ventures and go forward with some alliances to get programming out to people, what services would you offer?

John Cooke
It's so good a question that I'm afraid I can't answer it. If I announced with whom we would like to make alliances, and what we'd like to make alliances to do, I'd be looking for employment. My colleagues at Disney would not appreciate my disclosing such information here. I hope you'll accept that answer. It's the best I can do.

Jonathan Seybold
I tried to get him to do that, too.

Marc Canter
I'm glad to hear that you guys think protocols are an issue of 1994-95. Some of us have been worrying about protocols since 1984-85, even longer than Microsoft. Yet, you seem only to talk to Microsoft and the big companies. I would reiterate what Carol Peters said. Some of us have ideas you might appreciate.

There's a real difference of reality between what General Instrument plans to ship and what you guys think you're getting. The type of compression has changed since John Malone started the stampede two years ago, yet the goals for those boxes are still the same. That's not what you're talking about. It's not the full-service network. Who's building the boxes we want? How do we get them?

James Cullen
We don't have the answer to that yet, as I said earlier. We have not settled on a solution. But one of my primary concerns is

development of a set-top box that is digital, interactive, and enables user-friendly access through something like a remote device. We're using some of the boxes that are shipping in a few of our locations, and we're working with Oracle developing the server software. I like the PC idea. I know a number of you endorse it. Just to put it in perspective, I'd say that when we can get a PC for $300 for every set-top or equivalent in the home, it will be a winner. Until then, it's going to have a more limited focus and application.

Mark Stahlman
Matt Miller can correct me if I'm wrong, but General Instrument, Scientific Atlanta, and Hewlett-Packard have all introduced programmable set-top converters. To the best of my knowledge, none have been ordered.

Matthew Miller
That's not quite accurate.

Mark Stahlman
No one in cable TV wants a programmable platform. People want compression capability, navigation, and a beefed-up internal operating system. Personal computers are necessary in our lives. They are in our kids' schools. They are in our offices. We won't be going to the office everyday. We'll need them at home as part of our work. We'll need them to talk to grandma. Personal computers are the only opportunity to be everywhere. They don't have to be service-subsidized. Consumers will buy them even if they don't cost $300. They're buying them now for $2,000.

Jonathan Seybold
But Mark, are you going to watch *Gone With The Wind*, or *Seinfeld*, or CNN on-demand on your personal computer?

Matthew Miller
There are obviously commercial matters we can't share, but General Instrument (and I think everyone else in this business) has a dual vision. We are actively pursuing putting a lot of brains in set-top converters, compression, working with customers, and building boxes in volume. (By the way, I think it's volume that drives standards, not conversely.) At the same time, we are working closely with Intel as a partner to cable-enable the PC. We're going to have blindingly fast networking at very low cost, with personal computers connected to cable networks. We are not ignoring the PC platform. To the contrary, our sense is that with parallel development, each one will learn from the other. Televisions and computers are different, but there are also similarities. Our goal is to get out in front of the pack. If we waited for international committees to decide what the appropriate standardized technology should be, the market would pass us by.

I think this debate of TV versus PC is inappropriate. It's going to be both, for different sets of applications. The objective is to have as much consistency as possible within this dual environment, so that you can go build the network once, not three times, so that you can go program software with maximal portability, and so that what you learn on one platform you can port to the other. That's the objective, but we're not perfect. Forgive me for sounding defensive, but we are not as narrow-minded as you may think.

Donald Brazeal
Part of the excitement about the information superhighway always stems from the expectation that there is going to be broad dissemination of high quality information. Yet when forums like this one turn to content, they invariably focus on games and video on-demand. I would like to know what you're doing to ensure that

there is serious information on the information superhighway, not just marshmallows.

James Cullen

This question is often asked, and is a good one. It's very clear to me that entertainment, video on-demand, and perhaps video games, home shopping, and improvements to the open-air zirconium market of QVC, are going to pay for much of these systems, as will improvements by telcos to the basic telephony networks. We need to recognize reality. Still, the applications in health care for which we are now running trials in West Virginia and other locations, might be most important, along with the applications in education that may change our lives, moving education out of the four walls and the 9 to 3 paradigm, and involving both parents and kids. It's very clear to me that these things are coming. It's equally clear to me, if I can make a gratuitous comment, that people like Bob Pepper and Al Sikes, who worked on the PCS ground rules and video dial tone, have set standards and provided a vision that go well beyond video on-demand. Important social, education, and health care services are a big part of what we hope to do.

Notes

[1] The "New World," a term connoting the Western Hemisphere, was first used by Italian historian Peter Martyr (1457-1526). His *De Rebus Oceanicis et Novo Orbe* chronicled the discovery of America.

[2] When asked in a newspaper interview whether the failed alliances in the past year mean the digital revolution has lost momentum, Seybold responded, no, it was entirely predictable, pointing out that people always overestimate the short run and underestimate the long run. He noted that the number of home computers equipped with CD-ROM drives quadrupled in the past year, and the Internet was gaining a million users a month. "So in the midst of all that hype, there was actually a lot happening." *Los Angeles Times*, June 1, 1994, "A Digital Visionary Scans the Info Horizon," page D6.

[3] On July 1, 1994, Robert Kavner left AT&T, which is where he was at the time of the Roundtable, to join Creative Artists, a powerful Hollywood talent agency.

[4] *Infoway* is a short form for *information superhighway* that would succeed in getting around the misleading connotations of *highway*. Other possibilities are *Infobahn*, *Iway*, *Infonet*, and *Internet* (not original but to the point).

[5] This happened at several different telephone companies, but Pacific Tel was the most visible.

[6] Bruce Ravenel of TCI was on the earlier *Great Expectations* panel.

[7] Two major telecommunications bills promoting open competition of the Baby Bells with the long-distance carriers, on the one hand, and with the cable companies on the other, swept through the House in late June 1994 on votes of 423-5 and 423-4. The Senate version was expected to meet much more resistance, partly because it barred the Baby Bells from entering the long-distance market until they demonstrate competition in their local phone business. "Landmark Bills Reshape Phone, Cable Industries," *Wall Street Journal*, June 29, 1994, p. A3.

[8] The FCC unanimously approved Bell Atlantic's application to offer cable-TV and interactive multimedia in Toms River, N.J. on July 7, 1994. On August 2, 1994, Bell Atlantic and Dallas-based Sammons terminated their video dial tone agreement.

[9] *Wall Street Journal*, "Washington Slows Speed on Information Superhighway," April 8, 1994, p. B-1.

[10] Mark Stahlman, "New Media: What's Real & What's Not," *The Red Herring*, Vol. II, #2, 1994, pp. 62-64. Also, "Backlash: The Infobahn Is a Big, Fat Joke," *Wired*, March 1994, p. 73.

[11] (Herbert) Marshall McLuhan, 1911-1980, Canadian cultural critic and communications theorist, maintained that the method of communicating information has more influence on the public than the information itself. McLuhan's best-known work is *Understanding Media: The Extensions of Man*, McGraw-Hill Book Company, New York, 1964. The book is sometimes referred to mistakenly as *The Medium is the Message*, which is the title of its first chapter and has become a McLuhan trademark.

[12] See the reference to the *Wall Street Journal* article above.

[13] For a discussion of pending legislation at the time, see "Landmark Bills Reshape Phone, Cable Industries," *Wall Street Journal*, June 29, 1994, p. A3.

[14] The original Gordian knot, an intricate knot tied by King Gordius of Phrygia, was cut by Alexander the Great with his sword after hearing an oracle promise that whoever could undo it would be the next ruler of Asia.

[15] The issue of long-distance is key to the Senate version of the legislation discussed in the article on "Landmark Bills" cited above.

Hail to the market! It motivates, it filters (it also caters to popular tastes and emphasizes the short term). Hail to constitutional freedoms and free enterprise! We can say what we wish and sell what we please (within limits, of course). Hail to the Internet and the information superhighway! It's an era of wide choice and easy communication (for whom?) Hail to fast access! Information can be gathered and distributed with lightning speed (wait a second, they're smothering me with messages).

The digital media industry is meeting up with old and familiar minefields. As on-line services enter the mainstream, Steve Case of America Online finds six public interest issues becoming critical: (1) telecommunications regulation, (2) access, (3) copyright, (4) security, (5) privacy, and (6) his greatest near-term concern, control of content. Steve wants to keep content uncensored. The Librarian of Congress wants to improve its quality and supply. Billington witnessed the awesome power of media technology firsthand during the 1991 Russian coup. The United States is in deep trouble, he says, as he deplores the "unnoticed and unmourned" decline of libraries and other great depositories of historical culture. We must not leave content to the market, he maintains. Sonia Jarvis, speaking for public-interest groups, joins with Billington in advocating partnerships with the private sector and attention to the general as well as the particular interest.

Communications entrepreneur Richard Neustadt outlines three different images of the information superhighway that often get confused, complicating discussions of the issues. He comments insightfully on the prospects for universal access. Philip Zimmermann, author of PGP, doesn't want the government getting in the way of his whispering in someone's ear, even when the whisper is over 1,000 miles of glass fiber. Moderator Stewart Brand, having to call the session to a close, observes appropriately that discussion of these sensitive matters is likely to continue for the rest of our lives. But the panel makes a very good start.

Back from the Summit

Martin Greenberger
Having considered the complex business issues of the information superhighway in the last session, we are now ready for part two of this discussion: the even more difficult political and public interest issues. The title, "Back from the Summit," comes from the UCLA "Superhighway Summit" last January at which Vice President Gore spoke (with an assist from Lily Tomlin). It was a media event that more than met the goals of its organizers, although its format did not allow the panelists to delve fully into the issues. Steve Case, for example, should have had more time to pursue the good points he was making. This session is intended to give Steve, and other Roundtable participants, an opportunity to get into more depth.

After the meeting at UCLA, the Benton Foundation ran a related "Public Interest Summit." Richard Neustadt chairs the communications policy project of the Benton Foundation. He was at both summits. The second summit took place a little over a week ago in Washington, D.C. It was successful in a different way. I was particularly struck by the concluding panel discussion, handled very skillfully by its moderator, Sonia Jarvis. I immediately called Sonia to invite her to join us for this session, and she agreed. The discussion we will now have presents an opportunity to follow-up on each of these two summit meetings.

Stewart Brand will moderate the session. He is founder of The WELL teleconference system, father of the *Whole Earth Catalog*, cofounder of the Global Business Network, and board member of the Electronic Frontier Foundation. Stewart is an innovator par excellence, with a long history of inventive ideas bearing on the public interest, ecology, and communication among people.

Stewart Brand

This session moves forward from looking at the information highway in terms of what's good for customers and investors, to looking at it in terms of what's good for citizens in general. It's a different perspective, and the playing field intersects at an odd angle to the concerns of business and finance.

This past year has been an important one in the life of the Internet. Remember a while back when it was hip to have a fax? Later it became stone necessity. It was impossible to be in business without it. For some time now, it's been important for scientists and scholars to have an Internet address, but just hip for people in business. That's changed. It's now becoming stone necessity to be on the Internet if you're in business. It's even attractive for private citizens as a way of connecting with interesting information, people, or ideas. The transition took place this year. For example, the TED conference several months ago had almost no discussion of the Internet, whereas Esther Dyson's PC forum a few weeks later consisted entirely of it. Reality is shifting, and politics is a big part of it.

For me, one of the most interesting bodies of lore coming to the Roundtable this year was Pavel Curtis' experience with *LambdaMOO* at Xerox PARC. His line that the "killer application of the 90's is people" reflects the experience of those getting on MUDs[1] via a variety of platforms and modems, collaborating to create whole universes. The experience is extremely entertaining, and very narrowband. The net has its own politics that evolves along the way.

There's been a debate about whether the TV is going to turn into a PC, or the PC into a TV, or both, or something else entirely, such as toys coming through the TV, taking over in another form. Phone companies describe their customers as consumers, but it is these consumers who create the product of the phone system, not the companies. That's the fact of the network. That's why the issue of citizenship on the network will be critical.

This is a momentous time. The decisions on a whole gang of issues facing us will be made for political as well as economic reasons. There's the issue of universal access. Does everyone get on? Accustomed as we are to universal service with telephones, we are unlikely to do without it. There's privacy. Once we're electronic, our life is accessible in ways it has not been before. How are we protected? There's copyright and intellectual property. When bits are bits, not only do these media transform into one another, they become very easy to copy and distribute. The creator may get lost in the shuffle. There's the global issue. We speak of a National Information Infrastructure, but how many of the 7,000 log ons to the Library of Congress over the Internet every day are from outside the United States? The number is increasing. When on the Internet, we know the language we are using, but not necessarily to whom or to where we are talking.

Then there is the issue of government. Its role is essential, but still unclear and evolving. The previous panel discussion dealt almost entirely with the business model for the information superhighway. It will be determined partly by business, partly by customers, and partly by people acting as citizens. Then there are issues of standards and protocols. All of these issues are simultaneously active, and they intersect. There is not much chance of settling any of them right away, yet we can prepare ourselves by identifying emerging concerns. That's part of our mission here today. We're not going to agree, but I hope we can disagree informatively.

Steve Case

I have to be honest. My expertise and interest in political issues is much less than my expertise and interest in some other areas related to this new medium. But I lived in Washington, D.C., and I was a political science major, so maybe I will have something to contribute.

The focus at my company for nearly a decade has been on trying to create a new medium. We are moving a niche computer enthusiast market of a few million people toward a mass market with tens of millions of people, using all kinds of devices to access many kinds of content.[2] So far, the skills needed to do this are first, an understanding of the nuances of what's happening with the technologies, so that we can package the service in a pragmatic way; second, an ability to establish a tapestry of alliances with lots of different companies in both the content and technology worlds; and third, a concentration on what at the end of the day is the only thing that really matters — providing individual consumers with an interesting mix of services through a fun and friendly interface at an affordable price.

The politics of the medium has not been at the forefront as the market emerged, which is good, because this has allowed a natural development. Political issues have occasionally surfaced, such as the big debate in the late 1980s on whether the pricing of local access charges should change with the growth of the market, but for the most part, the concern has been with the technologies and with trying to build customer services. Unfortunately, the transition from niche to mainstream business will get the attention of lots of people and move us into another phase over the next ten years, a phase in which problems like standards and regulation will start rearing their ugly heads.

Many politically related issues are likely to impact this medium. I've picked six to talk about very briefly. First is the whole issue of telco-cable regulation. Since the previous panel covered it, I will only say that how it gets played out will influence the direction of this medium very meaningfully. Second is what we call the access troika. Local, open, and universal access are all swirling around the debate. Copyright is third. There's anxiety about how to get paid for content on the Internet and on other on-line services. We discussed the copyright issue in considering the remote digital services at the Library of Congress.

Fourth is security, about which Philip Zimmermann knows far more than I. It is a challenge to build a business on the Internet with digital cash, preserving a secure mode of communication. Fifth is privacy, a time bomb, which will be one of the big issues of the next ten years. Privacy does not relate to just the on-line medium, but also to direct marketing, telemarketing, and other areas where people are increasingly resentful of intrusion and of how much data companies are collecting on them. We need to strike a balance in tracking the services people use. Such tracking can yield wonderfully valuable information to marketeers for targeting messages, but going too far will create a huge backlash where people say, "This is not what I signed up for." Having the capability to track too much is going to lead to abuse. The privacy issue is likely to blow up sooner rather than later.

Sixth is regulation of content, which does not get a lot of attention, but is the most disconcerting issue to us in the near term. As we heard from Pavel Curtis and others, this new medium is as much about community and people interacting as about content, which raises very difficult questions on what is and is not appropriate. At one end of the spectrum is The WELL and Internet, where the mindset is, anything goes. People can say whatever they want. There's no regulation, editing, censoring, or filtering. At the other end is the publisher mindset, which is what Prodigy was initially, but backed away from. When anything posted is considered part of a publication, the editor can pick and choose what to allow and what not to allow, effectively controlling what is said.

America Online is trying to walk a very difficult middle ground between these two extremes. It's a challenge. I'm almost certain that in the next year or two we, along with other companies, will be appearing before a Congressional subcommittee looking into people talking dirty on chat lines and the vulgar remarks on some message boards. I think the kinds of debates that took place recently on violence in video games will happen in the on-line medium. This troubles us greatly, because we do think this medium is about empowering people to communicate on whatever they'd like to in whatever way they'd like to. At the same time, if it is too freewheeling and has no guidelines, it is likely to blow up. We need to work together as an industry in a responsible way, providing tools and trying out controls, in the hope of delaying the day when a Jesse Helms asks us to testify on the content of personal communications in this new medium.

Stewart Brand

We're going to move now from a completely new institution, America Online, to a very old one, the Library of Congress. I went to the Library of Congress six or seven times in the last four years to find photographs for a book I was writing on buildings.[3] It is the most pleasurable place to do research I know. People I encountered in the permanent collection are world class in their knowledge of historical buildings. I learned a lot from them. There were open bins with tens of thousands of photographs taken in the

1930s, and sequenced photographs of buildings over time, which is exactly what I was looking for. But it was shocking. I was often only one of two or three people using the prints collection.

This is an absolutely fabulous resource in the largest library in the world. No other nation has anything like it. If there is a National Information Infrastructure coming, this is where the national information is. For the Library of Congress to be losing budget in the age of information is crazy. Whitewater is not a scandal, but 41 million unclassified items in the Library of Congress is. What puzzles me is why the Library of Congress is so invisible to people. People providing content should go to this great content trove and put it to work. Its resources should be used to benefit everyone. Sorry I had to say that, Dr. Billington.

James Billington
I want to talk about the power and importance for society and the world of the whole media transformation taking place. As a special illustration, I will consider Russia, a country totally transformed — the jury is still out on whether it is for better or worse. Then I want to talk about our own society, and speak to Stewart Brand's intimation that the Library of Congress, like all the libraries and great depositories of our historical culture, are dying, unnoticed, unmourned, uncovered by the media. I will be rather blunt in my remarks.

First, why did the most powerful empire, the most powerful political machine in modern times, the most powerful secular ideology of our secular era, fall and implode in such a very short space of time? I have written a book about this, and there is much to be said.[4] Having been in Russia during the putsch attempt of August 1991, I see the effects in the transformation of that society of the sudden media explosion. In ways they did not understand, it all came together on those two nights, those 48 hours in Moscow, when a million mobilized troops (the numbers were far larger than ever reported in the press) faced 150 armed people. It was a massive imbalance of forces in the capital of the empire, with the entire political system and almost all the intellectuals supporting the attempt. It did not succeed, largely because of the media transformation that people had not understood. The pieces came together then.

There were multiple modes of communication out of the White House[5]. A very systematic attempt to cut the positional lines failed because of communications. The high altar inside the White House was the Xerox machine at Exit 8 of the Parliament. People were literally running up, reprinting things, and going out. The most dramatic moment for those of us who were around the White House during those 48 hours was not when the tanks approached, or the first tanks crossed over, but when the Xerox machine broke down. A call went out. "Is there anyone who knows who to fix it? Does anyone know?" It was almost complete chaos, because so many skilled technologists were there along with the entire news media corps, which was making television documentaries of what they were in fact doing as it was happening. Instantly and afterwards, the whole set of events was mythologized.

The basic issue was very unclear on the first two days, when there was almost a complete blackout of traditional media. The idea to defend the White House with a human circle was not anyone's program. No one called for this. It happened as a spontaneous reaction to an image emblazoned in people's minds of the Lithuanians doing the same thing earlier in the year. The image had just been broadcast, after previously being blacked out from television. People were responding instantaneously to visual images rather than to anyone's program.

Two images determined the outcome on the very first day. One was the only television appearance of the *putsch* — at the center a picture of Yanayev with trembling hands and shifting eyes.[6] The other, badly reproduced on the Xerox machine at Exit 8, was the major picture of Yeltsin on top of the tank with a confident smile.

Russian icons, the spiritual message of this coded visual linguistic system, forms a subliminal base for all Russian thinking. Eastern Christianity is like Buddhism in this respect. Hands and gestures give the basic message of what the Buddha is conveying in a particular position. The same is true of an icon. Yanayev, who happened to be an alcoholic, was on one of his heavy spins at the time. His hands were shaking and his face was agitated. The images of him and Yeltsin were the two pictures everyone had. No one knew what was happening, but they knew who the good and the bad guys were. It was extremely visceral and visual, an old command-and-control system pitted against a new fluid e-mail system and other forms of instantaneous communication inside the White House.

As the Russians now embark on a democratic experiment, having overthrown the regime in the most implausible of ways, a sudden mobilization of previously suppressed reactionary sentiments and dark ethnic hostilities appears in a figure like Zhirinovsky.[7] He is the only one who knows how to use television. Everyone is analyzing his political ideas. He has no ideas. He's a figure of visceral resentment produced by the new media, coached by a man named Anatoli Kashpirovsky, a well-known spiritualist and faith healer who used to hypnotize people on television, the first person to use television for mass semi-psychotic social purposes. Zhirinovsky and Kashpirovsky are communicating through the new media, producing as much evil as the previous wave produced good.

We are dealing with tremendous power that we don't know how to analyze. Yet we do know what it is doing in *our* society. I would like to respectfully disagree with one of the previous panelists (Mark Stahlman) who said we need more studies. We have any number of studies, but no one takes them seriously. They generally show that educational standards, literacy, and test scores are all falling. They indicate that this country is in far deeper trouble than it realizes.

What struck me most in the otherwise very intelligent discussion of the business side of the information superhighway was the almost total lack of interest in content. Discussions of process and investment have little to do with content. I tried to explain very simply last evening the core of what the Library of Congress is trying to do. The particular example is not as vital as the general principle. Do we want a national digital library of information important educationally and morally, so people know something about their common heritage in all its diversity? Is there a body of non-entertainment content, not commercially viable immediately, that people ought to see? Prediction, investment, calculation, and manipulation are important and relate to the dynamics of the economy, but they do not help with the the deep trouble we are in as a country.

I am not professionally apocalyptic. I've been a student of Russia too long to believe in apocalypticism. The Russians do it with their evening meals, and it is not healthy. But there are many objective signs, empirically documented, that our country is in all kinds of trouble. With the unexamined media explosion, we could very well produce some Zhirinovskys of our own as the political product of a totally amoral approach to the future.

Like everyone else, I tend to reflect the self-interest of my own institution, but what is key about the governance of the Library of Congress is that its board of trustees is the Congress of the United States. As the oldest Federal cultural institution in the country, the Library has a mandate to try to serve the general good. At my address last night, many people made pleasant comments, some made not so pleasant comments, but no one really responded to my theme. Maybe a national digital library is not the way to do it, but do we or do we not want a major campaign to accumulate content of intrinsic educational value? If we leave it to the market, and to the kinds of discussions and criteria I've heard so far, it simply is not going to happen.

Whether the Library of Congress, the New York Public Library, or the other great repositories do it, the question remains, who's going to pay for it? I don't think it will be the general taxpayer through appropriated means and the political process. Even though we have an Administration that is probably as favorably inclined toward this need as any we would ever get, budgetary constraints are taking their toll.

Why not, then, companies like those represented here? With everything venture capital is going into, this community should have a sense of shared concern and lead the initiative. Drawing in people who are doing other things is fine. Their engine will generate the revenues that make it possible, through entertainment and commercially viable services with a significant return. But unless a percentage of this return goes to producing knowledge of intrinsic educational worth, we will simply be disguising entertainment and advertising as education, attempting to make it an extension of normal business.

This takes concern for the general rather than the particular interest. Because of preservation rules and the basic dynamics and economics of the nonprofit library business, I can tell you that we will not have these collections to turn to in ten or twenty years if something is not done about them now. I don't see it happening. If I am wrong, I would be very happy to be so instructed.

Stewart Brand
This is worrisome. The library is one of the main pillars of civilization. If these pillars are not supported, the whole edifice is in jeopardy. Richard Neustadt will now discuss the diversity possible in various forms of broadcast and network activity. He is himself living proof of the diversity that is already possible. He will also consider issues of universal access.

Richard Neustadt
Bismarck[8] said there are two things we should not watch being made if we want to appreciate them — sausages and laws. This applies emphatically to the current remaking of communication policy in Washington. Nevertheless, I think it would be useful to sketch out what's going on and what's likely to happen in two areas — industry structure and universal service.

Industry structure is an old issue. In an environment of scarce transmission paths, the challenge has always been to figure out who should get these paths and under what terms. Should they serve the public interest? Should everyone have access? Should the government intervene to ensure "good" content?

The immediate political context is the Clinton-Gore campaign pledge in 1992 to build an information superhighway. There is a widespread assumption in Washington that to get the capital to build that highway, we have to change the rules and allow players to enter each other's businesses and aggregate services. The difficulty is that people have three completely different images of what the information superhighway will be. Many of the conversations tend to go past each other, since people rarely spell out their assumptions.

What are these three images? One is the *star* model, with the information superhighway consisting of fiber to coaxial to the home, carrying 500 channels of television plus telephony. A public policy concern is that the person who owns the wire will be able to overcharge. Hence the debate over cable regulation. Another concern is about access to the wire. Hence many appeals in the last six months for special lanes on the information superhighway. The commercial broadcasters want a lane; the public broadcasters want a lane; the educators want a lane; the librarians want a lane; everyone wants a lane. Congress is struggling with these problems. Even with lots of bandwidth, there are limits. How should the finite bandwidth be allocated to provide a good mix of services?

A second and entirely different image is the *mesh* model, which tends to be adopted by those with Internet experience. Whether one physical wire to the home or two, each will have virtually infinite bandwidth, since fiber has a lot of bandwidth and the lines will switch. In this model, the server, not transmission capacity, is the bottleneck. Telephone companies are indeed planning to sell server capacity rather than channel capacity.

In the mesh model, the television channel goes away. A meaningful consumer guide for 500 channels is impractical. No one wants that many channels anyway. They want an electronic book store, where an abundant supply of programs is constantly refreshed, and intelligent agents help shop for programs to watch. Here the concern is not with lanes on the information superhighway, but with whether a company controlling both transmission path and server will be obligated to provide interconnection and meaningful switching, so that a programmer who cannot get on one server will have other ways to reach the public. The issues focus on the standards for interconnection.

A third image, which I'll call the *spaghetti* model, has many paths to the home, including both narrowband and broadband wireless. (I'm working on a project, for example, involving 50 MHz wireless channels. There's a lot you can do with 50 MHz of microwave). In this vision, people will buy telephone service through PCS or cellular, disconnecting completely from the local telephone company, and get their television service from DBS, wireless cable, terrestial cable, telephone, and so on. With many paths to the home and low barriers to entry, there would be much competition. The real worry would not be about discrimination and concentration of power, but about the transmission industry's resembling the airline industry, with zero marginal cost once the capacity is installed, and no one able to make any money. (Then, ten years from now, the only people able to afford these conferences might be the programmers).

With people carrying these three completely different models of the future in their heads, it is hard to agree on what the issues are, never mind the outcomes. Still, it is reasonably clear where we are heading in public policy. We're heading toward a new set of rules (as James Cullen said in the last panel) that basically permit anyone to do anything. I believe Congress will pass legislation this year opening all services to competition by all comers. The debate centers on the transition. How long before the local phone companies are allowed into long distance? How long before others are allowed into video services? There will be passionate debate over such issues in the next few months.

When the dust settles and we get to building this information superhighway, however, its shape will be driven almost entirely by the market, hardly at all by the regulators. To decide how to position in this world means deciding first which image will be the future.

Let me switch to universal service. This issue was characterized by Vice President Gore at the UCLA Summit as making sure we don't have a world of information haves and have-nots. Of course, we've always had information haves and have-nots. The poor have less access to information than the rich. Information technology, if anything, has tended to narrow the gap. The question is, when is it appropriate for the government to intervene to try to redress the gap?

The tradition in this country, going back to the Constitution, is to make some basic channels of communication and information provision available to all. We did it first with the postal service, then public education, then public libraries, and most recently with telephone service, used as a luxury for its first fifty years. During the Depression, we adopted a series of policies to promote the universal provision of basic telephone service, not as a formal adoption of public policy, but rather as a coming together of the self-interest of telephone companies and their regulators. It still doesn't fully work. Only 94 percent of U.S. households actually have phones. Half of single-parent families below the poverty level do not. Before worrying about depriving people of the benefits of new technology, we should concern ourselves with the single mother who cannot call 911, or be reached on the phone by her kids' teachers. Society has not solved that problem yet.

The problem is about to get worse. As we move toward competition, the fundamental economics of the phone industry changes. The system that worked well in a monopoly environment, keeping basic residential rates low by raising rates for businesses and long distance, goes away as competition forces everyone toward marginal cost pricing. In the short run, there may be fewer poor people with phones. Longer run, the problem is likely to be solved by a new universal service fund created by a tax on telecommunications revenue. The struggle will be over how much it should be and how it should be allocated. Should we keep all residential rates low, or have a kind of phone stamp targeted at people who most need help? Even harder is the kind of question to which Dr. Billington refers. Should an additional system of subsidy provide advanced technology to connect broadband networks to schools and libraries, or to go into the home, so that we can have, for example, home health care using broadband networks?

What Congress will do on this almost certainly is a Hail Mary pass to the FCC. Congress does not itself have the faintest idea about how much subsidy is appropriate or what it would cost. Over the next few years, we will see a series of studies by the Commission to figure out whether we should raise the bar on basic telephone service and pay for more universal coverage. The question of how much of the technology society should make available to everyone would be a good one to discuss at the Roundtable next year.

Stewart Brand

I suspect we'll come back to this question several times today. Another regulatory issue being debated is how privacy can be protected on-line, on phones, and in general, electronically. More than a regulation, the government is offering the Clipper chip, initially to provide privacy for the telephone, but with a slight rider that makes it possible for law enforcement or national security officers to intercept messages and decrypt them. The great debate concerns not only what happens in Washington, since in typical Internet fashion, the customers have already come up with their own unregulated cryptography, thanks to PGP and its author, Philip Zimmermann. PGP is out there and is much better than Pretty Good Privacy, which is what it stands for. It may or may not be breakable by the NSA, but it is unbreakable by just about everyone else. Philip Zimmermann is a privacy activist who exemplifies how things can happen in the Internet version of the world.

Philip Zimmermann

There's been much talk at this conference about multimedia coming from CD-ROMs. I prefer to think of it as two-way communication between people, like videophones or videoconferencing. In the days before technology, face-to-face was the only way to have a conversation. We still do that, but we also have a growing number of conversations in virtual reality, where we may be talking to someone a thousand miles away. As technology advances, it becomes the next best thing to being there. We can have lunch with people far away, and do everything but reach over and grab the food off their plate. I think a conversation over lunch should be private, whether it is face-to-face or a thousand miles away. We should take that privacy with us when we move into virtual reality. That means the conversation has to be encrypted with strong cryptography, out of reach of anyone. The government should not be able to prevent me from whispering something in your ear, even if there is a thousand miles of glass fiber between us.

As Stewart Brand mentioned, the Clipper chip is the government's effort to create a new encryption standard. Encryption keys are put in the chips when they're made, then a copy is placed in escrow. The government promises not to use these keys unless we've been bad, or at least it thinks we've been bad. The government is putting forth a full court press with its spending power by buying lots of Clipper phones from companies whom it persuades to make phones for the rest of us. Doing business with the government would eventually require having a Clipper phone, so the government would be able to change the facts on the ground without changing the laws — via the tyranny of the installed base. If we wake up one morning with a hundred million Clipper phones installed, it would not matter what laws are passed. We would be stuck with an infrastructure from which we cannot escape.

PGP is a program that encrypts e-mail. It has become a de facto worldwide standard. It is available commercially from a company in Arizona, and is fully licensed. With paper mail, the government can only open our mail if we are targeted for investigation, examining one person at a time. With electronic mail, government computers can, in theory, scan tens of millions of pieces of e-mail everyday, looking for subversive keywords and political troublemakers. When the economy takes a wrong turn, as it did in

Germany in the 1930s or Russia in the 1990s, who knows what kind of leadership may arise? Who knows how an infrastructure built today will be used twenty years hence? We should not deploy technological tools that could be used to strengthen the hand of a potential police state. This is just a matter of good civic hygiene.

They tell us that Clipper is a voluntary device. We do not have to buy it. They claim they will not forbid other kinds of cryptography. But these claims seem to be at odds with what is happening with PGP. PGP has triggered a criminal investigation to find out how the software came into use in other countries. There are export control laws that say encryption software cannot be sent abroad.

The government is taking the position that electronic publication of this software is the same as exporting it. I am the target of this criminal investigation. This area of the law carries a federal mandatory prison sentence of approximately four years. Judges cannot deviate from these guidelines very much. (I do have a legal defense fund for those interested in the political issue.) I'm not indicted yet, and hope I won't be. I don't think I will, because I haven't done anything wrong.

We need to take steps to ensure our privacy in the information age. One is to pass a bill introduced by Rep. Maria Cantwell of Redmond, D-WA, that would lift all export controls on encryption software.[9] If the bill passes, it would energize our domestic encryption software industry, allowing it to compete in international markets, and probably lead indirectly to the eventual demise of Clipper.[10] I'm working on a secure telephone product that will turn any multimedia PC into a "military-grade" secure telephone. Another step is publishing freeware like PGP, if we can only find a legal way to do it. I'm not sure what's legal and what's not. The First Amendment is apparently not entirely operative in the face of export control laws.

I want to read a letter received from Latvia that relates to Dr. Billington's story about the Russian *putsch* . It arrived in October, on the day that Boris Yeltsin was shelling the Parliament building. "Phil, I wish you to know, let it never be, but if dictatorship takes over Russia, your PGP is widespread from Baltic to Far East now, and will help democratic people if necessary. Thanks." That was my best PGP fan mail. Last week, I received some fan mail from PGP users in Burma, which has a horrible government that tortures and kills people in large numbers. Some opposition groups are trained to use PGP there in jungle training camps on portable computers. It's quite a story. I didn't write PGP to be exported, but am finding the most inspiring examples of its use coming from overseas.

Stewart Brand
This gives us another model of what's happening. Pretty Good Privacy was neither a marketing or hierarchical event, but a political event coming up from the grass roots in a very powerful, compelling, and immediately useful way. It shows how these technologies are changing the political, economic, and sociological landscape. Drop PGP in the pond, and the whole pond is different.

Sonia Jarvis may have an angle on this, since part of her background is as associate general counsel for the National Security Archive, which negotiates with federal agencies for the release of information pertaining to national security and foreign policy. Since 1987, she's been executive director of the National Coalition on Black Voter Participation. She has a particular interest in universal access.

Sonia Jarvis

I'm delighted to be here, although it's a little daunting to be last after two days of fascinating discussion about some very important issues. I want to begin by explaining how I came to be here, aside from Martin's gracious invitation.

This past July, I attended the annual meeting of the Secretaries of State who conduct elections around the country. It was their conclusion that within ten years all voting would be done from home. I found this a rather startling assumption on their part, and asked them how it was going to be accomplished. They said the information superhighway would provide the means. That's when I started paying a lot more attention to this whole notion of an information superhighway. It could represent a fundamental change in how we conduct the business of government. Voting is already being done experimentally by mail, phone, and fax on a local level.

At the National Coalition, I represent 88 black organizations working on issues of community and civil rights. We analyze statistics and, in the past, were accustomed to receiving large thick articles containing data from the Census Bureau. Recently, the Bureau has moved to offering the data solely on CD-ROM, and consequently, without a CD-ROM drive, we no longer have access to it. Nor does my Board of Directors understand why we need a modem. I mention this to give you some idea of how far the nonprofit organizations have to come. We do not have extra money for what some have called "toys for the rich." I was content to work on a 286 PC at the office, with basically just WordPerfect and Lotus. At home, I have much more advanced equipment, because I'm a musician and need a sound card and other neat things, which helped me learn about what was going on in the on-line world.

Many public interest groups feel they are being left out of the type of debate we have had here over the last two days. A number of these groups recently came together in Washington, D.C. for the Public Interest Summit, a meeting called by the Benton Foundation, other foundations, and the Telecommunications Policy Roundtable, to raise the level of interest in these issues by the public.

I would like to ask this audience, since it is not one I get to talk with very often, what is the appropriate role of government? We've heard about how legislation and regulation can get in the way of innovation, but I'm also interested to know how the public interest is protected? How do we address the privacy concerns raised by Philip Zimmermann and Richard Neustadt? If this system is going to be the way we communicate with each other, how do we ensure that anyone can have access to it, regardless of race or socioeconomic standing? And how do we address the perennial issue of affordability? People like the equipment; they like the software; they just can't afford it.

The National Coalition would like to be a place where people can come to see how on-line access works, and what information is available in the Library of Congress and other depositories. We're very concerned about issues such as content versus conduit. We see a lot of attention being given to hate speech codes on college campuses, but wonder how that will be translated to the public access channels when some people want to talk about issues that are uncomfortable for others? Is the best way to protect the public interest a series of set-asides, as with radio? Or does the public broadcast model make more sense, or the cable model? Each has its problems, but at least the common-carrier model has some provision for universal service.

One thing I do on a regular basis is organize people to register and vote, which requires me to conduct phone banks. Phone service penetration is a lot closer to 75 than 95 percent in the areas I service. I'm concerned that universal access of the type seen before — whether in the post office, public education, or even with phones — has serious problems of basic infrastructure. Our schools are simply not the type we heard discussed yesterday by the education panel. Their models make sense for private education, but not for our schools, which are now even more segregated than they were before Brown vs. Board of Education.

I raise these issues because one way to move forward is for us to develop public and private partnerships. The nonprofit community is certainly interested in this, yet when the Vice President comes to talk to us, he does not acknowledge that the Administration's goal to connect all schools, libraries, and health clinics may not make sense so long as libraries are closing, schools are falling apart, and health care is a major problem for more Americans than we care to admit. How do we make sure these discussions about consumers, end-users, and networks will also apply to citizens, at a time when we are fundamentally changing the way we communicate with each other?

Stewart Brand
We'll start with questions for the panel. I have one for Steve Case, inspired by Sonia's remark about hate speech. Steve, you may run into hate speech before you run into bad language and pedophiles.

It is a deep and difficult issue, as we have seen clearly in academia. It relates to the issue of privacy and anonymity on-line. There are cutouts an e-mailer can use to be anyone, send e-mail in that person's name, take that person's on-line personality, and say something truly outrageous, including, for example, hate speech. Systems like *LambdaMOO* have pseudonyms. A person gets on, assumes a name, and that name sticks. There's only one of that name around. Whatever people do in the MOO, they are held responsible by the other people in the MOO. There's no sliding out from under it.

We found full anonymity so disruptive on an earlier widespread system called EIES (pronounced "eyes"), that when we started The WELL, we set up the software so that the login ID would remain attached to every remark made on-line, whether in e-mail or a comment. Each ID can have twenty names or *handles* associated with it, but people know that anything said with sbb in parenthesis is me, or with hlr in parenthesis is Howard Rheingold. That, plus the regionality, has produced a sense of community responsibility. When people do something really unpleasant, stupid, or hateful, community peer pressure can say, "Come on, straighten out." This is often corrective. In only a very few cases has The WELL had to kick someone off for being a totally destructive force.

Stephen Case

We're somewhere in the middle. That's usually where we are on these issues. In a cleaner world, it might be black or white. We think there are reasons for anonymity, but on the other hand, I think you're right that holding people responsible for what they say does create a greater sense of community. As with *LambdaMOO*, we provide pseudo-anonymity. Everyone has a unique name on our system. I'm SteveC. No one else is SteveC.

Therefore everyone knows that everything posted as SteveC is linked to me. I could have created an anonymous name like JoeD. That's why we call it pseudo-anonymity. Everyone is responsible for their remarks, but not necessarily in the person's real name.

I'll give one example of why in this new media we believe some level of anonymity is important, so long as people are held responsible. If a person is gay, but still in the closet, and wants to participate in the gay forum that we and other systems have, we don't think we should require a real name. At the same time, we don't want to go to the extreme of letting a person get on briefly as one individual, then an hour later as someone else. That would destroy the fabric of the community. This is why we're sitting in the middle.

David Nimmer

I'm a copyright practitioner, formerly a federal prosecutor. I listened with some incredulity and horror to Philip Zimmermann's description of the specter of his possibly being indicted. I presume that reason will prevail and this will not come to pass. But I do take Dr. Billington's warning seriously. The United States is not immunized against the rise of a Zhirinovsky on our own shores. We do have to be vigilant to protect our liberties.

I have a question for Philip Zimmermann. Granted the government may want to decode and review ten million e-mail messages a day, how much ability does it really have? From my experience as a prosecutor, I remember that when criminals spoke on the telephone about counterfeit money, they had the sense to refer to it as Gummy Bears or some other code word, rather than saying, "I'm bringing over $10 million in counterfeit money." I presume on-line criminals and spies will be smart enough to devise some minimal code words to camouflage their activities. Does the government have the artificial intelligence to determine that seemingly innocuous conversation is in fact espionage or crime in progress? How much do we really have to worry about the Clipper program?

Philip Zimmermann

I don't know how much criminals making counterfeit money have to worry about the Clipper program, but I am concerned about ordinary citizens, political opposition groups, future war protesters, and civil rights workers. Martin Luther King's phone was tapped. Peace and justice groups against America's policy in Central America were targeted for burglaries in the 1980s. We have a poor track record, doing bad things to political groups that disagree with government policy. COINTELPRO, a counter-intelligence program of the '60s, '70s, and '80s could come back. Something like it may be going on right now. (Someone suggested a sticker for Clipper phones with a circle around it saying, COINTELPRO INSIDE). We usually don't find out about these programs until many years later.

For a healthy democracy, political opposition groups have to be able to function without this kind of harassment. Privacy in communications is an important part of democracy. I'm not so worried about whether criminals get away with the Clipper phone. The government has other investigative tools to track them down. Each year there are less than 1,000 federally authorized wiretaps out of the millions of cases handled. We put the entire population at risk for the sake of a tiny number of wiretaps. To spend a billion dollars for 1,000 wiretaps a year, there must be more to it than meets the eye.

Richard Neustadt
I want to speak to stupidity for a minute. David Nimmer may not have had this experience as a prosecutor, but the number of stupid things criminals do is truly amazing. The reason the NSA is going after Philip Zimmermann so hard is that most foreign governments, the Russians and West Europeans excluded, tend to be amazingly sloppy about communications security. This has given our government the ability to listen in on foreign communications for years, and decrypt them very easily. The reason our government is reacting to PGP in a basically silly way (it won't feel silly if they indict you) ...

Philip Zimmermann
The word"silly" is not what comes to mind.

Richard Neustadt
... the reason the NSA is so passionate about this is that it has been able to break an amazing amount of the communications of the foreign governments that have been stupid about security.

Philip Zimmermann
I think foreign governments can afford to hire their own cryptographers.

Richard Neustadt
You would think so, but they don't.

Stewart Brand
One reason I like something like PGP is for authentication. What if Phil had gotten a letter from the mob saying, "Thank you very much." Would he have read it to us? The letter from Latvia could

have been from anyone. So we need authentication, and for authentication, we need this kind of technology.

Another possible application for it is electronic cash, which is untraceable, just like real cash. John Perry Barlow, a cohort at the Electronic Frontier Foundation, suspects that with all money in the form of electronic cash, taxes may have to be voluntary, because transactions will happen out of sight. If the Library of Congress has problems now, imagine how it would be if taxes were voluntary.

Michael Watts
I'd like to commend Phil Zimmermann. What he's talked about is the most important subject in this entire conference. Everything else we've discussed, like finding markets and educating kids, is rendered moot if a police state emerges. What the government is slyly trying to do is very dangerous. I'm absolutely relieved that Phil has done what he has with PGP. I think it is a matter of public record that the NSA now monitors the messages on all communication satellites, not just international ones. I've had some involvement with it. The NSA runs these communications through supercomputers that look for keywords. When it gets permission to do a wiretap on a domestic conversation, it's just permission to pay attention to an individual record from data it has already collected.

Philip Zimmermann
Thank you for your kind remarks, but so far as I know, and I try to follow this, the NSA does not have the technology to capture everyone's voice. It is a very computationally-intensive operation. Silicon is getting cheaper, and with the performance/price ratio doubling every year, I could imagine a time in perhaps ten to

twenty years when the government could have millions of chips doing voice recognition. It could happen. We have to inoculate the body politic to head off the government's temptation to develop tools of tyranny. There's only a narrow window of opportunity right now to put in place encryption standards to which the government does not keep the keys. This opportunity will close. We are stuck with the TV standards we have today because of decisions made over a short interval of time years ago. We have to plug this narrow window of opportunity we have today with tools of our own making before the government fills the niche for us.

Michael Watts
To clarify my comment, I was involved strictly with data communications. To my knowledge, nothing I've been involved with applies to voice.

Philip Zimmermann
Ah, yes. I'm sure they monitor all the data traffic in and out of the country. I'm told that it is illegal to monitor data communications inside the U.S., but I don't have any idea whether this law has real effect.

David Bunnell
I was struck during the last presidential election with the impact that new media type technologies had on the politics: Jerry Brown's 800 number; electronic town halls; and the whole Ross Perot movement, with access to people through television advertising, 800 numbers, and phone banks. I think we have a real opportunity to use new media technology to give people more direct access to government, providing them with information about government and involving them in the way decisions are made. We can cut out the middlemen, the lobbyists and big power interests, and give the

individual citizen the ability to become involved. We might start to develop a true electronic democracy. It would be a killer application for this technology. Would the panelists address some of the positive ways in which new media technologies could be used to improve our society and government?

Sonia Jarvis

We did see new media being used in 1992, but it was not very high tech. It was radio, telephone, and television, especially public broadcast stations and cable. When people felt they had a new way of reaching politicians, whether it was Bill Clinton or any of the other candidates, they responded. One of the consequences was the first increase in voter registration and voter turnout in about twenty years. Clearly, people felt more connected to the process than with the normal approach to politics of ABC, NBC, and CBS. The National Coalition held ten town meetings around the country, and learned firsthand how difficult that can be. What came out of it, though, was a new sense that communities could come together and work effectively on issues affecting them. We support this trend across the board, but let us remember the power of radio, basic television, and existing technologies, then add on the Internet and other means.

James Billington

The Library of Congress is part of the legislative branch of government. We make our bill digest service available free on the Internet, and we work to render intelligible the legislative process, which is pretty unintelligible to ordinary people. The day-to-day business of government that people can affect is the legislation that is shaped, formed, passed or not passed, and modified by the Congress, matters with which most people have little contact.

Many of the 7,000 or more people now logging in to us on Internet every day are asking about this.

Part of the Library of Congress is the Congressional Research Services, 800 people doing a great deal of direct sophisticated research. This is not a partisan political activity using new media, but it does provide a means for ordinary people to relate to the legislative process on matters not reported in their local newspapers. People have no idea what's happening in Congress. Congressional newsletters are increasingly public relations exercises designed to assure reelection. The Congressional Record and Federal Register are almost incomprehensible to the naked eye. The techniques we developed to help the Congress know itself can now be shared more broadly with the nation. If we're concerned about a police state, we not only need to protect privacy, but we need to educate the populace. Merely having access to information does not help, if the information is not rendered intelligible. This is an educational process.

Richard Neustadt

An example of what technology can do is the Right-to-Know Net, a project funded some years ago. What we did was help EPA create a database of information about toxic substances around the country, and then made this information available through CompuServe. Now it is accessible through the Internet and other on-line services. Environmental activists can easily find out what types of substances are being emitted in their neighborhoods, and organize locally to do something about it. The concept is being adopted by HUD for violations of fair housing laws, and by other federal agencies. It puts a new set of tools in the hands of local activists.

That's the good news. The bad news is that the spread of communications technology tends to provide more and more information to those who already have it. C-Span lets people who already care about what's going on in Congress watch it. I helped start the California Channel, which does the same for the State Legislature. There are all kinds of proposals for more on-line information services about politics. Public broadcasting is trying to create more political services. This is great for upper middle class people, but the people who are not registered and do not vote are precisely the people who are not watching.

It seems to me that electronic democracy pushes the problem to its logical conclusion. What we say is, "Okay, anyone who can afford to have a PC can use it to vote." What about those who do not have a PC, or do not know how to use it? Furthermore, if we could somehow magically solve the problem, if a federal program put a piece of technology in everyone's home to enable universal electronic voting, we would then get the kind of marvelous political system we have here in California, where the really important political decisions on where the freeways go, the tax rates, and so on, are made by plebiscite. This is not a good way to run a large democracy. There are reasons why representative government was adopted. Direct democracy with people making instant ill-informed decisions is a dangerous idea.

David Bunnell
The Ross Perot movement was not upper middle class. The people who responded through 800 numbers and got involved were more working class. If we want people to be educated, we have to let them be involved. This is key. Once they're involved, they'll become educated. If we take the elitist view that people are too ignorant to participate in the affairs of their lives, that's not

democracy. Representation is fine, but letting people be involved gives them a motivation to become educated, not only in how to use the tools, but in how to read, think, and debate.

Stewart Brand

This discussion will probably continue for the rest of our lives. If we can find a way to market discussion on-line, we'll have a killer application. Thank you all.

Notes

[1] MUD originally was an abbreviation for Multi-Use Dungeons, named after the game of Dungeons and Dragons. More recently it has been referred to as Multi-Use Dimensions.
[2] The number of subscribers to America Online as of June 30, 1994 was 903,000, up from 302,500 a year earlier.
[3] *How Buildings Learn*, Viking, 1994.
[4] James H. Billington, *Russia Transformed: Breakthrough to Hope*, Free Press, 1994.
[5] The White House of Russia is what the Russian Federation's government building came to be known as during the putsch. Built during the Brezhnev era and resembling a wedding cake, it was to be transformed from a symbol of the bureaucracy to a symbol of the struggle for freedom.
[6] Gennadi Yanayev, rising through the ranks of the Young Communist League from a peasant family, held a series of official posts before being nominated by Gorbachev at the end of 1990 to the vice presidency of the U.S.S.R. "Rumors have it that on the morning of August 22, when the coup attempt had fallen apart, Yanayev could not be reached at his office or at home. When he was finally found, he was in a drunken stupor — it took several hours before he could even begin to understand what had happened." Vladimir Pozner, *Eyewitness*, Random House, 1992, p. 13.
[7] Vladimir Zhirinovsky is chairman of Russia's Liberal Democratic Party, which won a staggering 25 percent of the vote in the party preference poll of December 1993, taking 64 seats in the parliamentary elections and dealing a severe blow to Yeltsin reformers. Nominated as the party's candidate for President in the next national election, Zhirinovsky has promised to replace democracy with dictatorship. His autobiography, entitled, *The Last Thrust to the South*, has been called by Dr. Billington "an even more psychologically unstable work than *Mein Kampf*."
[8] Prince Otto Eduard Leopold von Bismarck, 1815-1898, called the Iron Chancellor, was the creator and first chancellor of the German Empire (1871-1890).
[9] Only Clipper is currently exempt from these export controls.
[10] In July 1994, Vice President Gore wrote Rep. Cantwell that the administration would not go ahead with its plan to require the Clipper Chip, and would work instead with industry to devise a new plan. The White House denied that this represented a significant change of policy.

Biographical Sketches

Participants Taking Part in the Discussion

ROBERT ABEL, president and director of Synapse Technologies, developed the *Columbus* educational project with IBM. Synapse is currently producing *Evolution and Revolution* for IBM, and a project about flight for the Smithsonian and the Air Force Academy. Previously, Abel formed AND Communications, which produced *Human Capitol* and *Ulysses*. He has produced and directed documentary films, feature films, commercials, and music videos.

PHILIP ABRAM is product manager of photo CD portfolio authoring products for Eastman Kodak Company. He has been with Kodak for 12 years, holding positions in quality assurance, research, development, and market and business planning. For the past 9 years he has been involved in the electronic printing and publishing industry.

STEWART ALSOP is editor-in-chief of *InfoWorld*, executive vice president of InfoWorld Publishing Company, and a member of the board of advisors to the *Los Angeles Times*. He has been involved with the personal computer industry since 1981. As executive editor of *Inc.* magazine, he was responsible for the first article on the personal-computer software industry to appear in a major business magazine.

GARY ANDERSEN is founder and CEO of Firstlight, Inc., a firm that publishes CD-ROM multimedia titles distributed worldwide and designed for corporate, home, and educational use. Firstlight is working to increase the effectiveness of multimedia communications through the presentation and acceptance of information structured around the physiological way in which people see, recall, and learn.

BURT ARNOWITZ is president and CEO of Arnowitz Studios, a design and publishing company for new media. Its products in the multimedia education and consumer markets include *Computervisions*, an entire curriculum without a textbook, adopted by the state of Texas, and *The Animals!*, a multimedia CD-ROM about the the animal kingdom and the environment.

MICHAEL BACKES is currently writer/associate producer on the film adaptation of Michael Crichton's novel, *Congo*. He wrote a screenplay for *The Stars My Destination*, served as the display graphics supervisor for *Jurassic Park*, and was the screenwriter, with Michael Crichton, for *Rising Sun*. Backes was one of the founders of Rocket Science Games, an interactive multimedia design company.

JAMES H. BILLINGTON, 13th Librarian of Congress, is an author, historian, educator, and administrator. He came to the Library from the Woodrow Wilson International Center, where he established the Kennan Institute for Advanced Russian studies. He is the author of *The Icon and the Axe* , *Fire in the Minds of Men* , and *Russia transformed: Breakthrough to Hope*. He accompanied President Reagan to the Soviet Summit in 1988.

SCOTT BILLUPS, a 25 year veteran of the entertainment industry, has worked on television commercials, industrial films, feature documentaries, and other film and animation sequences. As the founder and sole employee of Billups Communications, he uses his computer-based production studio to create special effects for motion pictures, including the original computer visualizations for *Jurassic Park*.

Biographical Sketches

BILL BIRRELL is senior VP and executive producer of Sony Pictures Imageworks. SPI develops state-of-the-art digital imaging for motion pictures, emphasizing pre-visualization planning, visual effects, animation, and digital post-production. Birrell oversees the group's business affairs, planning, sales, marketing, and relationships with the creative community.

STEWART BRAND is founder of the *Whole Earth Catalog*, The Hackers Conference, and the WELL teleconference system, and is a co-founder of the Global Business Network. He is author of *Two Cybernetic Frontiers, The Media Lab: Inventing the Future at MIT*, and *How Buildings Learn*. He serves on the board of directors of the Electronic Frontier Foundation and the board of trustees of the Santa Fe Institute.

DONALD BRAZEAL is editor and publisher of Digital Ink Co., a subsidiary of The Washington Post that develops and manages electronic and information products. Digital Ink will be offering an online service that includes most of the Post's newspaper content, as well as services specifically designed for computer delivery. It is pursuing development of products for distribution internationally and for delivery via interactive television.

DAVID BUNNELL is a publisher and entrepreneur whose career is linked with the personal computer industry. He started *Personal Computing* magazine, following it with *PC Magazine, PC World, Macworld,* and *Publish*. After being named chairman of HyperMedia Communications Inc. in August 1991, he launched *New Media* magazine.

MARC CANTER recently started Canter Technology, working in the area of interactive TV content, specifically the "MediaBand" project. He is also founder of MacroMind, now called MacroMedia. His published articles include columns in *Macintosh Today, CD-ROM,* and *The New Papyrus*. He has been cited on a number of occasions in *Newsweek* as an innovator in the field of multimedia.

STEVEN CASE is president and CEO of America Online, Inc., a consumer online service. Case has created a customer-focused and market-driven enterprise that is highly regarded for its innovations in product development and marketing. He has been responsible for forging strategic alliances with dozens of hardware, software, media and communications companies, including IBM, Apple, Time-Warner, and The Tribune Company.

CHING-CHIH CHEN is professor and associate dean of the Graduate School of Library and Information Science, Simmons College. She is author and editor of numerous books on subjects related to optical technologies, multimedia, and new information technology applications in libraries.

JAMES H. CLARK is founder and former chairman of the board of Silicon Graphics. He left the company in March of 1994 and later formed a new venture called Mosaic Communications. His goal in starting Silicon Graphics was to make 3-D graphical computer systems that were as inexpensive and realistic as possible but were also capable of drawing pictures interactively in real-time. He patented the "Geometry Engine" at Stanford in 1981.

Biographical Sketches

TIMOTHY CONROY is executive-in-charge of the KCET Interactive Media Center. His involvement with interactive media dates from 1988 when he served on the board of directors for the Interactive Video Consortium, Inc.

JOHN COOKE is president of The Disney Channel. Prior to his appointment Cooke served for more than ten years with the Times Mirror Company, ending as vice president of Times Mirror Cable Television. Cooke is a member of the board of many prestigious institutions including The Johns Hopkins University, the Constitutional Rights Foundation, and the RAND Institute on Education and Training. He is also Chairman of the Board of Governors of the UCLA Center for Communications Policy.

CHUCK CORTRIGHT is president and CEO of Graphix Zone. He has twenty-five years experience in corporate level computer systems, with the last fifteen devoted to multimedia, computer graphics, and high performance microcomputer development, marketing, and sales. He is responsible for setting the strategic direction of Graphix Zone in the multimedia and prepress markets.

JAMES CULLEN is president of Bell Atlantic Corporation. Prevously he was president and CEO of New Jersey Bell. Cullen began his Bell System career with New Jersey Bell in 1964. He served a number of assignments in data systems and operations. In 1981, he was appointed as director of corporate planning at AT&T. In 1983, he was appointed vice president of strategic planning for Bell Atlantic, and in 1984 served as vice president for sales.

PAVEL CURTIS has been at Xerox Palo Alto Research Center since 1983. His current work centers on LambdaMOO a social virtual reality project he founded. He is investigating the implementation, application, and implications of systems that allow multiple simultaneous users to communicate and interact in pseudo-physical surroundings.

RALPH DERRICKSON is vice president of engineering and product development at Starwave. His responsibilities include engineering and product development. Prior to Starwave, Derrickson served as director of systems engineering, director of NeXTedge and regional manager at NeXT Computer.

JOHN DOERR is a partner at Kleiner Perkins Caufield & Byers, a venture capital firm. Since joining the company in 1980, he has sponsored a series of investments that include Compaq, Cypress, Lotus, Sun Microsystems, Symantec, and Xilinx. His new areas of interest include wireless communications, education, the "full service interactive network," and genomics.

JOE FANTUZZI is the general manager for Autodesk, Inc.'s Multimedia Division. He is responsible for charting the Division's strategic direction and building Autodesk's presence across various multimedia business segments. He joins Autodesk from Macromedia. As Macromedia's vice president of marketing, he was responsible for introducing more than 40 new and upgrade products, establishing strategic marketing partnerships, developing channel and OEM programs, and acting as primary spokesman for the company.

Biographical Sketches

BRAN FERREN is senior vice president of Creative Technology for Walt Disney Imagineering where he acts as liaison with other Disney groups to promote communications, corporate synergy, and new business relationships. His mandate is to seek future technologies with strategic value to the organization.

LUCIE FJELDSTAD is president of Fjeldstad International, a multimedia consulting company specializing in strategy analysis, industry evaluation, and partnership definitions. During a 25-year career with IBM, she held positions in planning, programming, development, marketing, finance and executive management. In the past four years she was accountable for IBM's worldwide strategy in the multimedia arena and in high performance network computing.

STEVE FLOYD is founder and president of FLOYDesign, where he has developed many projects featuring state-of-the-art multimedia technology. He has served as a special consultant to General Motors and was instrumental in helping Delta Air Lines set up a multimedia network, DeltaStarView, which supported its automated reservation system in travel agencies.

PETER FORMAN is president and CEO of New Video Corporation, a company which he co-founded. He has been involved in the development and exploration of multimedia tools and systems for over nine years. He has played an integral role in establishing strategic alliances with Intel and Apple, and in co-developing multimedia solutions for use on the Macintosh desktop.

FRANK FOSTER, a computer filmmaker since 1972, has consistently pioneered new entertainment technologies. This includes digital laser projection, MIDI software, and digital audio. His credits include effects and title design for dozens of commercials and feature films. Foster is currently the vice president of previsualization and multimedia at Sony Pictures Imageworks.

STANLEY FRANK was executive vice president of Encyclopaedia Britannica, Inc., responsible for electronic publishing, acquisitions, joint ventures, new product development, and investigations of new technologies. He was also president of Compton's Multimedia Publishing Group, whose divisions publish and distribute floppy disks and CD-ROM software such as Compton's MultiMedia Encyclopedia. Frank's retirement from these positions to pursue other interests in publishing was announced on September 30, 1994.

BERNARD GIFFORD is Chancellors Professor in the division of mathematics, science, and technology at U.C. Berkeley, where he is concerned with the design and development of technology-based autonomous learning support systems. He also serves as chairman and chief instructional officer at Academic Systems Corp., which he founded two years ago.

GEORGE GILDER, senior fellow at the Discovery Institute, is the author of numerous books, including *Life After Television*, on the future of computers and telecommunications, and *Microcosm*, on the quantum roots of the new electronic technologies. His new book on computers and telecommunications entitled, *Telecosm*, is being serialized in *Forbes Magazine ASAP*.

Biographical Sketches

MARK GORENBERG is a partner in Hummer Winblad Venture Partners, a venture capital fund dedicated exclusively to software investments. He has spent over 20 years in software development and has been software manager in both large corporations and entrepreneurial environments.

MARTIN GREENBERGER has been IBM professor of Information and Policy at the UCLA Anderson Graduate School of Management since 1982. At Harvard University he worked with Mark I, the first automatic digital computer. While on the faculty of the MIT Sloan School of Management, he helped establish Project MAC, now the MIT Laboratory for Computer Science. This is his 11th book.

JOHN GRILLOS is managing partner with Robertson, Stephens & Company, and is responsible for the venture group's software and information services investments. Prior to joining the company, he worked with two leading east coast venture capital partnerships and an investment banker doing computer software company buyouts. Earlier, Grillos served as president of two software companies, Tesseract Corporation and SPSS, Inc.

WILLIAM GROSS is the founder and chairman of Knowledge Adventure, Inc. Prior to starting the company, he created software products for the Lotus Development Corporation, including Lotus Hal and Lotus Magellan. From 1984 to 1986, Gross was president and founder of GNP Development, a developer of software after-market products that was later acquired by Lotus.

MARTY HARRIS is manager of technical development with the Getty Art History Information Program, an operating program of the J. Paul Getty Trust, where he manages the design and development of information systems for the humanities. His research interests are interface design, retrieval strategies, agents/knowbots and the internet, multimedia/hypermedia, and VR technologies.

CHRISTOPHER HEROT is director of Advanced Technology for the Lotus Notes Division of Lotus Development Corporation. He is in charge of incorporating new technologies into Lotus Notes, including video, audio, and interfaces to telephone networks. Prior to joining Lotus, Herot was vice president of product development for Bitstream, Inc.

LAURIN HERR was vice president of SuperMac for Asia/Pacific at the time of the Roundtable, having served the company earlier as director of business development in Japan. He previously was founder and president of Pacific Interface, Inc., a consulting company providing business development, marketing, and research services to the computer graphics, electronic imaging, and television industries.

DANNY HILLIS is chief scientist of Thinking Machines Corporation, which he co-founded. He is the architect of the Connection Machine super computer. At Thinking Machines, he has concentrated his research on methods of parallel programming, applications of parallel computers, and computer architecture. His current research is on evolution and parallel learning algorithms.

Biographical Sketches

JAC HOLZMAN is senior vice president and chief technologist of Warner Communications, Inc. He co-wrote Warner's business plan for early entry into the home video field and into interactive cable (Qube). He was founder, CEO, and creative head of both Elektra Records (1950) and Nonesuch Records (1964). He has helped set both operating and business standards for the optical videodisc and the compact disc.

MAX HOPPER is chairman of SABRE Technology Group, a unit of AMR Corp., and vice chairman and CEO of AMR Information Services Inc. Prior to American Airlines, he worked for Shell Oil Company, EDS, and United Airlines. He currently participates in the Information Technology Advisory Committee of the OMB.

DAVID H. HOROWITZ is an entertainment and communications industry consultant and investor. He is a director of the 3DO Company, a principal in several interactive multimedia start-ups, and an owner and executive publisher of SPIN magazine. Previously he was co-chief operating officer of Warner Communications Inc., and president and chief executive officer of MTV Networks Inc.

DENNY HYLTON is vice president of Broadband Multimedia Network Implementation for Bell Atlantic Network Services, Inc.. He was previously assistant vice president of research and development for Bell Atlantic, and assistant vice president of engineering, planning and capital management. He previously worked with C&P Telephone Companies.

SONIA JARVIS is executive director of the National Coalition on Black Voter Participation, a private, nonprofit organization based in Washington, D.C., committed to electoral equality for black Americans. Jarvis also works regularly with national organizations on issues such as civil rights.

HAL JOSEPHSON is president of the Interactive Media Festival. At the time of the Roundtable, he was director of industry relations with The 3DO Company. Josephson also founded and was president of the marketing/communications firm, MediaSense, Inc. He is an instructor at the Multimedia Studies Institute of San Francisco State University.

ROBERT KAVNER, at the time of the Roundtable, was executive vice president and CEO of the Multimedia Products and Services Group of AT&T, overseeing global business communications systems, consumer products, and federal systems advanced technology. He has since left AT&T to join the Beverly Hills talent agency of Creative Artists.

ALAN KAY has been a fellow of Apple Computer since 1984. Before joining Apple, he was a founder and fellow of Xerox Palo Alto Research Center and later chief scientist at Atari. One of the pioneers of personal computing, he was the designer of the overlapping window user interface, and of Smalltalk, the first completely object-oriented language. Kay has worked with children for most of his career. He strongly believes that the media which powerfully shape our way of thinking must be made accessible as early in life as possible.

Biographical Sketches

JOHN KERNAN is chairman and CEO of Curriculum Television Corporation, which develops and publishes interactive, multimedia curricula for elementary grade students. Kernan was formerly the chairman and CEO of Jostens Learning Corporation, which he founded.

BRENDA LAUREL works on the research staff at Interval Research Corporation coordinating the investigation of how design can better accommodate human diversity. She previously worked at Atari Research developing software architectures for dramatic virtual worlds.

CLAUDE LEGLISE is multimedia marketing manager at Intel. He has held a variety of marketing and management positions with the company. He directed the introduction of Intel's first 32 bit microprocessor, and managed the team that launched the Indeo video technology. Leglise is currently serving as a director of the Interactive Multimedia Association.

DAVID LIDDLE is president of Interval Research Corporation, which he founded two years ago with Paul Allen. The company performs research and development in the areas of information systems, communications, and computer science. Liddle also spent ten years at Xerox Palo Alto Research Center.

JAMES LONG, president of Starlight Networks, founded the company with Charlie Bass in 1990 to develop products to enable digital video networks and servers. In the previous 10 years, Long worked as a venture capitalist with Fred Adler and with a number of high-technology start-up companies.

GILMAN LOUIE is chairman and chief technical officer of Spectrum HoloByte Inc., the parent company of four distinct divisions: Spectrum HoloByte, Bullet-Proof Software, MicroProse USA, and MicroProse UK. Spectrum Holobyte is a manufacturer of interactive and networked games.

ROBERT LUCKY is corporate vice president of applied research at Bellcore. He began at AT&T Bell labs studying ways of sending digital information over telephone lines. He then rose to executive director of the Communications Sciences Research Division, where he was responsible for research on methods and technologies for future communications systems.

ANN MARION co-founded StonySoft with her husband to develop titles for CD-ROM. The Voyager company recently published their CD-ROM, "Society of Mind," based on the book by Marvin Minsky.

ANN McCORMICK joined Nueva Center for Learning in 1988, where she set up experiments in telecommunications, library automation, and multimedia. With Nueva, she founded Media 3, a multimedia development company that creates programs in reading and mathematics.

ROGER McNAMEE is a general partner of Intergral Capital Partners, a partnership investing in the information and life sciences industries. Launched in 1991 in collaboration with Kleiner Perkins Caufield & Byers and Morgan Stanley & Co., Integral focuses on growth-stage private and expansion-stage public companies.

Biographical Sketches

MATTHEW MILLER is vice president of technology at General Instrument focusing on business and technology strategies, with special emphasis on building relationships in the world of digital interactive multimedia communications. He provides technical advice and expertise to the CEO and corporate staff, and serves as the corporate representative in technology licensing, partnership, and development.

CRAIG MUNDIE is vice president of advanced consumer technology at Microsoft. He is responsible for managing the design and development of advanced consumer hardware and software, including core technologies such as multimedia operating system architecture, graphics, compression, and authoring system technologies for interactive television.

NICHOLAS NEGROPONTE is a founder and the director of the MIT Media Laboratory, an interdisciplinary research center focusing on study and experimentation with future forms of human communication, from entertainment to education. He also founded MIT's Architecture Machine Group, a combination lab and think tank searching for new approaches to human-computer interface.

DOREEN NELSON is the director of research for educational reform, and a professor in the College of Environmental Design at California State Polytechnic University at Pomona. She is involved in redesigning the content of the School of Education and Integrated Studies, and developing a curriculum for the International High School on Campus.

RICHARD NEUSTADT is a telecommunications entrepreneur who helped launch *USA Today* Sky Radio, DCT Communications, Private Satellite Network, General Magic, ShopperVision, and El Dorado Communications. Currently he chairs the communications policy project for the Benton and MacArthur Foundations, which is working on the issue of universal service.

DAVID NIGUIDULA leads the research on technology applications for the Coalition of Essential Schools at Brown University and its new parent organization, the Annenberg Institute for School Reform. The research focuses on how technology of all forms may best be used to serve schools that are seriously rethinking the way students and teachers work together.

DAVID NIMMER is of counsel to the law firm of Irell & Manella in Los Angeles. Previously, he was assistant U.S. Attorney in the criminal division for the central district of California. Since 1985, he has been responsible for updating and revising *Nimmer on Copyright,* the standard reference treatise in the field. In addition he represents clients in the entertainment, publishing, and high-tech fields.

DONALD NORMAN is an Apple Fellow at Apple Computer and professor emeritus at UC San Diego, where he was founding chair of the department of cognitive science. He was one of the founders of the Cognitive Science Society and has served as both chair of the society and editor of its journal, *Cognitive Science*. Three of his books have recently been issued as a Voyager CD-ROM, complete with video commentary and supplementary readings.

Biographical Sketches

ALAN NOVEMBER is an author, educator, and consultant. Much of his consulting work and writing involves the management of educational technology as a catalyst for restructuring schools, including curriculum, teacher training, and school/business partnerships.

JIM OLSON is general manager of Hewlett-Packard's Video Communications Division. He wrote the company's business plan for entry into the video products business, with major emphasis in production studio and post production activities, as well as the transmission and distribution of real time video images.

RUTH OTTE was president and COO (at the time of the Roundtable) of Discovery Networks. Her efforts helped transform a small entrepreneurial venture into an international multimedia company that operates the fifth largest cable network in the United States. She took over as president of Knowledge Adventure in September 1994.

SEYMOUR PAPERT is a mathematician and an expert on educational computing and artificial intelligence. He co-founded the Artificial Intelligence Lab with Marvin Minsky, and is one of the founders of the Media Arts and Sciences Program and the Media Laboratory at MIT.

ROBERT PEPPER is chief of the Office of Plans and Policy at the Federal Communications Commission. He has been at the FCC since 1986. Pepper has held several other communications policy positions, and served as policy analyst for the National Science Foundation's division of policy research and analysis.

CAROL PETERS, chairman and CEO of daVinci Time & Space, is developing an interactive environment for children that will be delivered over two-way broadband networks. Earlier, she spent four years at Silicon Graphics, Inc., where she led the project team that created the Iris Indigo workstation.

BRUCE POLICHAR is an independent consultant involved in the development and implementation of business and programming strategies aimed at merging traditional media content with new interactive technologies. His is assisting KCET in establishing an Interactive Media Center.

W. ARTHUR PORTER is president and CEO of the Houston Advanced Research Center, a nonprofit, private research consortium with major research interests in materials science, lasers, high-energy physics, supercomputing, geotechnology, space, and policy studies.

BRUCE RAVENEL is vice president, technology, at Tele-Communications, Inc. He is responsible for technology strategy and business development in broadband communications, interactive services, and telephony. Prior to joining TCI, Ravenel was director of strategic alliance management for U S WEST, Inc..

JONATHAN SEYBOLD has been a leader in using computers to communicate information for 30 years. He co-founded the Seybold Report newsletter, the Seybold Seminars, the Digital World Conference, and the Digital Media newsletter. The Seybold companies were acquired by Ziff-Davis in 1990 .

Biographical Sketches

ALFRED SIKES is vice president of The Hearst Corporation and president of Hearst New Media & Technology. The group creates, guides, and manages the company's growing interests in new media and associated technologies. Sikes was previously chairman of the FCC. He was also responsible for the NTIA TELECOM 2000 report, a comprehensive U.S. communications policy assessment.

KENNETH SILVERMAN is vice president and COO at Synapse Technologies, a producer of interactive multimedia. Mr. Silverman has 25 years of experience in the entertainment and communications industries, and was a member of the original Warner Communications task force that created Qube, the nations first interactive cable system.

MARK STAHLMAN is president of New Media Associates, Inc., a media research and financial services company. The firm develops business strategies for the emerging new media industry. He previously spent 8 years on Wall Street as a technology analyst, and15 years in the computer business, where he launched several new products, led standards activities, and managed a venture fund.

ROBERT STEIN is one of the founders of The Voyager Company, a publisher specializing in interactive media. Voyager uses new technologies to develop and publish works of significant content. At Voyager, Stein has overall responsibility for product development. He initiated the Criterion Collection, a series of definitive films on videodisk, and has worked intensively on Voyager's most innovative titles.

THOMAS STOCKHAM JR. is a professor of electrical engineering at the University of Utah. He joined the computer science faculty in 1968, and worked with his students on signal processing. In 1975 he founded Soundstream, Inc. Under his direction, the company developed digital commercial sound recording and editing technologies, leading to the establishment of these practices industry-wide.

CONNIE STOUT is the director of TENET, the Texas Educational Network. She manages the Texas Education Agency telecomputing program, which includes operation and expansion of statewide telecomputing networking. She is also an advisory committee member of the Federal Networking Council, and an executive board member of the International Society for Technology in Education.

SHINOBU TOYODA is executive vice president and CFO of Sega of America, where he oversees product development, licensing, and third-party licensees. He presided over the creation of Sega's Multimedia Studio and he also spearheaded the launch of Sega's 16-bit Genesis system in America. Toyoda prevously worked for Mitsubishi, where he was instrumental in the company's CD-ROM development efforts.

DOUGLAS TRUMBULL is vice chairman of Imax Corporation and CEO of Ridefilm Theatres Corporation. His firsts include developing modern electronic motion-control photographic techniques, the capsule simulator ride, and the simulation theater. Trumbull also directed the first commercial movie ride and he invented the revolutionary Showscan process.

LOUISE VELÁZQUEZ was president of Quincy Jones Productions and Publishing at the time of the Roundtable. Recently, she has moved to Oracle Corporation. Having worked with many forms of media, Velázquez has an extensive background in the business and strategic issues of cross-media projects.

JOHN WARNOCK is chairman and CEO of Adobe Systems Inc., a company he founded with partner Charles Geschke. Previously he was principal scientist at Xerox Palo Alto Research Center, where he led research on interactive graphics and the development of graphics imaging standards.

MICHAEL WATTS is president of Frox, Inc., a manufacturer of high-end home theater systems based on the SPARC chipset. He previously worked for several high technology companies including National Semiconductor, Dynabyte, Hughes Aircraft, and Coherent Radiation.

PEGGY WEIL began working with interactive multimedia as a member of the Architecture Machine Group, which has since evolved into The Media Lab at MIT. She created and produced the Voyager title, "A Silly Noisy House," and has done computer graphics animations for movies.

MAX WHITBY is a founding director of the MultiMedia Corporation (MMC), a publisher of interactive multimedia software associated with the BBC. During the past four years, MMC has created more than forty projects, with Whitby as the executive producer for many of them. Recently he chaired the BBC's Program Strategy Team reviewing new technology.

HARRY WILKER is vice president of publishing for Broderbund Software, responsible for leading the definition, design, development, publishing, and marketing of software products. He is also co-foundeer of Sentient Software, a computer-game developer.

ROBERT WINTER is a scholar, pianist and raconteur. The first of his four titles, Beethoven's Ninth Symphony, is a pioneering work in multimedia publishing. He recently co-founded Calliope Media in order to devote more time to interactive authoring and producing.

KRISTINA HOOPER WOOLSEY is distinguished scientist at Apple Computer, with interests in interface design and the design process. She co-founded and directed the Apple Multimedia Lab, which spawned a rich array of projects and talent during its six years. She has produced a wide range of multimedia titles.

STRAUSS ZELNICK is a senior entertainment executive with a varied background in managing creative and distribution organizations. He became CEO of Crystal Dynamics after serving as president of Twentieth Century Fox. He was recently appointed CEO of BMG Entertainment North America.

PHILIP ZIMMERMANN works as a software consultant in cryptography, authentication, and data security. He is a leading advocate for public access to strong cryptography, and authored PGP (Pretty Good Privacy), a public key encryption software package that has become the worldwide de-facto standard for the encryption of e-mail.

Index

Index

Index

Index

Index

Index

Index

Index

Index

Index

Index

Acknowledgments

Thanks to Didacus Ramos for his boundless energy and dedicated assistance with the directory, Roundtable, transcripts, and book.

Thanks to Stuart Volkow, a valued colleague, for the coordinating role he played at the conference and his welcome counsel.

Thanks to David Hines for his faithful and continued help with preparations for the conference and its execution.

Thanks to Bill Brown, Maroun Harb, and Bill Bartram for their keen eye and professionalism in answering questions on design layout.

Thanks to John Auld for his quick turnaround and even temperament in bringing the directory and book to print.

Thanks to Dylan Charles for his editorial assistance, sound ideas, and invaluable support in the final months of writing and editing.

Thanks to the corporate sponsors for their generosity and faith in making the Roundtable and its documentation financially possible.

Thanks to the Roundtable participants -- an extended family -- for their excellent suggestions, friendship, and loyalty.

And a big hug to Liz and the kids for everything else.